D1545571

ANY NUMBER CAN PLAY

Also by Clifton Fadiman

PARTY OF ONE

Any Number Can Play

by

CLIFTON FADIMAN

Cleveland   New York

The World Publishing Company

PUBLISHED BY The World Publishing Company
2231 West 110th Street, Cleveland 2, Ohio

Published simultaneously in Canada by
Nelson, Foster & Scott Ltd.

Library of Congress Catalog Card Number: 57–9282

© 1953, 1954, 1955, 1956, 1957 The Curtis Publishing Company
© 1956 The New Yorker Magazine, Inc.
Grateful acknowledgment is made to Harper & Brothers for permission to
include "In Praise of Quotation"; to Bantam Books, Inc., for "War and
Peace, Fifteen Years After"; to Random House Inc. for parts of "The
Cheese Stands Alone" and for "Crime and Punishment"; to *The Saturday
Review* and *The New Yorker* for parts of "Cleriheulogy." With the exception of "Any Number Can Play" and the greater part of "Cleriheulogy,"
the balance of the material originally appeared, although in a different
and in many cases shortened version, in *Holiday*, to whom grateful
acknowledgment is made.

THIRD PRINTING

3HC158

FOR

Jono, Kim, and Anne

Contents

Contents

Prefatory: Any Number Can Play

The best test of the quality of a civilization is the quality of its leisure. IRWIN EDMAN

Real civilization cannot exist in the absence of a certain play element. J. HUIZINGA, *Homo Ludens*

By all means use sometimes to be alone;
Salute thyself; see what thy soul doth wear;
Dare to look in thy chest, for 'tis thine own,
And tumble up and down what thou find'st there—
GEORGE HERBERT, *Church Porch*

ONE OF THE MARKS identifying a revolutionary period is the speed with which a shocking statement changes to a boring one. It has taken us only about five years not merely to become used to, but to yawn over, the repeated announcement that—barring war, revolution, or economic bust—the age of leisure is at our doorstep. It is all so

9

accepted: the thirty-hour work week is around the corner; the twenty-hour work week is around the next corner; automation is solving the problem of production; Father Time is sitting expectantly on our hands.

There is a certain danger in everybody all at once hearing about something as crucial as the imminence of leisure. This danger was less dire in former days when communication was subject to normal and perhaps advantageous delays. Now there is a tendency to absorb the instantaneously received idea, mentally file it, and proceed to the next message transmitted by the tireless mass-communicators. With so many signals crowding in upon us, there is no time, and soon no inclination, to arrange them in order of importance, reflect upon them, and take proper action. Eventually the alert reception of the signal suffices. We delude ourselves into thinking that because we know a thing we have done something about it: our equivalent of the primitive's belief that to name is to control.

Perhaps we might be stirred to more useful action if it were made clear that wholesale leisure is not only an opportunity but a peril. Just because the word leisure has traditionally pleasant connotations we may fail to realize that it presents us with a critical as well as a novel state of affairs. It is like peace. Peace is associated with calm, rest, harmony: it sounds like a passive state. But if we should ever really be pitchforked into a universal peace we would in a daze wake up to the fact that it is a dynamic state, and that the proper use of peace necessitates the calling-forth on a vast scale of human energies that have hardly been stimulated, much less tapped.

Some of the vastest changes in man's wayward career

have swivelled on a shift in the meaning of a word. When we decided that God meant not Many but One, we grew into different human beings. It is such shifts that make the dictionary an absorbing historical work, more a story of the life of man than a column of word-correspondences.

Upon an acute understanding of the meaning of the word *leisure* our lives during the next hundred years may well in part depend. For words are not only words. They are motors, often prime motors.

For twenty years I have felt vaguely that *leisure* is a much bigger word than is commonly thought; that it is not necessarily identical with *recreation*, in the sense that playing golf is recreation; that it involves the opposite of rest; and that if mankind ever truly engaged in it he would become a different animal, just as he did after the Fall of Man, when seemingly unto Eternity he forsook leisure, and went to work.

But it was not until I came across an essay by the distinguished philosopher and educator Mortimer J. Adler that I began to understand myself. This essay is called "Labor, Leisure, and Liberal Education" and appeared originally in *The Journal of General Education*, October, 1951.

Mr. Adler's main concern is, first, with the distinction between *labor* and *leisure*, and, second, with the proposition flowing from that distinction: that, in an industrial democracy like ours, adult liberal education, from which we graduate with our final breath, is to be understood *only* in terms of leisure. By liberal education for free men Mr. Adler means something distinct from "vocational training," which is the education of slaves or workers. (Since Adam's Fall and up to Automation's Rise the human race has been composed mainly of slaves or workers.) Liberal education is a large, high-ceilinged word: it includes physical training, which liberates the body; moral training, producing good moral habits or virtues; and intellectual training, producing the free mind.

To understand the tie between liberal education and leisure we must now ask ourselves what leisure is. It is important for us to come up with the right answer because ours is the first era in which it is possible to ask the question. Up to now most of us have spent our lives in labor, engaged in for purposes of bodily survival or profit, sleep, and other biological necessities, such as elimination, washing, hygienic exercise, nourishment, sexual intercourse (considered as a need rather than an art). The time left is free time or spare time.

Now free time can be used in two ways. One is "play," which includes all ways of killing time. The other is engagement in leisure activities. Mr. Adler includes among these leisure activities "such things as thinking or learning, reading or writing, conversation or correspondence, love and acts of friendship, political activity, domestic activity, artistic and esthetic activity." I should add creative travel, which is a kind of conversation with what is past or new or alien. These things are engaged in *for their own sakes*— that is why they are not labor. Work is done under compulsion. Leisure activities, however, we engage in freely; they are not "externally compensated."

In redefining leisure Mr. Adler is really going back to its original meaning, which we have obscured by confusing it with amusement or diversion or recreation—all excellent things that have little to do with true leisure. In Greek the word "leisure" is *schole*. Sounds like "school"? Exactly. In ancient Greece the word *schole* had two meanings. Primarily it meant time free from labor. The second meaning tells us what men should *do* with this free time—and, strangely enough, that meant learning and discussing. "School" and *schole* are related.

Now learning or study, says Mr. Adler, is neither play nor work. Play is pleasant but static. No change in the human being flows from it. To engage in it to excess, as children do by nature, is a kind of regression to childhood. Nor is leisure work; work is compulsory, for the sake of leisure.

Thus, briefly, Mr. Adler's argument, which he caps with a demonstration that leisure activities, in this sense, *are the same as virtue*. Only in the one-class leisure society lying in our immediate future does a qualified Utopia become more than a dream. Or, as Mr. Adler puts it in his perspective-opening essay, *The Capitalist Revolution*, "The ultimate aim of pure capitalism, beyond the establishment of economic justice, is the enjoyment of leisure for all men in the major portion of their life's time."

From the severities of Mr. Adler's logic I should like to rescue only one word. That word is "play," which (perhaps because he is himself a strenuous mental athlete) he is not inclined to use as an honorific. And yet I should imagine that even he would admit that the notion of mental play is involved in most of the leisure activities he mentions. With this shift in accent my thesis now marches with Mr. Adler's: that an important key to the use of leisure lies in the large-scale production of mental players or—let us take the bull by the horns—of both professional and amateur

intellectuals. There lies the paradox: the one country that
has gone all out for the production of material goods is
now, as a consequence of this same productive genius,
forced to go all out for the production of nonmaterial
goods. We who have proved magnificently that any number can work are now compelled to prove that any number
can play.

The title of this essay and of this book, by the way, were
decided upon before I encountered an essay by David
Riesman in which he touches on the same notion and
with the same phrasing. Alluding to the function of intellectuals in our society he speaks of "the possibilities of
democratizing that function so that any number can play."
And there, precisely, is our task.

I plead for the play of the mind not on the ground that
it is pleasant but on the ground that it is necessary. And,
if this seems to verge on the puritanical, we might consider
that a certain infusion of puritanism was helpful in both
the founding and the development of our country. No great
pioneering effort is devoid of a tincture of seriousness; and
the kind of wholesale, pervasive mental exercise I am
talking about is in the exact sense pioneering.

I said it was necessary, and I believe it to be so, unless
we are prepared to accept tedium as an integral part of our
lives, just as the Russians accept domination as an integral
part of theirs. For we are indeed beginning to be afflicted
with a new kind of tedium. It may make us quite ill.
To prevent or cure it will soon become an urgent neces-
sity.

This twentieth-century tedium is a curious one. It is
rather unlike previous tediums. The medieval monk, his

soul sunk in *acedia*, was in part suffering from monotony, from a lack of stimulus, from an insufficiency of active control of his environment. Our trouble is the precise contrary. We are suffering from an excess of control, or apparent control, of our environment, and from an excess of stimuli, available everywhere and at all times. The lack-luster face of the subway rider reading his newspaper; the vacant look of the moviegoer emerging from his dark cave; the unexpectant countenances of the citizens swarming along Broadway: these are all pictures of a special boredom. Not unhappiness, not fatigue, and certainly not aristocratic ennui; but that odd modern *stunned* look that comes of a surfeit of toys and a deficiency of thoughts.

One of the most interesting ways in which our illness reveals itself is in our passion for motion. Chrysler, for example, has designed a car that will travel 130 miles per hour. This will be bought by those who are weary of cars that travel only 80 miles per hour. The appeal is, though lunatic, profound. It strikes deep. Machinery *applies* power; therefore, we reason, it should give *us* power. It does not. We refuse to admit it. We will *force* it to make us feel powerful. And so poor Françoise Sagan fractures her skull in an imbecilic accident because in her sickness she is willing to mistake motion for emotion. The case of James Dean is similar; and it is more than a coincidence that he should be the cult-object of the most profoundly bored generation of youngsters in all history. The current excesses of these miserable children stem in part from the frustration of having the simulacrum of power without the reality. For the unconscious knows that no one is enhanced when he presses a switch, turns a dial, or jams down an accelerator. But the conscious refuses to admit it; one's pride would be hurt.

Motion mania may assume queer forms. The Anglican Bishop of North Queensland recently suggested church-run "antiboredom clinics" to counteract the gambling craze of Australians. Because they are bored, they gamble; and gambling is but a way of communicating swift motion to money instead of to one's own body.

The United Nations has discovered another problem on its hands, that of relieving the growing boredom of the world's first international police force. It is meeting it with boxing gloves, radio quartets, and so on—all the paraphernalia of the spiritual vacuum from which the boredom emerges.

The Crusades were stimulated in part by the love of God, in part by the love of loot, in part by the tedium of daily life. So in the future in highly industrialized countries boredom may expand to such proportions that it can release itself only though mass aggression. Wars may be fought less between nations than between rival systems of ennui. The hyperbomb of that day will have lost meaning as a weapon and gained meaning as a complex substitute for Françoise Sagan's "sports" car, as this death device is so playfully named. That being the ultimate logic of the situation, we may contrive to kill boredom and ourselves at one and the same time.

And so we have these two vast and powerful forces, matching each other in the speed of their growth, rushing toward each other to what would appear an unavoidable, head-on collision. Of this potential disaster there exists a general uneasy sense. As yet it has hardly reached the con-

scious level. Already we feel, and correctly, that the use of
the coming leisure, as well as the neutralization of the coming tedium, are somehow connected with a fresh understanding of the idea of play. Being however animals first and
rational animals second, it is natural enough that at the
outset we should associate play with Mr. Adler's conception of the word—that is, with diversion, mass excitement,
violent activity, accelerated motion and the pleasures the
large muscles and the epidermis are eager to supply. And
so, with a magnificent efficiency translated from our commercial and productive skills, we are mass-producing
laughter, entertainment, speed, sport, colored images, loud
noises, excitement. For all this there is something to be
said: I am not arguing for gray solemnity. But it does not
touch the heart of our dilemma. The solution does not lie
in the multiplication of external stimuli in the area of pure
diversion.

Hence in a blind, almost instinctive way we seek it in
other areas. One of these areas is that of business, in which
as a nation we are supremely competent and in which as
individuals most of us are supremely interested.

Psychologists use the term "elation" in its generally
accepted sense—an emotional state of intense, joyful excitement. But they also frequently give it a special coloration whereby it becomes a distant cousin of mania and is
linked to a partial loss of the sense of reality. We have all
been struck, I am sure, with the way in which elation, as
thus conceived, has entered advertising, that accurate
barometer of our unconscious social pressures. The cigarette jingle implores us: "Don't miss the fun of smoking."
"It's fun," we are told, "to save at the Federal Savings

Bank." "Just luxury and fun while you fly," says one of the
larger airlines reassuringly, brightly. And a tooth-paste
maker, using pictures of laughing, playing children as
illustrations, seeks to persuade us that brushing is fun.

I have no quarrel with the object of these advertisers.
They are trying to sell perfectly honest goods and services.
I am concerned only to point out the new note of elation
that shrills through such advertisements and a thousand
like them. For clearly there is something excessive in as-
sociating "fun" with sober, habitual actions like brushing
one's teeth and filling out deposit slips; something akin to
hysteria about the hordes of wildly grinning figures who
gesture and scream their manic messages concerning
prunes and refrigerators. The disquieting effect on the
nonenthusiastic observer proceeds, I think, from a sense
that we have here a case of emotional displacement. Seller
and buyer are co-operating, to a degree in all innocence,
to insert into the world of detergents (Be *Happy* with
Didey-Wite!) and chewing gum (Try This *Exciting*
New Gum with That Fascinating Artificial Flavor!) the
emotions linked to true play. They are trying to climb over
the tedium-leisure roadblock by using the ladder of consumption, by forcing the mere tools of daily living to take
on tedium-relieving functions.

The same rather touching introduction of the play element can be noted in the business office itself. Here we
have a whole ritual of play, compounded of coffee breaks,
office parties, first-naming, martini lunches, padded expense accounts, golf course deals, and Roman circus annual conventions, now a growing branch of show business.

In the "technique of ideation" known as "brain storming" the play tendency may also be discovered. Here is how brain storming is played: a group of sales or advertising executives sit around a table and think up ideas, as rapidly as possible, as farfetched as may be, through a chain reaction of association. Later on these furious fancies are winnowed and the best ones applied to the promotion of the product. One brainstorm enthusiast, who has tried the game on women, finds that they take to it as "more fun than bridge or canasta." Here, in playing-to-order and with a specific commercial objective, we have an interesting mutation of the essence of play, which is spontaneity. J. Huizinga, the author of a classic dissertation, *Homo Ludens*, would call such behavior "false play" or "puerilism."

To the same puerilistic universe belong: educators who regard the child as a "personality" to be made happy rather than as a mind to be made mature; the George Patton view of modern war as an improved football game; the gospel typified by the radio evangelist who announces as his motif "Living Should Be Fun"; "Togetherness," substituting for the oversevere domestic disciplines of our Puritan ancestors a consciously relaxed "fun morality" in which the barbecue pit and let's-all-watch-television replace family prayers and solitary reading; such linguistic growths as jive talk and adman jargon, springing from the same make-believe impulse as does the child's private language; and, most important, the religious prestige now enjoyed by sport, so marked in some communities that nongolfers are regarded as an inferior caste. (This is also true of those rash enough to confess they have no hobbies.)

One is ill-advised either to ridicule or condemn these

tendencies. On the contrary they should be viewed seriously and even sympathetically. They are all symptoms of a vague collective conviction that the age of leisure is almost upon us; that we should do something about it; that this something is linked to the play impulse in all human beings; and that therefore we should (a) intensify diversion and (b) introduce play into areas where it formerly had no function.

Of these propositions only the last pair are questionable. We have seen, however, how human, how natural it is at first to assume their viability. Only within the last few years, I think, have we begun to see just how questionable they are and to make a few tentative gestures in the direction of an alternate mode of action, more difficult, more rewarding; the cheerful, unaffected but conscious training and exercise of the mind.

Superior leisure class societies based on slavery discovered this mode of action in ancient Greece, developed it, and produced a unique culture. Our own society, which will be a leisure class society based on machinery, may if it wishes do as well. The day may come when Presidential proclamations will state the civic duty of keeping our minds, as well as our bodies, fit; when, incompetent plumbers having given birth to the do-it-yourself movement, dispensers of canned opinion will give birth to the think-it-yourself movement; when the constructive use of leisure will prove attractive not because we're filled with an urge to become highbrows, but simply because we're bound to find out that a healthy mind, like a healthy body, is more interesting than a sick one and infinitely more interesting than a dead one.

Two considerations incline me to this sanguine view. The first is that unless we figure out ways and means of making the play of the mind salable to the great majority of us, we will have to face the boredom we have already noted, a boredom that may lead to social disaster.

The second consideration is more positive. It has been expressed by many, most clearly perhaps in an essay entitled "A Fortieth Reunion in 2156," by the distinguished psychoanalyst, Dr. Lawrence S. Kubie, appearing in the *Harvard Alumni Bulletin* of September 29, 1956. Peering into the possibilities held out by the next 200 years, Dr. Kubie sees "signs that we stand on the frontiers of [an] exciting new existence." This will come about when we have learned (as we are now learning) how to use all or a large part of our minds. "It is literally true," writes Dr. Kubie, "that no man has ever used more than a small fragment of his brain power. . . . And why is this? It is because [the brain's] psychological products are so organized that almost from birth we are continuously blocked by conflicts among internal factions. Each man grows up to resemble a pair of moose with horns locked in battle. He dies of a struggle which he wages with himself."

I think it only fair to assume that if we can be shown how "to free our enormous latent creative powers from the crippling and paralyzing domination of unconscious conflicts," we may develop almost as much enthusiasm for the play of the mind as we have already developed for driving a small, white ball into a slightly larger hole.

I am further encouraged by Dr. Kubie's second prophecy which is no more and no less than that biological science is bound eventually to discover a means of stopping the process of physical decay. With an immortality of leisure facing us, I cannot believe that we will consent to degenerate into Struldbrugs.

Chesterton once said, "If a thing is worth doing at all, it is worth doing badly." These essays were, for me, worth doing, even if badly. They represent an imperfect attempt to see what my own mind could come up with, if allowed free play. They are not (using Mr. Adler's terms) the products of work, but the products of leisure. A good many of them touch more specifically upon the thesis outlined in this prefatory word. I am not a professional thinker, merely a citizen who finds it pleasant to think, on however small a scale. Perhaps these elementary finger exercises may encourage others to take up the instrument.

American Yeas and Nays

Who Wants To Be Alone?

FROM TIME TO TIME one's ears catch the sound of penny whistles, calling attention to the private pleasure of having a mind of one's own. *The New Yorker*, for example, has for years been attacking that peculiar institution, the captive audience. The philosopher Lewis Mumford suggests that homes be equipped with a built-in lay cloister to which distracted signalees may ritually retire for lone meditation. Professor R. M. MacIver, the eminent sociologist, after a lifetime of studying society, publishes a book, *The Pursuit of Happiness*, devoted in part to the charms of staying outside it. In one essay the professor laments that there exists today "a many-sided assault on privacy," a Macedonian phalanx spearheaded by various energetic committees of investigation. No man can live well, he thinks, unless permitted, even encouraged, to withdraw at times into an inviolable self.

Angst over privacy came to a boil in the July, 1955, issue of *Harper's Magazine*. Here William Faulkner, after defining the American Dream as "a sanctuary on the earth for individual man," declared flatly that the sanctuary has been violated, in particular by the press, to such a point that the Dream is becoming "lost." He believes artists and scientists feel this loss most keenly; only the writer's work, not his personal life, should be in the public domain. Mr. Faulkner was understandably bitter at the indignities he had himself suffered; but, beyond any private resentment, he was terrified for the future of the Republic. He was sure that once the right to privacy is withdrawn, the individual ceases to be.

On the whole, the Think-It-Yourself movement would seem to be, as Madison Avenue might put it, clicking masswise. The public clamor for privacy shows a marked increase in decibels. Pleas to be yourself are so insistent that it is getting hard to find an uninterrupted half-hour in which to ponder them. A million book-buyers eavesdrop on the soliloquies of Anne Lindbergh. What with all this excitement over the quiet life I assume a few more noises can do no harm, even though I merely pour turmoil on troubled waters.

Switch off the radio and TV sets. Cut your telephone wire. Muffle your doorbell. Throw away your mail and morning paper. (Hold on to this book.) Steal away to your Mulling Corner and mull over these random facts:

1. Charles Lindbergh, a world hero, suffered a marked temporary decrease in popularity when he once forcibly tried to prevent a cameraman from photographing him and his family without permission.

2. A friend of mine, who stumbled on "fame" some time ago through his appearances on the radio, has ever since been trying to get his name *out* of *Who's Who*. The edi-

tors politely but steadfastly refuse to excise him. His only recourse is year by year to trim his biography. This he does, hoping to be represented eventually only by name and birth date.

3. On August 18, 1955, a wounded gunman was caught by Chicago detectives. John Chancellor, WMAQ's reporter on that station's "Night Desk" program, scored a scoop by catching with his microphone the interrogation of the wounded man by the detectives. *Variety* called this performance "one of the top radio reporting jobs of this or any other year." Private pain provides public pleasure.

4. On October 6, 1955, the Senate Internal Security Subcommittee announced that it would open an investigation of a University of Chicago Law School project in which a microphone was concealed in a jury room.

5. The family car is being stripped of its modesty. As the wall falls before the picture window, so does the carport oust the garage.

6. A score of traditional arts rooted in privacy, from the minor one of letter writing to the major one of prayer, suffer from anemia.

7. Modern building techniques make possible the construction of apartment walls thin enough to transmit sound perfectly without quite collapsing.

8. No one is interested in banning that most hideous of all contemporary sounds, the ripping scream of the jet plane as it invades one's home and one's heart.

9. As of September, 1955, a Portland, Oregon, city ordinance against phone solicitation (what hath God wrought!) was up for repeal. I'll bet it's been repealed too.

10. Recent careful reports in *The Wall Street Journal* point to a rise in successful door-to-door and telephone selling. The Fuller Brush campanologists, for instance, have done about 10 per cent better each year since 1952. Even large department stores ("Get the consumer before he has shopped around") are using missionaries who know how to wedge their foot in the door. Never send to know for whom the bell rings; it rings for thee.

Like Mr. Faulkner, Mr. Mumford, Mrs. Lindbergh, and Professor MacIver, I, as a privacy-lover, am but a vestigial piece of antiquity. However, I take no pride in the fact, any more than I take pride in my vermiform appendix. I differ too from the Jeremiahs in that I do not deem privacy a natural right. In a noncommunicating society it may have seemed so. In a society where every man's mouth is at every man's ear it is transformed from a right into an ideal. To fight for privacy, if you favor it, is proper enough. But to be indignant at its denial is to misinterpret the nature of your contemporaries. There is a vast difference between the atomic age (that is, one in which men were by and large atoms) and the Atomic Age in which men are linked by an endless chain of signals. Indeed we may call it a signal difference.

Communication starts by being an aid, a convenience. It grows, grows, grows—like a tree if you like it, like a cancer if you don't. In any case, it ends as a way of life. The transmission and reception of messages, almost irrespective of meaning, becomes an activity fascinating in itself. It can be deeply satisfying to certain temperaments that are outgoing, social, manipulative, present-minded.

But it yields its last measure of satisfaction only if pushed
to its last degree of development. This involves an "assault
on privacy," or rather, as I believe, a common unconscious
willingness to be assaulted.

Such a point I think we are nearing today; but that it
necessarily involves the death of the individual or the
decay of our liberty is doubtful. Both these words are
abstractions continually being redefined. The Chinese
does not consider himself less of an individual because he
lives in a noisy, semipublic compound along with forty
or fifty kinsmen. Nor do the majority of Americans feel
their liberty threatened by intrusions upon their privacy.
When certain specific liberties guaranteed by law are in-
fringed, we do protest. But—let's be honest—how *many* of
us protest? And how loudly? It is not that we are indifferent to the ideal of liberty. It is that the general understanding of the meaning of that ideal has undergone a change
during the last century. One may not like the change; but
it is there.

Early in our career we Americans produced a pair of
privacy-loving types: the gentleman and the frontiersman.
(Mr. Faulkner, a high-level merger of the two, is thus a
double-barreled privacy-lover.) The gentleman and the
frontiersman did much to create this country. Gentlemen,
for example, wrote the Declaration of Independence.
Frontiersmen put it to work.

If you want a symbolic date to mark the first body
blow received by privacy, try May 10, 1869. On that day a
group of determined antiprivacy men—helped out by a
more numerous and more detached group of Chinese
and Irishmen—hammered in a Golden Spike just north-

west of Ogden, Utah. From that day every forward step
in communication has lessened both the prestige and the
utility of those two admirable types, the gentleman and
the frontiersman. The communicator takes over. The fly
of privacy is trapped in the network of communication.
The particular kind of individualism that interests Mr.
Faulkner yields to the hookup that interests 100,000,000
Americans.

However distressing this may seem to more traditional
minds it's pretty much what we wanted. The fact is that
only a (possibly invaluable) minority want more than a
modicum of that specialized kind of liberty known as privacy. What most of us want is a generalized kind of liberty
that will permit us to work freely with and even intrude
occasionally upon our neighbors. As the architect Bernard
Rudofsky reminds us in *Behind the Picture Window* (an
amusing attack on the conventional modern house) our
Puritan forebears employed "tithing men" to watch other
people, one for each ten families.

The Englishman enters a parlor car, sits down, draws
his newspaper around him like a cloak of invisibility. To
us a parlor car is just what its name suggests—a parlor on
wheels suitable for social intercourse. How many of us
would not be perplexed by D. M. Low's remark (in his
introduction to a recent selection from the works of Norman Douglas) that Douglas felt "all interrogation, all
social curiosity is vulgar"?

Always excepting those two obsolescent types, the gentleman and the frontiersman, we are a social folk and
always have been. We are more than social: we are natural organizers of communication. Indeed we are geniuses

at it. Genius, it is often said, is an infinite capacity for *not* taking pains: you can't write *Hamlet* by trying hard. By the same token we haven't become wizards of communication because we wish to enslave each other's minds (though that happens on occasion) but almost because we can't help it, any more than bees or ants can.

That is why it is not entirely accurate to ascribe the assault on privacy to callous journalists, profit-minded advertising men, snoopy politicians, and vulgar press agents. Some are, it is true, callous, profit-minded, snoopy, and vulgar. But in a larger sense they are merely smart professionals. And what they profess is what we profess too. All they have done is to exploit commercially a contemporary American hunger, just as the brothel-keeper does with a permanent universal one.

The urge for privacy is not innate, like the impulse toward self-preservation. It is a social phenomenon, like feudalism or bubble gum, subject to erosion by the moving waters of history and the winds of fashion. Where it is not needed, as among certain primitive tribes, it does not exist. Perhaps in our own more complicated way we are approaching this condition.

A few paragraphs ago I threw out ten random facts. Think them over. On the whole do they not finger-post either a passive acceptance of the nonprivate life or, among our more energetic types, an active distaste for it? And is it hard to call to mind dozens of other instances, all pointing in the same direction?

We accept the telephone pollster's intrusion because, to tell the truth, we're not doing anything much more interesting at the time anyway. With avidity we read gossip columnists, not in the least critical of the fact that they, having discovered infinite riches in a little rumor, make a good living out of name-dropping. We like air shows tinged with exhibitionism, and many engage in them without any feeling of embarrassment. Indeed television has changed the meaning of the phrase "I'll match my private life with any man's." It is now less a proud claim to virtue than a lively challenge to competition. For many of us publicity has become a natural form of self-expression, as whittling or writing poetry are to other temperaments.

Apathy toward privacy may take subtle forms. Why, confronted with a menu, do most of us choose steak? Of course there is always the possibility that we like steak, but such a supposition gets a familiar essayist nowhere. Look at it this way: complex or unusual choices are privacy-linked. In a way they are gestures of exclusion—not snobbery, merely signs of a private life with all its unique standards and prejudices. Choosing steak is a gesture of inclusion, a public statement suggesting that I am not handicapped by such odd standards and prejudices. We are inveterate selectors of steak not because we're "standardized" but because we're social-minded, free of the shameful lust for privacy. On the other hand, when objects designed for public exhibition, such as motorcars, are involved, we are knowledgeable and choosy. For one mildly competent connoisseur of ideas we can boast one hundred thousand truly competent connoisseurs of public domania such as baseball, movies, or juke-box balladry.

Even our domestic architecture—with its picture windows and its movable glass walls, its ranch style calculated to place all the inmates on a single level, its ambition to "integrate" outside and inside, to force a shotgun marriage upon lawn and living room—emblems our drive to set nature and ourselves under one vast Plexiglas dome, echoing with intercom. Our very notions of good and evil undergo change: soon we will suspect guile in any bank that does not announce its probity with a glass frontage. Even today the fiscal honesty of our public servants is not properly established without the help of a coast-to-coast television hookup.

Men of imagination and intellectual ability, such as Mr. Faulkner, are in a particularly bad spot. For one thing they are not dull enough to be let alone. For another they are not rich enough to buy being let alone.

It is an unfortunate fact that writers, artists, thinkers, and heroes are simply more interesting than bankers or railroad presidents. They have more of the leaping stuff of life in them. Indeed that is why they become what they are. We, the public, are quick to sense this. We want a little of what they have, their secret, their mana. Just a little. Not much. Just enough to make their lives miserable.

The only consolation one may offer them is this: it is the paradoxical nature of modern publicity to veil rather than reveal the object; and the subtler, the rarer the object is, the truer this is. Mr. Hemingway, for instance, has been widely publicized, but it is unlikely that we really know anything important about him that we cannot guess from his books. The organs of publicity are so vast, so complexly intermeshed, so powerful that they cannot afford to lie quiet with a view to ambushing the essential truth about a superior human being. Thus most "public figures"—or

rather the public projections of the private figures—are apt
to be synthetic. Either the figure himself, in a kind of animal self-protectiveness, constructs a synthetic image for
public consumption; or the publicizer, who is more efficient at it, constructs one. There are no "revealing" interviews. All interviews by their very nature succeed only in
drawing a picture of the dead, not the living, part of the
interviewee. The very word is apt: an interview is the
place to inter a view. Thus, while Mr. Faulkner is bound
to be subjected to annoyance, in the end he retains private
ownership of himself.

To be free of mere annoyance, however, he must be
wealthier than most creative men are apt to be. Privacy
is becoming a luxury product, a buyable commodity for
those who are both wealthy and out-of-step. It already has
an established market value: one hears of million-dollar
invasion-of-privacy suits slapped against film companies.
The settlement of Exurbia, an exotic country described
elsewhere in this volume, is due to the efforts of a minority
of prosperous Americans (most of them communicators
who get enough of public living from nine to five) to buy
a little privacy with cold cash.

In general, however, I think intrusion is here to stay
and I think most of us want it that way. That is what I
must remember when momentarily I am irritated by the
shutter-snapping of the street-corner photographer. After
all, this good citizen is merely engaged in earning his living in a manner as socially approved today as piracy or
chattel slavery once were. He is part of a gigantic communications system by which many of us (and more of
us all the time) live, continually taking in each other's

publicity. He is no more to be condemned than, say, the television M.C. who invades your living room or the pilot of the plane that falls upon your house and kills your children in cold steel and aluminum. None of this is imposed upon us. We made it.

Vous l'avez voulu, Georges Dandin, vous l'avez voulu.

Horatio Alger, Fare Thee Well; or, The Road to Success

ACCORDING TO HERBERT MAYES, author of the standard and sole biography, Horatio Alger, Jr. began to struggle upward almost exactly 125 years ago. His natal day fell, all too patly, on a Friday the thirteenth, in the month of January, 1832. His birthplace was Revere, Massachusetts. In the neighboring town of Chelsea his clergyman-father tended those souls who had elected Unitarianism. When I knew Chelsea, a little over forty years ago, it was a plug-ugly town, clamorous with sailors from the Charlestown Navy Yard, awash in saloons that grew more and more numerous as one neared the Revere boundary (Revere had local option). It had a lot of character, Chelsea did. But in the elder Alger's day it must have been a hotbed of virtue.

The father of our hero was a perfect example of what happens when the power to interpret and spread Christian doctrine is vested in men incapable of understanding it.

By the time his son was ten years old he had efficiently maimed young Horatio's soul, pretty much in the manner described by Samuel Butler in *The Way of All Flesh.* He had made out of a potentially healthy boy a weak, confused, guilt-ridden fumbler. Little Horatio, of course, could not have known that he was better off dead. So, in a state of dull bewilderment relieved only by sharp moments of misery, he lived to be sixty-seven and conceivably the most popular author who has ever existed.

He wrote perhaps 135 books, and it is hard to say how many tens of millions of copies have not only been bought but read. His influence during the last thirty years of the Innocent Century was incalculable. Millions of American boys thought of Horatio Alger not as a real person but as a kind of institution touched by divine grace, much as we are instructed to regard General Motors today. Thousands of them, spurred on by reading his books, at least got a few splinters in their hands from climbing the ladder of success. And out of all his triumph this pale, pudgy hack, good in heart, a bit soft in the head, contrived to fashion one of the most pathetic careers in literary history. The man who defined the meaning of life for two generations of American boys died without being quite certain why he had lived. He started scared and wound up the same way, meanwhile managing to instruct millions in the virtues of courage, manliness, and independence.

In 1852 Alger was graduated from Harvard, after an education undetectible in his books. He then fled to Paris where he sowed two wild oats (one oat named Elise, the other Charlotte) in a manner that suggests he didn't quite know what he was doing at the time. Escaping from the oats, he returned to America where he footled around for a few years, managing to fail even in his halfhearted, half-witted attempt to join the Union Army. In 1864 he was ordained a clergyman of the Unitarian Church. But it was not until 1867 that his life-mold suddenly hardened. Encouraged by the famous writer of boys' books Oliver Optic, Alger wrote *Ragged Dick*. For thirty years he wrote *Ragged Dick* over and over again, maneuvering his unchanging hero from rags to riches.

Most of his time he spent at the Newsboys' Lodging House in downtown New York. It was simultaneously church, office, club, and funk hole. Here he achieved status acting as confessor and benevolent uncle to hundreds of Phil the Fiddlers, Paul the Peddlers, and Mark the Match Boys. Though his books show no indication that he understood boys (it is a small sad irony that *Tom Sawyer* and *Huckleberry Finn* appeared during Alger's high noon), he does seem really to have loved them. When his favorite, a Chinese lad named Wing, was run over by a wagon, his heart broke along with Wing's frail body. No sexual abnormality would appear to be involved. It is more probable that Alger centered his emotional life on boys, as Lewis Carroll did on small girls, because he was incapable of dealing with grown-up men and women. He never matured; neither did he retain any of the grace and spontaneity of the child. He was a joyless Peter Pan.

One fantastic episode alone colors his dun life. Like almost everything that happened to him, it was anticlimactic: Alger was as unskillful in rounding off his own experiences as he was in ending his books. Returning from a

Midwestern trip, he stopped at Peekskill, New York, where, through a comedy of errors, he was mistaken for a wanted murderer, and arrested. As a consequence of the embroilment he became acquainted with a married lady named Una Garth, with whom he fell in love very much as teenagers do. Mrs. Garth removed to France. Alger followed. By his lunatic behavior he almost succeeded in breaking up a marriage with which it would seem Mrs. Garth was moderately contented. Frustrated in his suit, Alger fell into a decline that landed him just this side of madness. But he didn't die of it; he didn't go crazy; he just went back to his Newsboys' Lodging House to endure an increasingly pointless, friendless existence. He spent his last years abstractedly acceding to his publisher's incessant demands and musing on the Great American Novel he hoped to write. Unfortunately he had sufficient intelligence to sense that his work was trash. Nor did he get out of it the satisfaction of a well-run business. His publishers pocketed the lion's share of the profits, and his own merely adequate competence he gave away to his poor street Arabs. About a year before he died, ailing in mind and body, he removed to his married sister's home in South Natick, Massachusetts. There during his final days he received a former secretary with the words "I shall be ready soon to get on with some work I have long had in mind." Shortly afterward Horatio Alger died, a nonentity whose name was known to millions.

I suppose my generation is the last to have been brought up on the Algerine virtues. From his books I learned that wealth is the direct consequence of honesty, thrift, self-reliance, industry, a cheerful whistle, and an open, manly face. Today (*now* they tell me) I *know* this to be untrue. But somehow I *feel* that there just might be something in it. I still try the cheerful whistle from time to time. I remain an irresolute, lapsed communicant of a dying church whose doctrine links sinlessness and solvency.

Some months ago I dropped into a briskly commercial bookshop in quest of a few algers. (This use of a proper noun as if it were a common one is associated with very few other authors. One does not buy a few balzacs or a couple of hemingways. But an alger is a *thing*.) I was surprised to learn from the bookseller that a mild Alger revival is current. There's a fairish demand for those rarer items that originally appeared in limited editions of 50,000 or so. Half a dozen standard titles have recently been reprinted for a quarter, and look rather uneasy in their slick glossy modern paper covers. In response to my query my bookseller friend said, yes, he'd sold quite a number. "To kids?" I asked. He looked at me kindly. "Nah," he said. "Fellows your age—sometimes even older—come in and buy an alger and take it home to their kids. The kids read a page and hand it back. They figure Pop is nuts. Then Pop gets off in a corner and reads it himself and goes all soft inside. Know what I call it? *Nostalger*. Pretty good, eh?" I conceded that it was pretty good and slunk out, furtively concealing in my coat pocket a reprint of *Strive and Succeed*. I am a fortunate man: my children, aged three and five, are illiterate.

But I—I am not. I have now reread this work which has

somehow, like unsinkable flotsam, survived for seventy-five years. I have also emerged glumly victorious over:

Struggling Upward; *Or*, Luke Larkin's Luck

Ragged Dick; *Or*, Street Life in New York

Phil, the Fiddler; *Or*, The Young Street Musician
Making His Way

Jed, the Poorhouse Boy.

With Jed (who within three months manages by pluck and luck to become Sir Robert Fenwick of Fenwick Hall, Gloucestershire) I felt I had reached my narrow limits, and gave up.

To make fun of algers is easy. But it is not hard to resist the temptation. They do not really make me laugh. In a wan, sickly way they make me sad. Trash? Yes, of course. Alger had no more writing talent than an Igorot. Yet the ostensible matter of his books, even though they carry no conviction, has a certain feeble nobility. Alger's heroes may be cutouts, but these cutouts make certain moral gestures that are at least pallid reflections of fine things: generosity, self-sacrifice, honor, manliness. It is true that these virtues do not win the jackpot for them. That is always the consequence of an accidental encounter with a passing philanthropist. But the philanthropist operates only when virtue presses his spring, never when villainy does. Goodness *does* pay off, if indirectly.

I have no wish to defend these books. Their qualities are few and dubious. Yet I cannot help wondering whether their moral world is so markedly inferior to that of our television shows for the young, in which a lust for violence and a passion for bad grammar struggle for domination. Is Tattered Tom half as much of a repulsive imbecile as Mr. Disney's Davy Crockett? Were the small fry of my childhood, innocently responding to Alger's bland Sunday school view of life, inferior except in point of sophistication to today's urchins so knowingly responding to the calculated sadisms of the comics?

I know that our higher-level juvenile literature is miles above Alger, more inventive, broader in scope, far better written. But it lacks something algers had. Though a foolish man, Alger is a *serious* man. For all his mandatory happy endings, he is not unaware that life is hard, even tragic. What writer of contemporary books for the young would think of including a scene like that in *Phil the Fiddler* in which poor little Giacomo dies of beatings and starvation? I am not demanding that misery be inserted into our bright juvenile literature. I merely wonder whether its doctrinal optimism is much more realistic than Alger's Calvinistic creed of work, with its corollary acceptance of the notion that even the young have to endure and suffer.

This brings us to what is really interesting in Alger Boys of today find him unreadable, not because he is a bad writer but because even if he were a good writer the things he believes in would no longer make sense. The entire Alger success-mythology, which we like to think a permanent part of the American character, is actually as dead as the moral system of feudal chivalry. Those who pay mechanical respect to it are paying respect to a corpse, a corpse that was alive, though moribund, as little as twenty-five years ago.

There is nothing novel in this statement. The gradual abandonment of the older American creed that linked hard work, virtue, and monetary reward has been apparent. It is apparent in the spate of recent business novels, whether satirical in tone or tenderly effusive, as with the *Executive Suite—Cash McCall—Man in the Gray Flannel Suit* school. The change has also been charted systematically in a series of recent social studies of which David Riesman's are the most brilliant, C. Wright Mills' the most choleric, and William Whyte's *The Organization Man* the most quietly factual. It is apparent in the shift in emphasis in our best primary schools, where, though a picture of Abraham Lincoln may still hang on the wall, the virtues stemming from independence have in actual pedagogy been jettisoned in favor of those stemming from co-operation. But to see just how dramatic the shift has been, the thing to do is to read Horatio Alger. In his books—simplified, moralized, sentimentalized—what Mr. Whyte calls the Protestant ethic is exposed with the clarity of a child-drawing.

The Alger books are essentially about money. On their low level they are part of the nineteenth-century literature of acquisition, just as are the novels of Balzac on their higher one. They do not tell you how money in quantity was actually made during the last half of the nineteenth century. Alger, living in a fog, knew nothing about this and would have been shocked at finding out. But he does put his finger on an economic fact of his period—the real *possibility* of accumulation, whatever the techniques may have been. The technique he stresses is the most elementary one, the only one open to his millions of lower-middle-class boy-readers: saving.

With the passage of the income-tax amendment, thrift, although we did not know it at the time, ceased to be a virtue. Within the last twenty-five years it has become a vice, or, more precisely, a peril. Our system now depends not on accumulation but on consumption. In *Luke Larkin's Luck* the millionaire solemnly tells Luke, "I am disposed to think that a boy's worst enemy is the one who makes it easy for him to run into debt." In *The New York Times* of November 4, 1956, the distinguished conservative economist Sumner Slichter, born during Alger's final decade, sums up our present view: "Consumer debt has become respectable, and the growth of personal indebtedness is being encouraged today by a large number of manufacturers, retailers, airlines and steamship lines with goods and services to sell and by finance companies and banks with money to lend." Installment buying replaces the penny bank, and even our children are given allowances, not in order to save, but in order to learn how to spend. My two small children look forward to opening their ten-dollar register banks around Christmas time as a prelude to the buying of presents. They are already unconsciously familiar with the idea of money as a medium of exchange, rather than as a treasure hoard. With Alger, money is a reward to be saved, it is associated with ethical values. In our time it is a switch, with no moral coloration, that sets consumption in motion. It is noteworthy that a well-known department store, endeavoring to encourage the modern view of thrift (advantageous consumption) associates it, not with Alger's *individual* morality, but with group fashionableness: it's *smart* to be thrifty.

It is possible that the shift is connected with the actual

value of the dollar. In Alger the dollar is made up of one hundred valuable cents; his heroes, when they are flush, continually buy "beef steak dinners" for fifteen cents. (Alger, very much like a certain type of contemporary businessman, seems to be unaware of the existence of any other food.) Today we are all psychological inflationists: the shrewd man is the one brainy enough to buy goods and services *quickly* before his airy dollars accumulate too dangerously.

In Alger genteel poverty is made much of not only because his plots turn on the vicissitudes of climbing the success-ladder, but because only by starting at the bottom can the hero really come to enjoy the delights of accumulation. Inherited income would defeat this pleasure. But it is now unfashionable (which is to say nonheroic) to have come up from the ranks. Our recently appointed Supreme Court Justice Brennan finds it necessary to defend himself against the indictment of being a rags-to-riches success: "A lot of baloney," says Mr. Justice Brennan, in that now mandatory we're-all-plain-folks-together phrasing so different from the prim language of Luke Larkin. "I'm no Horatio Alger. My father paid all my expenses till he died, then I was lucky enough to get a scholarship to finish Harvard." The middle-class man who has been able to consume from the moment of his birth enjoys a prestige denied to the poor man, who has had to waste a lot of the community's valuable time before getting to the point at which he can perform his social consumption-duty.

The shift in viewpoint extends even to such minor matters as expense accounts. "Luke meant to keep a careful record of his disbursements and report to Mr. Armstrong

without the addition of a single penny." On the whole I
think this sentence expresses the attitude of the well-
brought-up small-time business agent of 1875. It does not
of course express that of today's account executive or
salesman. The swindle sheet is not only a legal tax dodge,
it is part of the morality of our time. Insofar as it is a mode
of consumption, increasing the sense of co-operation between buyer and seller, enhancing the happiness-quotient
of a business transaction, it is praiseworthy. Up to a point
(of course) the free spender of the firm's money is preferred over the rigidly honest Algerine penny pincher.
Business, again up to a point, has shifted from warfare to
welfare as part of a general socializing process.

Now that thrift is generally felt to be either un-Ameri-
can or impossible, controlled, intelligent gambling gains
in status as an outlet for our residual acquisitive instincts.
Of one unfortunate who went to prison Mr. Armstrong in
Luke Larkin's Luck says gravely, "The cause was Wall
Street speculation. This is more dangerous than extrava-
gant habits of living." Wall Street today, whose ups and
downs millions of perfectly moral Americans share daily,
is popular, not only because wise legislation keeps it reasonably honest, but because it has lost almost completely
its old Algerine aura of sin. It is "right" in much the same
way that baseball, golf, and fishing are "right." That is, its
"rightness" flows from communal participation. There is
something *infra dig* or eccentric about not owning "a share
in America."

Just as Alger's view of money as something to be made
and kept no longer generally operates, neither does his
view of how it should be given away. There is a great deal

of "charity" in Alger, but it is always man to man, even palm to palm. It is a gesture in the tradition of the New Testament, a retail transaction between two individuals, spiritual in essence, monetary in form. The adjective that comes first to mind when we think of it is "Christian." The adjective that comes first to mind when we think of charity today is "organized." This does not mean that we are less charitable. It is certain that, *per capita,* and making the proper allowance for the dollar's changed value and the general increase in wealth, we give away more money than we did in Alger's time. But we do it wholesale, via drives, community chests, red feathers, because such methods raise the consumption index of charity-destined money: we can give *more away more quickly.* At the same time the primitive-Christian heart of the process, man-to-man giving, is weakened. The generosity is still there, but it is an item in the budget. We *allow* for generosity instead of having it overcome us, as in Alger's world. Warmheartedness is communized; it has shifted from being a part of the Protestant ethic to being a part of what Mr. Whyte calls the "social ethic."

No one as yet knows which ethic is preferable. The Protestant ethic of individual enterprise produces an Alger hero at one end of the moral scale and a robber baron at the other. The social ethic produces the broad-gauged big businessman with a highly sensitive social and intellectual conscience; and it produces the smoothie who has displaced God in favor of the Organization. We cannot measure the change on an ethical scale; but we can measure its dimensions, and they are considerable. The Model Boy gives way to the Man in the Gray Flannel Suit. Team co-operation is preferred to individual self-reliance. The employer is thought of less as a boss, in the old-fashioned manner, and more as the captain of an athletic team. No politician dares run for office unless he can command the language of the football coach rather than that of the independent-minded statesman. Alger's virtues of "grit" (one hardly hears the word nowadays) and perseverance seem less essential than the art of getting along with people and the ability to make contacts. Even mere industriousness has lost much of its market value. The man marked for success is not the one who burns the midnight oil at his desk but the one who plays the right kind of golf with the right people at the right club. The Calvinist idolization of work gives way to that of properly manipulated leisure.

Alger's heroes are quiet-mannered, but the manner conceals an intense aggressiveness; they burn with competition. They *want* to be Number One Boy; they *want* to excel in class; they *want* to be noticed. Contrast these urges with those unconsciously acquired by any American child in a "good" school. He learns to co-operate long before he learns to read and write. In fact, if he gets his "A" in socialization, it often does not seem to matter whether he *ever* learns to read and write. Good marks have little prestige value; in many schools marks and examinations, those temptations to competition, have been abolished.

The Alger hero is conventional enough, agreed; but he is conventional within an agreed-upon competitive framework. His aim is to forge for himself a standardized "character" which will enable him to dominate people. The aim of the up-to-date modern child and young man is to build up a standardized "personality" which will enable him to manipulate people. Both the "character" and the "personality" are constructions unrelated to the inner real person; and the discrepancy gives rise, as Dr. Riesman points out, to the guilt feelings characteristic of the nineteenth-century "inner-directed" society and to the anxiety neuroses peculiar to our own "other-directed" society. Thus, probably the worst offence in the Alger moral calendar is dishonesty, whereas among the more knowing teen-agers of our own time it would probably be the desire to be better than or different from the other members of their "peer-group" (Dr. Riesman's phrase). In the same way, "ambition" gives way to "antagonistic co-operation," cheerfulness to smoothness, greed for wealth to a passion for security, self-reliance to group-reliance. With respect to external, uncontrollable factors the Alger hero placed his faith in luck, as was proper in a period of seemingly unlimited possibilities. We place no reliance on luck, not to speak of providence, but have worked up another, less tenuous *mystique*: trust in the Organization, provided we have the good sense to Play the Game.

Lip service is still paid to the Puritan ethic, because not to pay it would be a kind of moral parricide. But Alger's nonsmoking, nondrinking, nonswearing heroes exist today only in outlying pockets of our culture, those still stuck fast in "inner-directedness." Advertising, consumption's brain, has made smoking and drinking social assets. As part of the co-operative consumer network smoking and drinking enjoy prestige upgrading and lose all moral stigma. The whisky-drinking Man of Distinction looks more attractive to us than Alger's Model Boy.

One of the most interesting differences between Alger's age and ours is the attitude taken toward education and "self-improvement." With Alger, to "stand low in one's studies" is a mark of inferiority. He makes a great fuss over book larnin'. This is plausible enough in a period when the illiteracy rate was, compared to our time, dismally high. We, on the other hand, have demoted the student in our iconography, unless he is that sacred cow, a "specialist." Actually our educational system by and large is far superior to that of Alger's day, but we lay stress on matters to which the little red schoolhouse paid no attention, such as learning about the world around us, getting along with one's fellows, laying the basis of good consumer habits, joining— and here we are even allowed to excel—in group sports. As for the traditional curriculum, it is perhaps as well taught as it was in 1875, considering that we need at least eight times as many teachers as are available; but the student is now not encouraged to measure his ability against that of his colleagues, on the ground that no one's feelings ought to be hurt and that no one, whether in the vanguard or the rear, should be compelled to experience the horrid shock of finding himself out of step.

One of the reasons for the popularity of algers is that, though they did not really deliver, they seemed to hold out the secret of self-improvement. The successful, respectable Mr. Whitney admonishes Ragged Dick: "During my leisure hours I improved myself by study and acquired a large part of the knowledge which I now possess. Indeed, it was one of my books that first put me on the track of the invention which I afterwards made. So you see, my lad, that my studious habits paid me in money, as well as in another way." Mr. Whitney lets the cat out of the school-bag. The cat is marked with a dollar sign.

We go in for self-improvement too. Few of us ever think of making a million dollars in any way whatsoever. But we can at least enjoy the satisfaction of seeing clearly that we certainly can't make it out of reading books. The consequence of this insight on the whole has been good: we are gradually forced to the realization that culture is its own reward, an insight that is the beginning of a higher civilization.

As for the sillier kind of self-help literature, even that is decreasingly materialistic. The stress is not on profit making but on getting along—getting along with others and, far more important, getting along with oneself. The typical self-help best-seller of our time is not descended from Horatio Alger or Samuel Smiles. It is part of the literature not of commerce but of psychiatry. It aims not to increase your income but to decrease your tension.

Finally there is the question of the small vs. the big town. Here Alger, poor chap, is schizophrenic. Most of his heroes come from small towns. Most of them "succeed" in New York. Now New York is by definition a bad place: "A city boy would not have had his suspicions so easily allayed; but Jed was unused to city ways, and, it may be added, to city wickedness." The small town had a monopoly of virtue, but the big town had a monopoly of dollars. God dwelt in the small town, but on the other hand all the benevolent philanthropists lived in New York. Alger was in a pretty pickle and he never really got out of it. He essays a half-solution by representing his heroes as bringing to Sodom the leaven of their home-town virtues. They improve New York's moral tone and in exchange New York makes them rich. In general however Alger is on the side of Main Street. He is never tired of advising his heroes not to leave home. They always do, but you can't say he didn't warn them.

In the last few decades a notable reversal has taken place. For one thing, from Sinclair Lewis to Grace Metalious, the small town has taken a beating. It is no longer a synonym for goodness. For another, Alger's opposition between the city slicker and the fresh-faced country lad has lost whatever basis in actuality it may have had. Everyone is familiar with the fact that the really sharp operators in New York, the ones who can cut your throat without giving you any sensation whatever, are all immigrants from out of town. The native New Yorker is a mere lamb standing around waiting to be fleeced by the narrow-trousered, striped-tied, worldly elegant from Tennessee or North Dakota.

For Alger there were only two places: "home" and New York. A boy left home at the cost of pulling up his roots, and all he got for it was a million dollars. But the contemporary Organization Man, who may be compelled to change his habitat every three years, sees his country's topography in an entirely different light. The home town is no longer a locus of sentimental yearnings. Nor is New York the Mecca of his ambitions. He is a man with detachable roots, designed to be plugged in functionally at any place in the United States or indeed the world. Both city and country have lost the symbolic values Horatio Alger attached to them. Today it is in the Organization that our hero's real birth begins. That is his true home town. It is

within the Organization that he grows, progresses, and
achieves some wealth and more security. That is his New
York.

We are far indeed from Tattered Tom. Today there are
more things in heaven and earth, Horatio, than were
dreamt of in your philosophy.

The Buried America

A COUPLE OF YEARS AGO a small group of professional
communicators, myself among them, contrived to smuggle
onto the airwaves a radio program called *Conversation,*
which at this writing is still leading an attractively precari-
ous life. The idea ("premise" is the imposing show-business
slang) is for me to act as "host" to two or three people
whose intelligence varies from the creditable to the superb.
We sit around a table for a short time, talking as well as we
can on some noncontroversial, nontimely topic. Then we
go home. As a certain limerick has it, we have received
numerous prizes. We have given quiet pleasure to a minority, and in a small way enlarged the constructive possibilities of radio. We have attracted a mentally alert audience
but no sponsor.

To blow *Conversation's* horn, however, is not the purpose of the subjoined remarks. As we are all talking animals, I thought it might be interesting to set down what
we have learned from three years of *Conversation*; wherein
we have failed or possibly succeeded; and what has been

the nature of the response to this eccentric attempt to revive a moribund and even somewhat discredited art, some random samples of which may be found as a kind of appendix to these remarks.

I say discredited. It is noteworthy that the play of the mind should be looked upon with more and more suspicion in proportion to the growth of our worship of the play of the body. During the last twenty-five years sport has evolved from a pleasant diversion to an article of faith. A fair part of the very general respect in which our President is held would, should he libel golf, disappear overnight. Is our attitude toward mental play a reflex of our attitude toward physical play? I don't know. However, the two attitudes, whether connected or not, have developed simultaneously.

Consider the case of a man who would like to revive the custom of settling differences by means of the duel. He would encounter opposition, not only because dueling is outmoded but because it is frowned on by the moral sense of the community.

That is the case with conversation. In many circles that set the tone and temper of our way of life conversation is looked upon as a waste of time, or even an antisocial practice.

Under these circumstances it was not at the outset easy for us to find good talkers. Or, rather, good talkers who were willing to talk in public, thereby running the slight risk of being considered odd characters. We found less difficulty as we proceeded. Apparently, though there is *some* peril involved in the display of the real, rather than the arranged, content of one's mind, people can be found willing to take the chance.

Willing; they are of course not all equally able. Yet of everyone, particularly the host, it may be said that he had to learn the art by doing. For conversation is a semiforgotten art and we found ourselves amateur revivalists. It is as if a group of men were to set out to learn the secrets of the art of making stained glass.

We learned first to shed certain national prepossessions. For example, we Americans place considerable faith in the question-and-answer technique as a means of eliciting what is loosely called the truth. We had to learn that, as far as conversation is concerned, the technique is unproductive. I do not believe that the interview method ever generates real answers. It may draw out public pronouncements. But it can never create good talk, and whenever on *Conversation* I find myself "spurring" my colleagues with questions, I know we're in trouble. The art of exchanging ideas has nothing to do with the art of interrogation. It is precisely in a country like Soviet Russia, where the exchange of ideas is forbidden, that the art of interrogation has reached its highest point of development. Especially in select secret police circles.

We also had to guard against our national predilection for the anecdote. The raconteur has his place in conversation but it should be a minor one. Nothing kills good talk more quickly than the creation of a can-you-top-this atmosphere. It is more important for the raconteur to know how to switch the talk back to a subject of general interest than to tell his story well. Unless this switch is made the talk becomes mere anecdote swapping, and bears the same relation to conversation that a page of Bartlett does to prose. I do not mean that the storyteller cannot be entertaining. He can be, and often is, but his function is not primarily conversational. He belongs to the same family as the parlor entertainer.

All of us on *Conversation* had to learn to control the impulse to substitute anecdote for opinion and jokes for wit. Similarly we had to check the perfectly natural desire to make conversation out of our personal experiences. The only thing duller than a man who tells you what once happened to him is the man who relates the funny dream he had last night. He may be a pillar of the community, he may be a hero, he may be a saint, but he was not cut out to be a conversationalist. Truth to tell, he should no more be permitted to engage in conversation than I should be permitted to wire a house.

We find on our program that on the whole women tend more than do men to intrude the personal. I do not think this is because they are more egotistic than men, for they aren't. More probably their tendency to express things in terms of personal reminiscence flows from the greater concreteness of the female imagination. Joan of Arc was one of the very few women who lived and died for an abstract idea, and I have always been a little uneasy about the absoluteness of her femininity. Women will gossip, often entertainingly, though quite uselessly. Men will speculate, often dully, and just as uselessly. But conversation can rarely be created out of gossip, however brilliant, whereas there's always a thin chance of creating it out of speculation, however crude.

But, whether it be male or female, we have noted that it is the trained mind that is least given to mere reminiscence, that is most capable of using its powers of comparison and generalization in order to lift the subject from

the lowlands of information-exchange to the high plateau
of general interest. The best talker the program has developed, in my opinion, is an academically trained historian
with a European background. He is used to judging experience rather than exchanging experiences; comparing
ideas rather than personal tastes; and striking wit from his
contemplation of character rather than from his recollection of the gossip column. The ones least able to engage in
general conversation are often men of a high order of
achievement and energy of mind but who have never been
tempted to view the spectacle of life in any perspective
wider than that of their own wills and ambitions. In talk
they are often forceful and persuasive, like a good debater,
but rarely playful and graceful, like a good dancer.

Little by little, week after week, we learned one of the
prime rules of conversation: he who is overinterested in
his own viewpoint spoils the game for everybody. It is not
enough to *listen* to the other fellow—that's merely good
manners. One must be *interested* in his mind, and for the
good reason that such an interest is the magic key that
opens one's *own* mind. Just as by loving we become lovable, so by a lively and sympathetic attention to another
viewpoint, we become aware of the pitch and quality of
our own.

We learned other things, too: how, in Addison's dry
old phrase, to "methodize" one's thoughts, that is, to depend less on the easy attraction of mere digression and
association of ideas; how to model one's sentences, choosing rather the intelligible, no matter how rigorously
phrased, to the vague, no matter how informally expressed;
how to curb the tendency most of us have when facing a

microphone to utter only smooth inanities that will displease and interest no one.

Theoretically a good conversationalist ought to be able to talk on any subject. He should not be handicapped by excessive information. It was the strength of his mind, not the copiousness of his memory, that made Dr. Johnson a great talker. We have discussed over a hundred topics, from puns to cyclical theories of history, and I have not yet come to the conclusion that the "expert" in any of these fields was necessarily the best equipped to carry on a conversation about it. Arnold Toynbee (with Eleanor Roosevelt, Bertrand Russell, and Adlai Stevenson one of our four most distinguished guests) was brilliant, but not by virtue of his erudition, which in any case could not be displayed in half an hour. It was not his "authority" that counted, but the depth, grace, and agility of his mind.

In sum, we began to learn a few first principles. Give us another ten years or so on the air, and we may develop a handful of talkers able to bear comparison with the great ones of the past. But I hardly consider that such a natural resource would be thought worth the attention that might be given, let us say, to the development of a new plastic.

In any case we still have a long way to go before we can be satisfied with ourselves. The program has its value, but that value should not be measured in absolute terms. It should be measured rather in terms of the social need it seems to fill.

A few million Americans seem to be getting something from *Conversation* that other and more expensive programs apparently do not give them. It is dangerous to try to profile this audience merely from the letters they write, but I shall attempt it.

There are a great many Americans—perhaps ten million or so—who live just a little out of the main stream of our contemporary life. They are not eccentric or highbrow or even particularly well educated. They are not rebellious or maladjusted or unsuccessful. They eat the same food the rest of us do, drive the same cars, vote for the same two parties. Nevertheless some hidden umbilical cord attaches them to an earlier and less restless America, to an America in which the values of the mind and the contemplative virtues played a larger role than is fashionable today. They are not professional intellectuals (high-grade intellectuals rarely look at television or listen to the radio, for the simple reason that they have more interesting things to do). They are men and women in ordinary walks of life, often of mature years, and frequently, to judge from their letters, slightly isolated by their interest in ideas. They are a buried, a silent America, rich in qualities on which at the moment no high market value is set. These are the Americans who listen to *Conversation* and other programs on the air that seem to satisfy their needs.

It's hard to say why they attend to our unimposing half-hour. In their letters they use complimentary adjectives such as "stimulating" and "thought-provoking," but these mean little. I get the impression that *Conversation* pleases them in part at least because it is quiet, well mannered—"gentle and pleasant" is the phrase one correspondent uses. They appear to be fed up with facts, with propaganda, with controversy, with the high-pitched utterances of authority. They are not looking for The Truth and they seem to be pleased, rather than disappointed, that on *Conversation* we never settle anything or arrive at an iron conclusion. One of them writes: "It's not enough to be right or wise. It's enough to be interesting and good-humored." Good humor would seem to be a microscopic virtue; yet, oddly enough, it is highly appreciated. The air is full of bad humor, controversy, charges and countercharges, resentful shouts and strident boasting. Or, on the other hand, it is full of synthetic sweetness, phony sentiment, cooked-up morality, and deliberate folksiness. Genuine good humor is rare.

They also seem to feel that they are part of the program, and this gives them a sense of "belonging." It is a curious paradox of radio and television that the more carefully a show takes into account the prejudices, the passions, the preferences of its mass audience, the less close, in any profound sense, it is to them. It may be a successful show and an entertaining one, to boot—but it remains a spectacle, something one looks *at* or listens *to*. It is the *artless* program that takes no account of the audience, that is nothing but the few people who compose it, which, surprisingly, draws its audience *into* itself. *Conversation*, in the world of TV and radio, will never be big-league stuff, and should never try to be; but this special quality of intimacy, of *naturalness*, it does by its very nature have, and a sizable number of Americans appear to respond to it. It makes rather small sounds but they are real sounds from the real throats of real people.

Finally, I think it pleases this audience precisely because it isn't "contemporary." Most of us enjoy the feeling of being up to date and we are encouraged in that feeling on every side. But there *is* a minority—quite decent folks too —who are tired of the endless struggle, who admit that they can no longer keep up with the latest gossip, book, play, or "personality." This minority would like to escape, not into some infantile dream-universe, but into the larger world of general ideas, ideas that may be half baked or ill expressed (they often are, on *Conversation*) but at least are not bounded by the confines of twenty-four hours.

There are any number of more ambitious programs that tell you what to think. *Conversation* is one of the few that shows you people thinking.

RANDOM SAMPLES OF CONVERSATION
FROM *CONVERSATION*

How To Waste Time

H. ALLEN SMITH: At my house the latest time-waster is two bird-feeders—

FADIMAN: What?

SMITH: You put birdseed in it and leave it outside your window.

FADIMAN: Oh, it sounded like a couple of elves—

SMITH: No, that's what I've turned into.

JEROME WEIDMAN: You mean you feed strange birds?

FADIMAN: That you don't know formally?

SMITH: Well, you put these things out, and you're supposed to get all manner of magnificent birds as guests during the winter social season.

WEIDMAN: Doesn't it depend on the kind of table you set?

SMITH: Well, you use two different kinds of food—

WEIDMAN: Good and bad.

FADIMAN: For upper-class birds and lower-class birds.

SMITH: No, you put birdseed in one feeder and suet in another. This attracts two different kinds of birds. This winter I've wasted in its entirety. I've looked at ten thousand chickadees, all exactly alike, and two woodpeckers.

WEIDMAN: What do the woodpeckers eat, suet?

SMITH: Yes.

FADIMAN: Naturally, the other food is unsueted to them.

WEIDMAN: Why don't you try pastrami?

FADIMAN: Then you'd get some peculiar birds from Lindy's.

SMITH: A lot of people waste time looking at birds, but they don't think they're wasting it.

FADIMAN: Take my friend John Kieran. He gets up around 3:30 A.M., rain or shine, to look at the birds. Of course, he has to wait around a couple of hours until the birds get up.

WEIDMAN: But Allen here just stares at the chickadees, whereas John goes home and writes a book about them.

FADIMAN: True, but that's not why he does it. I think John finds it more amusing to waste time with birds than to waste time with people.

SMITH: Well, I'm a confirmed people-watcher.

FADIMAN: Next Christmas don't forget to remind me to give you a couple of people-feeders.

Basic Fears

DR. JOHN SPIEGEL: It's important to live with reality, endure it, so to speak, for a long time, in order to find out in the end whether it was good or not. It is precisely this uncertainty about reality that we fear. The personality wants definite answers, engineered answers that you can get by pushing a button.

FADIMAN: Do you think this hunger for certainty ties up with our growing unwillingness to accept dogmatic answers in the field of religion?

CHARLES SIEPMANN: No, I think it's connected with our technological genius. We've made an unconscious psychological transfer: because in technology we can lick things, we think we can do the same with the problems of living. We're a black-and-white culture; everything is soluble. . . . Look at the best-seller lists, and note how many books offer short cuts to God and simple answers to insoluble problems. . . .

SPIEGEL: Well, religion can be thought of in two ways. One is the notion derived, as Dr. Siepmann says, from technology, that it can provide you with the answer to your insecurities. The other has to do with the values themselves, apart from any particular creed, the values that give us confidence, that tell us that in spite of whatever dangers and troubles may at the moment exist, things, over the long pull, are going to work out for the human race. . . .

Friendship

BERGEN EVANS: Is there something mystical and eternal about friendships? Or are they practical relationships that, as Dr. Johnson says, one must keep in repair?

NORMAN COUSINS: It seems to me that my best friends are those who wear well over the years. I may not see them from month to month, yet when I do see them, it's as though there had been no lapse of time.

FADIMAN: Ah, but how much lapse can you afford? I heard a woman saying the other day: "Why I hadn't seen Helen for twenty-two years, and when I met her on Fifth Avenue it was just exactly as if we were back in Vassar."

Now these people may be declaring themselves friends. But they're also declaring that they haven't grown much in twenty-two years.

COUSINS: Maybe they both grew at the same rate.

EVANS: When I was a student at Oxford, a wise older woman once said to me, "I do not want friendships any more, I only want acquaintances. I cannot stand the strain of death breaking up friendships." This shocked me rather— not because it was an expression of a cold nature, but because it showed that she had given *too much* to friendship. . . .

Eras I Should Like To Have Lived In

DR. ARNOLD J. TOYNBEE: The individual is so tied, so bound by our huge, complicated society. A small society like a Renaissance Italian city-state or an ancient Greek city-state would have given Mr. Barzun more of a chance to live as he describes.

FADIMAN: But my eighteenth-century Polynesian society is still simpler.

JACQUES BARZUN: Disagree; there'd be no incitement to do anything.

TOYNBEE: Well . . . oceanic voyages in canoes. . . .

HENRY STEELE COMMAGER: But the difficulty of doing things isn't only a large-scale difficulty. It's the day-by-day difficulty. It's curious, here are we four, all longing for the days before labor-saving devices, the days when the scholars, writers, artists—and statesmen as well—had time to do everything they wanted to do, without interruptions by timesaving mechanisms.

TOYNBEE: Look at Macaulay, for instance. On his three months' voyage to India he took a pile of books with him. Thanks to this long voyage, he could work out a scheme of education for India, as a consequence of which he changed the official language from Persian to English when he arrived. He couldn't do that now. Wouldn't be allowed to.

BARZUN: No, he'd be on the phone most of the time.

TOYNBEE: He'd be on a jet plane too.

FADIMAN: And arrive, in the approved modern manner, in a magnificent state of diplomatic unpreparedness. . . .

Cataclysms

FADIMAN: I wonder whether it isn't true that imminent cataclysm, if sufficiently vast, makes little impression on the mind.

JACQUES BARZUN: If anything, it's exhilarating.

FADIMAN: Here we are, all living with the possibility of imminent catastrophe, that of the explosion of H-bombs.

DR. ALFRED GOLDSMITH: Or even of lava crawling into the ocean bed.

FADIMAN: But do you find your day-by-day conduct affected by this knowledge?

GOLDSMITH: No, as long as grandfather wasn't bothered by it, you assume you won't be, and your grandchildren won't be. But if the catastrophe becomes fairly frequent, it begins to be more serious. During the recent floods in New England, many small towns reported that they doubted whether they would rebuild at all.

BARZUN: That's because floods are relatively novel. But for centuries, Italian peasants have been engaged in making delicious wine on the slopes of Vesuvius. Yet they know that it's a volcano in eruption.

GOLDSMITH: Well, the fertility of the Vesuvian soil may be greater than that of New England.

BARZUN: You mean there's a kind of temptation to defy the lava. . . .

How I'd Like To Live My Life Over Again

FRED ALLEN: You can't take it with you. No matter what kind of life we lead, we accept that.

GILBERT SELDES: I wish there were some way of denying it. That phrase has always irritated me. That, and "It's later than you think." I hate that one.

ALLEN: All the same, you've never seen a Brink truck in a funeral procession. . . .

People I Would Like To Have Met

FADIMAN: If you had Lincoln at your disposal, what would you like to ask him about?

J. B. PRIESTLEY: Well, in Lincoln there is some unknown element entering all the time, some other dimension.

FADIMAN: He's our one mysterious figure.

JACQUES BARZUN: The mystery is connected with his being apparently so plain; and also, we must remember, he lived in an age when people perhaps never went below the surface to see what it was about him that was so magnetic.

PRIESTLEY: Everything about the man is very curious, the death, the prevision of the death, everything.

BARZUN: The black dream he used to have. . . . And his speech—so remarkable. He must have spoken unlike any contemporary. His was an age of inflated diction, of bad schoolboy rhetoric—and he spoke and wrote utterly differently.

FADIMAN: Curious that we should all want to talk with Lincoln—but not because he was a great statesman or because he was involved in earth-shaking historical events. . . .

The Nonconforming American

FADIMAN: Don't statesmen and politicians find it a real handicap to show undue unconventionality?

ADLAI STEVENSON: Well, it has its dangers. In my judgment a statesman or politician should be a teacher. In a government by consent you have to understand what you're consenting to. That means it has to be explained to you by the politician, who is the spokesman of democracy in action. That makes politics sufficiently hazardous. It becomes more so when the teacher runs counter to conventional opinion. I believe we asked Socrates to swallow hemlock.

ALISTAIR COOKE: That's never happened to a Democratic candidate yet. . . .

STEVENSON: Well, in a way it's happened to a lot of Democrats. . . .

BERGEN EVANS: Of course many politicians often assume a sort of superficial eccentricity. . . .

FADIMAN: But that's just brand-name stuff—the ten gallon hat—

COOKE: Or the Indian headdress.

STEVENSON: Well, the point I was trying to make is that conformity becomes almost compulsory in politics. If you depart too far from the norm, you become an eccentric, and so a fellow of questionable wisdom. On the other hand, if you conform too rigidly, you can't teach because you can't express new ideas courageously— It's one of the prices you pay.

The Death of the Private Life

FADIMAN: What I'm trying to find out is whether the average person hasn't become perfectly resigned to the notion of having less and less of a private life.

JACQUES BARZUN: Yes, because of a sense of obligation to the community. But also out of obligation to all sorts of other ideals. For example, notice the way parents have given up a great deal of their privacy to children. The children come into the room as they wish, interrupting anything whatsoever. We say it's good for the children, they must always feel free. But for everyone who feels free in that way, someone else feels constrained.

BENNETT CERF: Ninety per cent of us not only don't resent invasion of privacy, but we actively seek it out.

King of the Tame Frontier

AFTER HAVING PASSED almost half a century trying to hypnotize myself into the belief that New York City was a proper habitat for *homo sapiens,* or even *homo stultus,* I recently threw in the sponge and removed to the pleasant town of New Canaan, Connecticut. Now, just as I am dancing cheek-to-cheek with a Locke mower, I am sandbagged by A. C. Spectorsky's *The Exurbanites.* The net effect of this book is to make a Seventh Avenue subway change booth look like the Ideal American Home. After a dose of Spectorsky many a man in a gray flannel suit will become not merely discontented with his lot but homicidally inclined toward the real-estate broker who unloaded it on him.

All of which is irrelevant to the virtues of *The Exurbanites.* They are multiple. Here is a social study that can actually be read by ordinary human beings. Mr. Spectorsky has marked out for himself a field of study that checkably exists; he has observed it with care, toughness, and compassion; and he writes about it with a negligent charm coating a basic seriousness. Even though he fills me with terror, I have learned much from him and urge him heartily upon all Urbanites, Suburbanites, and Ruralians who contemplate removal to my own land of Exurbia.

Mr. Spectorsky's term is already part of the language. What is an Exurbanite? Here is Mr. Spectorsky's answer. He is a man originally from New York City. Scorning the suburbs as neither fish, fowl, nor good green country, he has settled in the Exurbs, perhaps fifty miles from Columbus Circle. The rhythm of his life is a function of the commuters' train. He lives in Fairfield County, Connecticut; or Rockland County, New York; or Bucks County, Pennsylvania; or Upper Westchester, New York; or on the North Shore of Long Island.

The typical Exurbanite is a member of a relatively new species, the Communicators. He deals in symbols—words, notes of music, pictures on paper. He sets the styles, thinks up the fugitive ideas, and glamorizes the objects by which we live. He makes a good deal of money—the *average* annual income in Fairfield County is $7,431. He is rarely solvent.

He suffers, says Mr. Spectorsky, "from a self-created exurban syndrome." In the first place, he is schizoid—"These short-haul expatriates really never leave town." He is a symbol-manipulator trying to live like a thing-manipulator. Continually seeking "status," he thinks to find it in liquor, foreign cars, and "regional stigmata" such as salt-box houses and Rototillers. He is Republican, conformist, and increasingly, though he lives by ideas, anti-intellectual.

He drinks too much, plays too hard, and is plagued by psychosomatic illnesses. Intelligent, witty, quick-brained, often charming, he is also at bottom baffled, even miserable. His wife is in no better case. She lacks the daily stimuli which her husband presumably receives in the big city. She is overworked, overbechilded, and underloved. Frustrated, she frequently seeks to side-step her frustration in liquor, infidelity, frenzied absorption in the children, housekeeping, or do-goodism.

The Exurbanites have made a partial escape from the city rat race only to find themselves confronted by a new set of problems—fiscal or emotional—which they strive courageously but with only middling success to solve. Their personal equation juggles three major factors: insecurity, obligations, and a sense that time is running out.

Mr. Spectorsky's analysis is, of course, far more detailed than this brief summary suggests, and is hedged about with qualifications and subtle distinctions. As mere description of a readily observable type his book is solid. His picture is confirmed by a whole spate of recent novels, of which *The Man in the Gray Flannel Suit* is a fair sample. He observes truly and acutely. Few have written about a commuters' train with an eye closer to the object. He knows the country-club set, the "genius" (the genius works at home), the Saturday-night parties, the creative people of Rockland County, the ingrown money-men of the North Shore, the conscientious school-improvers of Westchester. His book is no fantasy, no tissue of generalizations. He seems to speak from much doleful experience. He has been there.

And yet there is something incomplete about his rueful thesis. I am not sure that I know what it is, but as an Exurbanite myself, I feel driven to place Exurbia in a perspective somewhat more encouraging than Mr. Spectorsky's.

In the first place, there are a great many pleasant, normal, nonfrenzied, nonalcoholic, sexually happy, and even solvent people in Exurbia. They don't rocket about in Jaguars. Their houses are not full of early American glass. They are glad to be out of the city for a reasonable part of the week. They read good books. They rear their children quietly and without tension. A few are even Democrats. In other words, poor copy.

Now, Mr. Spectorsky knows these people exist and admits that they do. But, he says, the *tone* of Exurbia, particularly in my home county of Fairfield, is set by the others.

He may be correct. But, even if he *is* correct, I would suggest that his correctness is that of a limited view.

Exurbia cannot be understood or adequately defended unless we are prepared to admit now what I believe we will all be forced to admit within fifty years: that the Big City, as a place to live, is dead or dying. New York is not merely a monstrosity. It is a dying monstrosity and, except as a commercial nexus, its only appropriate form, is on the way to extinction. We have killed it ourselves, of course, by our stupidity and our greed, which is merely stupidity in a state of acquisitive excitement.

The Big City is an invention. But it is not an invention like the alphabet or the number zero, whose utility is inexhaustible. It is more like gunpowder or the kerosene lamp, which are mortal. It began a long time ago, perhaps in Thebes or Babylon. It has had a fruitful, glorious career; and it has come to the end of that career in the choked, stinking, clamorous, and increasingly hideous streets of New York or Chicago. The Big City will continue to grow.

But its citizens will not, for the condition of their survival
is the deepening of their anesthesia. As a generator of
poetry the city is dying: Dickens, Balzac, Whitman, even
Dos Passos and Thomas Wolfe, considered as celebrants
of the city, already begin to sound like historical novelists
or composers of classical epics.

About thirty or forty years ago a few began to see the
ugly handwriting on the dead, concrete wall. Not many;
just a few. But these few were men and women with a
unique ability to sense the future. There are specialized
minds that can sense the future of the stock market; they
understand money. There are specialized minds that can
sense, often without being able to put it into words, the
future of a gigantic invention like the Big City; they deal
in ideas and feelings. These people do not *make* history;
they merely feel it coming. They are, after the saints, the
clearest-sighted people in the world, because their business
requires them to deal with the nontransitory. They are
artists, makers of permanent goods.

These people years ago settled in Westport, New City,
New Hope, Woodstock. Without quite knowing what they
were doing, they founded Exurbia. They fled the city because they could work better and (at that time) more
economically in the country. But underneath this simple
drive lay a vague prophetic consciousness that the Big City
was accursed, accursed not only for them but, in time to
come, to be accursed for all men and women.

They were numerous enough to found New York's Ex-
urbias, but not numerous enough to settle and develop
them. This was reserved (Mr. Spectorsky is perceptive on

this point) for another class, a kindred class of semiartists, or quasi artists, or even pseudoartists. These are the Communicators: commercial writers, TV and radio people, song writers, advertising men, Broadway playwrights, comic-strip creators, illustrators, the manipulators of symbols, styles, slogans, and popularizable ideas. To a limited extent these folk, for all their brashness, instability, commercial obsessions, and questionable taste, have the same *kind* of spiritual antennae possessed by the creative artist. Just *because* they work with symbols, even if the symbols are often fake ones, they have a lucidity, a quickness of mind that is not so frequently the property of those who work with three-dimensional objects or with money. They are nervous, triggerish, energetic, and—oddly enough—physically enduring, as they must be to survive the New York, New Haven and Hartford.

These people have a thousand weaknesses, but they also have one remarkable quality—the capacity, like their serener, abler cousins, the artists, to sense the future. Thus they knew, a little in advance of the rest of us, that the future included the gradual obsolescence, as living quarters, of the Big City which supported and will continue to support them economically.

The Communicators are the frontiersmen of the twentieth century. They have made the dizzy necessary half-leap (for remember, their economic base still remains Megalopolis) into the wilderness of Exurbia. It does not matter that this is a tame wilderness of washing machines, golf clubs, croquet, bonded rye, and MG's. It is, as against New York, a genuine frontier in the sense that it requires a new kind of living if one is to survive.

The original pioneers were full of hopeful, mixed-up dreams of adventure, material wealth, privacy, and living near to Nature. For some these dreams were fulfilled; but all of them also encountered back-breaking toil, flood, drought, loneliness, and mental starvation. Some did not have what it took; the others settled the country and forged a new way of life. Most of them did not live to enjoy the fruits of their labor, but their sons and grandsons did.

I believe firmly that the man in the gray flannel suit, the brief-case carrier, is an absurd figure only to the professional satirist, and sometimes to himself, his wife, and his children. To the eye of the Muse of history he is no more absurd than Daniel Boone or Kit Carson seems to us today.

He, too, has a dream, a dream of trees and stars and green grass, of privacy, of ordered, small-scale, communal living. He has a vague vision of combining the philosophy of Henry Ford with that of Rousseau. He is having a hard time making that dream come true; and, because of the refractory nature of dreams, he is baffled, frustrated, often in despair. So were the other pioneers, whose experiences, including boredom, physical exhaustion, and lonesomeness, he is repeating in terms suitable to the mid-twentieth century. But just as the original settlers smoothed, by their own laborious efforts, the path for their descendants, so the Exurban pioneer, himself perhaps a failure, is making it easier for the next generation. (That accounts for his almost feverish concern, so non-Megalopolitan, for the welfare of his children.)

His sons and daughters will inherit the good that will flow from the bankruptcy of the Big City.

Daddy may kill himself to pay off the mortgage, but his progeny will own a mortgageless home. The motorized gimmicks that Daddy operates so clumsily they will handle with ease and efficiency. They will use the helicopters that will make the industrial wen of New York easy of access. And they will inevitably have worked out the four-day or even three-day work week that will finally make Exurbia viable.

I prefer to believe that the frictions Mr. Spectorsky so well describes are ad interim frictions, the sacrifice a frontiersman has to make in order to found a new culture. Boredom, excessive drinking, frenzied play, vulgar display, infidelity—these are not intrinsic to the Exurbanite, nor to the Exurban situation. They are the growing pains, odd ones, I admit, that are inevitable whenever an old institution, like the City, is dying and a new one, the Exurbia of the twenty-first century, is striving to be born.

So do not smile at us, at our chatter about "roots," at our fumbling gestures of do-it-yourself, at our silly status-competitions, at our shiny-new, small-town patriotism. We may be the most ludicrous frontiersmen in history. But we are blazing a trail and marking out new country. The 8:10 is our Conestoga, the electric hedge-clipper our ax, the portable sprayer our rifle. And make no mistake: we may complain, we may despair, we may go under—but we are not going back. We are little men confusedly engaged in something big, and we know it.

Eggheads, Intellectuals,
Ideologues, High-Brows

SEVERAL SERIOUS OBSERVERS, including David Riesman
and Jacques Barzun, have recently concluded that the
current fashionable attack (for there *is* an attack and it *is*
fashionable) on the man of ideas is a kind of inverted
tribute to him. Mr. Barzun writes: "We think we are riding
a wave of anti-intellectualism because certain such men
are attacked; the fact is they are attacked because they
have become important." Perhaps, if I may employ a nonintellectual expression, the intellectuals never had it so
good. But let us not fall into an occupational weakness of
intellectuals by pushing this notion too far.

If the mind-man needs further consolation he can always
remind himself that the "wave of anti-intellectualism" is
nothing new. If it is a wave of the present, it is also a wave
of the past and will doubtless be a wave, one wave, of the

future. (It is part of the nature of the intellectual to think anything tolerable if he can only convince himself that it is recurrent.)

In 1876 Senator Simon Cameron helped to quash the nomination of Richard Henry Dana to the Court of St. James's with the comment, "One of those damn literary fellers." Long before that, in 1837, Emerson had looked forward wistfully to the time when "the study of letters shall no longer be a name for pity," thus pointing indirectly to the dismal state of affairs in his own era. Indeed the American intellectual was in the doghouse during most of the nineteenth century. As I have elsewhere suggested, it is as though we were rebelling against Papa. For the fact is that this country was set going by a bunch of calm-eyed intellectuals, otherwise known as the Founding Fathers, and we have remained a bit embarrassed ever since by the cerebral immaculacy of our birth.

It is also true that our nineteenth century was in no position to make good use of men of ideas. We had a continent to conquer and a bare century in which to conquer it. The nonintellectual's "Let's do it" or "Let's get it" made more apparent sense than the intellectual's "Once we've done it and got it, what have we got and what do we do with it?" That was Thoreau's question and for some time he kept on talking to himself.

It was only with the closing of the frontier, roughly in 1914, that the intellectual's question, even when his answers were wrong, became obviously useful. The election of Woodrow Wilson marked a hesitant return (on a lower level) to the kind of mentality of which Jefferson, Madison, and the two Presidential Adamses provide early examples. Ever since then the intellectual has played an increasingly conspicuous role in our national life. He has suffered that normal consequence of conspicuousness, abuse. He irritates us, not because we dislike him (we are merely *told* that we dislike him or should dislike him) but because we need him. It is natural enough to resent a support of which all along we had supposed ourselves independent.

I suggest that we can slightly decrease the sum total of bad temper in our land by separating four words. Currently these are violent words, full of unnecessary or carefully built-up heat. Let's see whether we can induce them to simmer down. The four words are intellectual, ideologue, high-brow, and egghead.

An intellectual is simply a man in whom is writ large what makes you and me specifically human—an interest in the rational mind and an ability to use it. As such he is nothing more nor less than the most important kind of person the human race can produce. One early intellectual figured out the use of fire. A recent one figured out how the universe hangs together. Between Ugug and Einstein stretches a long line of intellectuals, great and small, able to supply nothing but ideas. These ideas, however, make everything else possible—including attacks on intellectuals, for these very attacks depend on a series of ideas dreamed up by such visionaries as the inventors of the alphabet or those nineteenth-century lunatics who worked out the equations that have made radio and television possible. In a way the rest of us, no matter how industrious or transiently useful, are parasites living luxuriously on the work of a handful of superior minds. In my own case Hertz and Marconi for some years paid my insurance premiums and grocery bills.

As I pointed out above we don't need these impractical chaps all the time. We merely need them in a general long-term way in order to keep the human race human. To attack intellectuals, as thus defined, is simply to attack what is best, after our immortal souls, in ourselves. It is a form of attempted suicide. Those in whom the death wish is unusually strong, such as Hitler, are precisely those who *really* hate intellectuals, as opposed to those who merely *think* they hate them.

An ideologue may be defined as a mad intellectual. He is not interested in ideas, but—almost the exact contrary—in one idea. When he erects this idea into a system and forces the system to give birth to a way of life, confusion often results, usually to his great surprise. Two examples are Robespierre and Lenin.

The intellectual is occasionally blamed for the work of the ideologue, which is like condemning the psychiatrist because he and the patient are both involved in the same thing, mental illness. The ideologue is often brilliant. Consequently some of us distrust brilliance when we should distrust the ideologue, a fact of which the ingenious inventors of the egghead were well aware. The ideologue is often more persuasive than the intellectual because he has a simpler line of goods to sell and never questions its value. Sometimes he achieves great success by *attacking* the real intellectual—Bryan is a good example.

The intellectual level of any society must be measured not merely by its ability to produce intellectuals but also by its ability to distinguish them at once from ideologues. On this double scale England ranks high, Germany low.

Both intellectuals and ideologues are pros. Both live by

ideas, just as the farmer lives by the soil. But the high-brow is not a pro. He doesn't usually work at the job, any more than the audience works at the writing of a play. He takes in and enjoys what intellectuals, particularly artists, produce. This is his avocation. His vocation may be anything. I have known high-brow house painters, and I once taught a class of high-brows of whom few made a living with their brains.

Like the low-brow, the high-brow is limited in his conversation. He will stick to Sartre or Stravinsky or Picasso because they are what his temperament permits him to enjoy. The low-brow will stick to Yogi Berra or Jackie Gleason for exactly the same reason. The high-brow *may* also be an intellectual; he is more often simply an appreciator. Asked what books he would take to a desert island George Bernard Shaw replied, "Some blank notebooks." There spoke the true intellectual. Equipped only with blank notebooks the high-brow would go crazy—though less rapidly than would the non-high-brow.

The high-brow is never an ideologue. Indeed, as with Bryan and Stalin, it is the low-brow who is more apt to be also the ideologue.

Except in the statistical sense there is nothing queer or eccentric about the high-brow. There are fewer cassowaries than there are sparrows, but both are equally part of nature, though the cassowary seems a little queer because we don't see him around much. At the moment we have fewer high-brows than low-brows, but it is easy enough to conceive of a society in which the reverse would be the case.

Of course there are phony high-brows but, oddly enough,

rather few of them. I have, when permitted, spent a good deal of time with high-brows, and I should say that what makes them difficult at times is not insincerity but rather the contrary—the whole-heartedness of their devotion to a fairly narrow range of interests. The same is true of the low-brow, whose avocational passion for baseball or comic strips is as pure-hearted as it is boring—to the non-low-brow only, of course.

The egghead is not an intellectual, not an ideologue, not a high-brow. He is not any of these things because he doesn't exist. He is a political invention or, better, a cartoon character. The egghead, I have been informed by both Republicans and Democrats, was constructed during the 1952 presidential campaign out of imaginary yolk and albumen. Certain qualities of those very different types—the intellectual, the ideologue, the high-brow—which some average voters could be persuaded they disliked, were built up into a synthetic figure who was then christened egghead.

The whole egghead controversy, now that its political utility is decreasing, is beginning to reveal its basic absurdity. By this time it should be apparent that Dwight Eisenhower is not the folksy, cracker-barrel tintype the publicity boys projected on their magic-lantern screen. He is a man of dignity and substance, perfectly open to the impact of large ideas and capable, as he has shown, of rapid mental growth. It should also be apparent that Adlai Stevenson is no utopian visionary, but a practical, highly intelligent politician, in the British sense of the word. He is not an intellectual as, let us say, Bertrand Russell is an intellectual. He is certainly not an ideologue. And I can't perceive that he's much of a high-brow. The worst you can say of him is that he's well-educated, but even that is a risky charge to make. Mr. Dulles is well educated too. It is true, however, that Mr. Stevenson's gift for language is considerable and that Mr. Eisenhower's is limited. This rather minor difference (hardly a matter on which one's vote should turn) was blown up, it would appear, by a group of able propagandists and given currency through the picturesque and meaningless term, egghead.

It would be a good thing to drop the word from the national vocabulary. It would be a good thing, too, to use the words intellectual, ideologue, and high-brow with some feeling for their different meanings.

One of the most diverting oddities about the egghead controversy is the notion, presently entertained by some bewildered elements of the electorate, that Democrats are by nature cursed with an excess of intellect and Republicans are by nature blessed with an excess of good old-fashioned American horse sense. The charge against the Democrats can be refuted easily enough by recalling that once one of their Presidential aspirants was given to such highly intellectual behavior as wearing a coonskin cap while campaigning. As for the Republicans, one hates to dig up old scandals but it is a fact that again and again they have produced leaders like John Hay and Henry Cabot Lodge, Sr., who, in addition to being able politicians, were also high-grade intellectuals. It took a good deal of probably deliberate clowning on Theodore Roosevelt's part to obscure the embarrassing fact that he was one of the best-read Americans of his day.

The truth is that intellectuality does not to any extent link with either party—nor indeed with any general political orientation. Liberals are not more intellectual than conservatives. As a matter of fact, at the moment more interesting political ideas are being produced by conservatives, though twenty years ago the reverse happened to be the case. In the long run intellectuals are above party. That does not mean that they are bad citizens or snobbish folk. It means only that they think most easily and fruitfully in long-haul abstractions, whereas party politicians (and the human race generally) think most easily in short-haul concretions.

Just as we should try to dissociate the intellectual from the political liberal, so we should try to dissociate him from the nonconformist. He *may* be a nonconformist—Bertrand Russell was one, at one stage of his great career. He may be a conforming nonconformist—Galileo was one. And he may be in many respects an outer conformist—as, to take two very different illustrations, Gladstone and Santayana were. But I should like to remark that few types are more typically *non*-intellectual than the village atheist, the reefer-smoking jive musician, Norman Mailer's *Deer Park* sex lunatics, and the Union Square soap-boxer: nonconformists, every man jack of them.

Nor should the intellectual be confounded with the pessimist. The most genuinely cheerful and well-integrated men I know are those whose lives are concerned mainly with ideas. Equations kept Einstein equable. Indeed this very equanimity may be one reason why some of us distrust intellectuals. Our distrust masks unconscious envy. As was pointed out in sublimer terms almost two thousand years ago, things, which you can hold in your hand, let you down, whereas ideas, which you can hold only in your head, don't. But the dismaying fact is that most of us own more things than we do ideas.

I am less convinced than I was some years ago that our civilization is endangered by the assault on the intellect. I do feel that at the moment the idea man is not generally admired. He is certainly not well-paid. Yet a great deal of attention is being given him, and, as we noted above, this may well be the first sign of a rise in his prestige. The next step may be a general and more thoughtful recognition of the probability that the twenty-first century is going to need him in vast quantities.

At the moment I am more inclined to think that the danger (probably a passing thing) lies less in a distrust of ideas by the naturally nonintellectual than in a distrust of ideas by the naturally intellectual. We are not in peril because George F. Babbitt prefers Marilyn Monroe to Dostoevski. But we are in peril when good minds, minds that might energize our educational system or raise our religious experience above decorous joinerism, bow down, in cynicism or fatigue, to lesser gods.

One weakness of intellectuals is that they are fascinated by any fresh idea. The current attack on them, though its roots are deep in time, does have a certain spurious novelty. Some intellectuals—and remember, we can't spare a single one—have been taken in by it. My experience has been that few Joe Doakeses talk cynically about the intellect but that a fairish number of presumptive or potential intellectuals do. It is no longer considered bright to be bright. Thus I am less disquieted by the instigated hooliganism of those whom some high-brows call primitives than I am by the occasional defection of those whom some low-brows call sophisticates. It is when an intellectual like Donald MacLean turns into an ideologue, when a man cut out to be a brilliant economist becomes a public-relations expert —it is then that one gets a hollow feeling. For mere stupidity can never kill the man of ideas. If he should die, it will be by suicide.

We Knew What We Wanted

WE KNEW, thank Heaven, what we wanted: a country house we could start living in five minutes after unlocking the front door. No authentic colonial suitable for remodeling. No white-frame, green-shuttered, shingle-roofed, road-fronting abomination, genuine down to the last splintered, dirt-collecting, wavy floor board. Not for us. We would buy a stone house with twenty-four-inch walls, slate-roofed, low in upkeep, and set far back from the main highway. Let birds, not people, dwell in wooden houses. Down with charm!

"Trouble with a stone house," said one of the thirty-seven brokers we lived with for twelve months, "is that they're always cold and damp."

"But," I objected, "Joe Robinson over in Westport tells us they're always warm in winter and cool in summer."

"Oh, Joe—" replied our friend, with that tolerant smile reserved by brokers for the moral peccadilloes of their colleagues. "He *lives* in a stone house, got to protect his own investment. Poor Joe."

But, being homeless, all we wanted was to be like poor Joe, with an investment to protect. We kept right on trailing slate-roofed stone houses. Well, we'd settle for a tile roof, if it came to that; no point in being difficult. As a matter of fact we *did* see a jim-dandy house with a beautiful tile roof. I was ready to buy it at once. I would have bought two houses a day if I had not been accompanied by my keeper, who doubles as my wife. In this case she pointed out that while the tiles *were* lovely, they were also breakable and could be secured only through a firm in Italy that had ceased operating shortly before the First World War. My wife's father had been a real-estate broker. My advice to any house-hunter is to sacrifice looks, breeding, character (I didn't have to) but marry *only* the daughter of a real-estate broker.

Don't get me wrong. I love real-estate agents. As a rule they are helpful, hard-working, and honorable. But all of them have a living to make. You have to take them as they come, which is what a few tried to do to us.

Of several we nurse fond memories. Mr. Haskins, who phoned us about the Jones place—"It's a dream house"—was, when informed that we'd already seen it through another agent, not in the least hurt. "You couldn't do better," he said warmly. "It's a dream house. Too bad though about that water in the cellar. Hard to get rid of. But except for that—a dream house." He was quite right. We *had* noticed some water in the cellar. Not much. Just enough, if properly drained off and piped, to maintain a small swimming pool. The trouble was that the dream house already *had* a swimming pool, and my wife hates waste.

There was also Mr. Calloway. Mr. Calloway really *knew*

the neighborhood, in time as well as in space. He would describe, let us say, the McNulty house. Sounded good. We were off to the McNulty house, a pleasant twenty-mile drive through lovely country. Once there, it was hard for us not to notice that some months previously we'd already seen the McNulty house. Only in *our* files it was listed as the Jackson house.

"Is *that* what you call it?" Mr. Calloway said kindly. "I always call it the McNulty house. The McNultys had it for years up to about 1921. Then they sold it to the Rolfes and the Rolfes died out and the estate claimed it and then some people named Lawson bought it and I suppose they must have sold it to these new people you call Jackson. But it's really the McNulty house."

We drove back twenty miles, through the same lovely country.

A touching trait of many brokers is that they are less interested in selling you a house than in making your fortune. This is accomplished by the Selling-Off process. Why, argued Mr. Holinshed (we called him the Sell-Off King) pay high for the four acres we thought we wanted when you could buy a place with forty acres *cheap*. He would sell off thirty-six acres for us, just like that, and work it so that we got the house for nothing. The offers were in the files. It was my wife who observed that these offers, when exposed to the open air of inquiry, evaporated like perfume. She would also notice that across the road from the forty-acre place lay a splendid domain of perhaps 650 acres, somebody else's property and apparently not yet overrun by would-be buyers. Anyway I didn't want to get our house for nothing. It seemed mean.

People who look for stone houses must get used to feeling inferior. It was Mr. Lipton who tactfully made that clear to us. Mr. Lipton, when we murmured "stone," would turn his head away as if from a gas leak. We once spent two days in the eighteenth century with him. During this time he showed us only colonial houses that had been properly restored by a locally famous antiquarian named Horner. He would point out a Horner as Bernard Berenson might point out a Fra Angelico.

"There's a real Horner. Right on the road—had to be in those days. No driveway snow-removal problem like you have in these pretentious modern places. Of *course* you can't stand up in the bedrooms; they have real charm. Look at those hand-blown old windowpanes. Look at these hand-hewn timbers, all hand-pegged, old hardware, wide board floors—there's nothing like a Horner."

Within two days "random width floors" and "H and L hinges" began to acquire in our minds the kind of sanctity usually reserved for Mother and the Flag. We liked Mr. Lipton and would gladly have bought a house through him, but he couldn't help making us feel that, when it came right down to it, we weren't worthy of paneling with old wormholes made by old worms. We just didn't measure up to a Horner. No background.

In Fairfield County, Connecticut, writers are a dime a dozen anyway and carry little prestige. If they are also radio and television entertainers they naturally carry none at all. In consequence I often felt guilty in the presence of real-estate brokers, like someone who's married above himself. Mr. Murgatroyd, for example, though always affable and courteous, sold houses as a kind of amusement. His real lifework was acting as a judge at dog shows. We often felt that we were selfishly exploiting abilities that should by right have been expended on the canines who in certain parts of the county are regarded as having reached the level toward which those lower animals, men, are slowly and painfully evolving. Mr. Murgatroyd took us to very nice houses indeed. He was always on first-name terms with the owners of these mansions, and we felt our vulgar purchase of the place would in a way disturb this intimate relationship. This we did not want to do. Anyway, we couldn't live up to Mr. Murgatroyd's offerings, which were generally attached to kennels only a wealthy dog could afford.

Mr. Murgatroyd, quite properly, overawed us. Miss Bannister, in a different way, was also too much for us. Though in a small way a professional talker myself, I am a sphinx compared with Miss Bannister. We spent many pleasant afternoons with her, learning a great deal about real estate, without ever being able to find an opportunity to tell her what we were looking for. Her rhetorical equipment was extraordinary, even godlike, for it created things out of a void. Vigorously pulling open the door disguising a shallow cavity in a bedroom wall, she would exclaim, "Endless closets!" In a trice, before we could poke our heads inside, she would be off into the next bedroom, opening and quickly slamming another door ("Endless closets!"). She moved so efficiently and talked so convincingly that at the end of the tour I was persuaded that I had seen a house simply honeycombed with closets. My wife, however, who is insensitive to mere language, had made careful note of the fact that there was ample closet space for a quiet midget couple.

Miss Bannister was master of a lightning logic that

quite overwhelmed me. For instance, when I feebly objected in one case that the taxes seemed excessive, she agreed energetically, going on to explain that precisely *there* lay our opportunity to appeal for a reduction, an opportunity that would not exist in the case of a moderate assessment. There was a time during our Bannister period when I was convinced that bargains were to be found only in highly taxed houses. Miss Bannister's optimism also applied to distances from the station. She had a fine contempt for merely linear measures. Her phrase was always, "You can make it in less than ten minutes," a phrase generally uttered as she drove us along the left side of the road at a pace that made it seem probable that we would make either Hell or Heaven in less than ten seconds. We shall miss Miss Bannister.

In Le Sage's old tale of *The Devil on Two Sticks* the fiend Asmodeus takes Don Cleofas on a flying tour over the city and magically reveals to his companion what is going on under the roof of each dwelling. A real-estate broker is Asmodeus, and any house-hunter, I suppose, is a Peeping Tom despite himself.

From the convolutions of the empty shell the marine biologist can deduce the inhabitant. So is it with houses: they are speaking shells. We saw in succession two similarly priced houses. In one a large sunny bedroom was decorated with cheerful nursery murals, furnished with scaled-down tables, chairs and bookcases, and supplied with a serviceable phonograph and even a small merry-go-round horse. In the next the broker threw open a moderate-sized closet and announced: "The child's room." Problem for a class in creative writing: sketch the later lives of the two children involved.

One home we saw had a mistress' dressing room complete with a wall of shoe and handbag racks, a vast assemblage of lined lingerie drawers, and six closets. Down the hall was a small cubbyhole jammed with the master's clothes.

Another house had a small, paneled chamber specifically designated The Coupon Room, with coupon shears neatly laid out upon the desk: a perfect set-up for the archeologist interested in a reconstruction of American civilization, McKinley Era.

On one and the same day we would come upon a gleamingly perfect house, with a sullen couple of domestics mechanically polishing the legs of the dining-room chairs —and upon another in which we would be greeted by a cheery housewife who would say "We're a little upset," and amiably show us bedrooms with beds seemingly unmade for weeks and piles of soiled clothing in solid strata over every floor.

We noted again and again—we examined two hundred and seventy houses—that people will apparently spend large sums of money in keeping two acres of lawn like velvet, and put up happily with a kitchen suitable for their great-great-grandmothers. As a matter of fact it may be laid down as a general rule that the more expensive the home, the more primitive the kitchen. The kind of house we couldn't possibly afford also almost invariably boasted a maid's room about six feet wide, occupiable only by a very short maid with a hinged back.

The house-hunter opens a hundred doors upon a hundred small tragedies and comedies: the lonesome little child, trailing after a maid too busy to notice him, while his parents are somewhere in the city being successful enough to afford a home for him to be abandoned in; the owner who insists upon telling you everything he has done to improve the place, and whose exhaustless memory invariably ruins a potential sale; the owner who looks doubtful when you ask the location of the furnace switch; the owner whose emotional identification with his house—a common, rather touching, and completely infuriating phenomenon—is so complete that, when a bona fide offer is made, he at once withdraws his place from the market; the poor chap who is forced every few years to sell out and move to larger quarters because of his wife's obstinate fertility; the divided homes (we ran across dozens of these) in which the husband wants to remain in the country and the wife can no longer resist the seductions of Fifth Avenue; the recently bereaved young widow who *must* sell; the quiet, sad couples in their sixties whose children are grown up and who look as though life had somehow betrayed them; the houses occupied by comfortable-looking bachelors and their extraordinarily handsome nieces.

In the course of our quest for the stone-and-slate dream house we learned a thousand things about human nature we had never before suspected. We learned also how to sniff a cellar for dampness; how to recognize a down-grading neighborhood; how to test underpinnings by jumping; how to shudder at the obscene phrase "galvanized iron plumbing"; how to handle garrulous caretakers; how to judge the sound-insulating properties of walls by flushing toilets in various parts of the house—my wife and I have probably between us achieved over a thousand purely academic toilet-flushings.

How did we make out? Fine. We're crazy about our house. It's a white-frame, green-shuttered, shingle-roofed, road-fronting colonial—remodeling shouldn't take more than six months—with quite a lot of landscaped acreage. This latter we intend to transform into the only jungle in Fairfield County. We may charge admission. The upkeep is terrible.

Boys and Girls, Come Out To Play

The Cheese Stands Alone

The cheese stands a- lone, The cheese stands a- lone,

Heigh- O the der-ry O! The cheese stands a- lone.

MANY YEARS AGO, having resolved to write a book about
cheese, I collected data on upward of five hundred varieties and accumulated specimens (often quite lively) from
many of the countries of the world—literally from China
to Peru. (China's soybean yields a courtesy cheese, *hoi poi;*
Peru's cheeses I cannot recall.) The specimens have long
since gone the way of all flesh and dairy products. The
data, however—so vast is the field—I have never been able
to digest, and so the book remains an unfulfilled dream of
my youth. For consolation I call to mind one whom I
resemble in no other outstanding respect, Casanova, who
also found his powers unequal to the task of writing a dictionary of cheese. Yet I think a man should from time to
time, in whatever poor phrases he may command, laud
those gifts of God which have filled him with most joy.
Let these rough notes, therefore, so ill-matched to the alti-
tude of my theme, serve as a kind of thank offering.

Universal hungers are few: who dreams hotly of soufflé? But wine, once loved, remains a passion; so too with bread, salt, perhaps meat. As for cheese, I range myself with the great connoisseur P. Morton Shand who deemed a love of it inherent in humanity. The Chinese, it is true, like it little, linking all milk products with their herdsmen-conquerors, the Tartars and Mongols. But Ben Gunn, marooned on Treasure Island, with his pitiful "Many's the long night I've dreamed of cheese—toasted mostly," emblems much of mankind; and I have heard that our men on besieged Corregidor, reduced to mule meat, split into two groups—those who dreamed of chocolate, those who dreamed of cheese.

Like its great brethren, bread and wine, cheese is born of a miracle. At the very instant when the milk is on the road to ruin, mysterious lactic acid or that more mysterious ferment, rennet (extracted—who knows first by whom?—from the fourth stomach of the suckling calf), works like grace upon it and raises it to the higher life of curd. Curd, pressed and treated, is touched again by grace, this time in the guise of bacteria or mold. Time passes. Now the curd, like Odysseus before Penelope, throws off its grossness, growing godlike in form and feature. It has become Cheese. It has voyaged in one superb celestial arc to the very end of the Milky Way.

Cheese is not the gift of the cow alone, but of the ewe, the goat, the reindeer, the zebu, the buffalo, the camel, the llama, the mare, the ass, the zebra, the yak. It may even be, if we are to trust Maurice des Ombiaux's droll anecdote in his *Les Fromages*, the gift of the human female. In color it shades from the delicate rose of a virgin's blush to the grand severity of Pentelic marble. In form it is protean: the ball and the brick, the cube and the cucumber, the disc and the dumbbell, the melon and the millstone, the bologna and the ostrich egg, the pineapple and the parallelepiped. On New York's First Avenue, near East 116th Street, there used to be and perhaps still is a veritable Cellini of cheesemongers who would sculpt your cheese to your fancy.

The eye of the turophile may consider the eighteen basic varieties of cheese or the thousand variations on those varieties. In either case he tries to classify. He may arrange them according to the quality of their resistance to life's onslaught: yielding, such as the chaste cream, the mold-matured Camembert, the bacteria-ripened Roquefort; firm, such as Gorgonzola or Münster; obdurate, such as Parmesan. Or, with André Simon, he may view them in terms of their aggressiveness: the gentle Petit Suisse, the strong Roquefort, the brutal Limburger or Marolles. Or he may borrow the late Edward Bunyard's division, based on their poetical style: the romantic cheese, like Brie, given to excess, even to tears; the classic cheese, such as Stilton, growing like Nestor nobler as it ages.

Ancient is the lineage of cheese. A legend, deeply unreliable, has it that some thousands of years ago an Arab merchant named Kanana, wandering over the desert, stopped for lunch, poured out the milk that he had kept in a skin bottle made from the lining of a calf's stomach, and found an odd but attractive-tasting mess, now known as curd. As a child, Queen Semiramis was fed cheese by the birds. Zoroaster, who flourished about 1000 B.C., lived, says Pliny, exclusively on a cheese for twenty years. (It has been deduced that this could only have been a Gibraltar of a Parmesan weighing about 1 ton, 12½ cwt.) The Greeks attributed the invention of cheese to the demigod Aristaeus, son of Apollo. In Book 9 of the *Odyssey* Homer describes the dairy techniques of the one-eyed Polyphemus, who seems to have gone in for something like our domestic Ricotta, a rather insipid by-product of Asiago or Parmesan whey. Hippocrates mentions it as being made of both goat's and mare's milk. The Old Testament (see I Samuel 17:18) speaks well of cheese.

The poet Martial tells us the ancient Romans were fond of the cheeses of Toulouse. The Emperor Augustus favored them, especially Salonite cheese, which he ate with small fish, brown bread, and figs. The learned Palladius, the more learned elder Pliny mention cheese. When British soil first shook under the tread of Caesar's legions, Cheshire cheese was already being made there. His affection for Roquefort, first mentioned in a monkish chronicle of 1070, ennobles the character of Charlemagne.

The genealogy of the literature of cheese is also venerable. The first important publication, Pantaleo de Confluentia's *De Laticiniis*, was issued at Turin as long ago as 1477. Since then earnest students of the subject have not been lacking.

Enfeebled, stultified, nay, *rotted* by the processed horrors of our time and country (what dolt said good things come in small packages?), we have forgotten that cheese is what Hilaire Belloc said it is, a profound matter. Only countrymen, leading quieter, wiser lives than ours, still know this. In England's remoter countryside, when a birth is expected, a vast cart wheel of cheese is piously set aside.

Day by day it is cut out at the center so that at last there remains a large ring through which on his christening day the fortunate babe is ritually passed. Switzerland's Saanen, an Emmentaler cheese, takes six years to ripen and will keep till the blast of Gabriel. In our culture, a privileged child is at birth put down for Groton and Harvard, but in Switzerland, when a baby is born, a wheel of Saanen is marked with his name. On all the holiest occasions of his mortality—christening, betrothal, marriage—his private cheese is served; and when he dies the mourners consume the last of this ceremonial Wheel of Life.

Provided it be well and truly made there is really for the confirmed turophile no such thing as a *bad* cheese. A cheese may disappoint. It may be dull, it may be naive, it may be oversophisticated. Yet it remains cheese, milk's leap toward immortality.

Edam's crimson cannon balls, for example, may seem, like their solid Dutch creators, a bit plodding. But a thick round of Edam or Gouda on the blackest of bread companioned by the blackest of coffee makes a muscular breakfast that puts to shame epicene toast-and-orange-juice. Nor does the more reflective palate disdain that rarity, Edam that is sharp, dry, and two years of age.

"Swiss" cheese, Emmentaler or Gruyère, would seem to have too obvious an appeal. But there is virtue in simple candor. (Simple candor is particularly good with beer.) Look to it, however, that your Gruyère betrays around its eyes that trace of lachrymose moisture which announces its ripeness, its readiness to be yours. Hardest of all to come by is the supreme Gruyère long past its salad days when it was green in judgment, Gruyère that is rich, salty, nutlike, and virtually holeless.

I will confess Bel Paese a neutral affair at best, but Taleggio shows to what it may aspire, and Pont l'Évêque seems to me the highest avatar of the type. Pont l'Évêque now appears rarely, but it has an attractive cousin in Mont Dore, a Rhône valley whole-milk cheese I have found in many New York shops. Soft, yellow, delicate without effeminacy, Mont Dore was the favorite cheese of Pascal, whose *Pensées* must owe some of their powerful grace to its ingestion.

Parmesan, the Carborundum of cheeses, is humble fare. Marry it to onion soup—and it is royal. One recalls Willa Cather's Bishop Latour in *Death Comes for the Archbishop* savoring such a parmesanctified soup, rich in its "nearly a thousand years of history." One bows the head in gratitude to Louis XV's father-in-law, the exiled Polish king Stanislaus Leszczyński, who made it famous. Mark well, however, that God did not make it in canisters. It was not born grated; it does not achieve gratedness; it must virtually at table have gratedness thrust upon it.

Gentlemen, let us raise our sights. Let us praise the immortal French triad, the Three Musketeers: Roquefort, Camembert, Brie.

Ewe-born, cave-educated, perfected by moldy bread, greenish-blue-veined Roquefort was called by Grimod de la Reynière "the toper's biscuit." So joyfully does it mate with wine that wine buyers will not use it as a palate cleanser lest it mask the wine's poorer qualities. The poet Baudelaire, liking perhaps its faint, tantalizing hint of decay, was an amateur of Roquefort, pairing it with that

Burgundy of beautiful balance, Corton. We receive great
Roquefort rarely, for it is often oversalted for export purposes. Though it lacks the true Roquefort texture, our
native Langlois Blue from Oregon is no bad substitute.

Esteeming Roquefort, I view it without passion. Yet I
can conceive why Émile Zola, in describing a cheese market, speaks of "majestic Roqueforts looking down with
princely contempt upon the others, through the glass of
their crystal covers."

For full persuasion Camembert, like a good orator,
should stop short just this side of fluency. Before this stage
it speaks of chalk; past it, of ammonia. For perfect Camembert the recipe is simple: go to Normandy.

I have recently, however, eaten good imported Brie.
(Domestic Brie, while pleasant enough, is not Brie at all.)
When you speak of Brie, uncover: Talleyrand called it the
King of Cheeses, the only king, it has been noted, to which
he remained faithful. In its subtlety, its delicacy, its beauty,
and its appeal to the intellect, Brie might quite as aptly
be called the Poet of Cheeses. Like many a fine poet, it is
hard to get at. The ordinary cheese knife, an abomination,
is powerless; a razor blade has been suggested; I have
found a small demitasse spoon the very thing for those
precious, cryptic corners. A perfect Brie cannot be produced by standardized methods; it is the end product of
a series of miracles. Essays are writ by fools like me, but
only God can make a Brie.

As for English cheeses, only one (but that the lordliest,
Stilton) seems to reach our shores regularly today. Cheddar, Cheshire, Gloucester, Double Gloucester—all could

after patient research once be found. Now, I hear, supreme examples of these cheeses are even on their native heath hard to come by. Pity; for, while England may well survive the falling away of her colonies, a falling off in her cheese whispers of some deep and stanchless inner wound.

Great Cheddar, I hope, Englishmen still enjoy. As for ourselves, domestic Cheddar lies around us in its infancy, and some in its maturity. I have found few domestic Cheddars more honest and upright, the consequence of clean living, than the sharp variety sold by Jack and Marion Ayres of Sugarbush Farm, Woodstock, Vermont. But even at its shelf-cured, three-year-old Vermont best, it cannot equal a fine English Farmhouse Cheddar. (Farmhouse Cheddar is satisfactory; the other kind merely Factory.) A good Cheddar, like a human being, needs nine months to round into decent enough shape to make a public appearance. I prefer a more elephantine period of gestation. A knowledgeable Englishman, John Houghton, once suggested two to five years—but his counsel was offered two and a half centuries ago when both men and cheese were allowed time to live. To Cheddar—as to all cheeses of character—Edgar's wise words in *King Lear* must apply: "Ripeness is all."

Of Stilton it is hard to speak without emotion. Its azure veins avouching its noble lineage, it thrones it as the world's most regal Blue, exerting, like any true aristocrat, authority without aggressiveness. A Stilton's self-confidence springs from its past (the richest milk and cream) and its future, which can only be one of glory. John Galsworthy in *The Forsyte Saga* refers to "grand years-old Stilton." Charles Lamb speaks of some Stilton as "the deli-

catest, rainbow-hued, melting piece I ever tasted." John
Jay Chapman recalls a morsel "that was like Agincourt.
It was sonorous, undying." Here Chapman strikes the right
note. There's such divinity doth hedge a Stilton as aureoles
no other cheese. It is magisterial.

See, however, that your Stilton be of a healthy cream
color, not anemic, with a hint of greenish-yellow, its edges
brownish, its veins wide-branching, its texture not over-
flaky, its vast interior uncrevassed. If you can, buy a whole
Stilton or at least a half. The grandiose gesture will repay
you; properly kept at room temperature a well-bought,
well-bred Stilton will for many months share with you its
nobility. With careful stroke remove the crown. Then cut
out a wedge perhaps one and a half inches high, and further wedges as required of exactly the same height, until
a new smooth top is exposed. Replace the crown so that it
fits tightly; keep truncating your Stilton in this manner till
you have disposed of the last bit. Then buy another Stilton.

Stilton, as I say, does reach us, as do many other fine
cheeses: the unctuous Stracchino, the subtle, feminine
Hablé Crème Chantilly, the devourable Provolone, the
mild Gruyèrish Banquet from Iceland, the carawayed
Christian IX from Sweden. Phil Alpert, the master cheese-
monger of East 10th Street, New York, offers hundreds of
"cheeses of all nations," but most of them are made here
in excellent imitation of their originals. To secure, however,
a wide and deep understanding of cheese one must and
should travel. The pleasure of a cheese tour are subtler
than those of a châteaux tour, for there is always the chance
that you will make a great discovery. Besides, cheeses taste
better on the home grounds.

We come now to our own land, with which from the cheese-lover's viewpoint we may merge our good neighbor Canada. A Rembrandtesque picture presents itself, a dramatic mingling of light and shade.

The blackest shadow, of course, is cast by processed "cheese." The word should always, like Soviet "democracy," be framed in quotes, for no matter what the law may say, I refuse to call this cheese. For me (though it is only fair to state that millions of us seem to like the stuff) processed "cheese" belongs to the same Kallikak family as ordinary commercial white bread, powdered coffee cellophaned cake, and our more popular carbonated beverages. The best I can say for it is that it is nonpoisonous; the worst, that it represents the triumph of technology over conscience.

In the preparation of this solidified floor wax—often the product of emulsification with sodium citrate, sodium phosphate, or Rochelle salts; of steaming and frequently blending odd lots of cheese; of paralyzing whatever germs might result either in loss of profit or gain of flavor—every problem would seem to be solved: packaging, keeping, distribution, slicing, cost. One problem alone is not solved: that of making cheese.

Bernard Shaw once warned us (he was speaking of mass entertainment) to be sure to get what we liked; otherwise we might begin to like what we got. There is the point—not that processed "cheese" is so bad in itself (though it is) but that its convenience, neatness, and cheapness give it so many advantages that it may elbow real cheese aside and in the end compass the death of our cheese palates. Let us not be fooled. My guinea-pig son, aged one year and seven months, was not: fed a "cheese spread," he spat it out; fed a tiny bit of Stilton he took to it like an angel. Give our American children the processed corpse of milk and they will grow (I dare not say mature) into processed men, all package and no character.

I can call to mind one exception to these strictures. But even that is not a native product. It is a Danish import called, regrettably, Littlefellow, a processed cheese spread, mild, creamy, with an interesting tang. As for other processed plastics, remember only that the wrappings of foil are the cerements of death.

But enough of bitterness. It is sad work and I take little pleasure in it. Processed "cheese," "cheese spreads," and "cheese food" (often hypoed with onions, garlic and similar horrors to mask the taste of the corpse) represent the baser element in an industry which also boasts honorable men. We have plenty of sound, decent domestic cheeses, most of it Cheddarish in nature, some of it an excellent aping of greater European originals, such as Gruyère or Roquefort.

Our basic trouble is that we are in a hurry and cheese is not. Honest, edible Cheddar is easily found, but really mature, shelf-cured Cheddar, dry and on the point of the crumble, is rare. Still, I have eaten good Cheddar from Canada, Vermont, New York, and Wisconsin; and I once tasted an Oregon Tillamook filled with both the goodness and severity of God. Sage Cheddar—Vermont's pride—can be a wondrous thing. It eats supremely well on a hot summer afternoon in the country (circumstances alter cheeses), especially if you mate it incestuously with its mother, milk, and load it on cracker-barrel crackers—even though for the most part crackers are the enemy of cheese, just as bread is its friend. (I mean real bread—pumpernickle, dark rye, stone-ground whole-grain bread, or crusty French loaf.)

The great war, as in other areas, is between the urge to standardize and the urge to create. More often than one would think, the creator wins. One of our finest native cheeses is the work of a creative artist, Emil Frey of Monroe, New York. This cheese offers a good example of serendipity. Frey was experimenting with a formula for a German-type cheese (probably Limburger, which is originally Belgian) and accidentally came up with something new. But it takes greatness to recognize greatness, and Frey, being great, knew he had something. He called it Liederkranz—one of the most beautiful (and odorous) soft cheeses in the world, and named after a famous New York singing society.

The roll of individualistic, ruggedly independent American cheeses is a long one. (No "process cheese," of course, can be included in the list.) Let me mention only a few. There is, for carefree nibbling, the plain, honest Jack from California. From the Colorado Rockies comes a little flattened sphere of black-rinded, whole-milk Cheddar, Mountain Blackie—an utterly delicious, subtly acid, eating cheese, imperfect for wine but otherwise a fresh and lovely thing. Poona, a Pont l'Évêque-like cheese made in New York State, has extraordinary breeding. Canada's Oka, lineally descended from Port Salut, can be superior, though I fear it is cured too quickly. The secretary of the Cistercian Abbey of La Trappe d'Oka (where the cheese is made) writes me that its unique flavor is due "partly to the special bacteria of our cellars, and partly to the rich pasture ground of our hilly country." The brother-abbey of Gethsemani in Kentucky makes a similar cheese I have found supremely good of its kind.

Yes, the mind that refuses to be processed still lives and flourishes, in our dairies as well as in our politics and arts and sciences.

Certain strange and wonderful cheeses of Europe I may never taste—Sweden's Prestost or Saaland Pfarr, whose curd is washed in whisky; Romania's Branja de Cosulet, a creamy sheep's-milk cheese, resinous from its pine-bark casing; Septmoncel from the Jura, ranked by some experts above Roquefort; England's esoteric Blue Vinny. . . . But no matter: there is enough fine cheese in my own country to last my time and give it edge, savor, and unctuousness. And there is always the hope that, like a new planet, a truly supreme American cheese will swim into my ken, and that, like Cortez in Keats' sonnet, I shall at last look

With a wild surmise,
Silent, upon a peak in dairyin'.

Do Not Destroy These Originals!

. . . I always took a delight in a singularity.
Margaret, Duchess of Newcastle

The idea of the Average Man was created by the brilliant Belgian astronomer and statistician, Adolphe Quételet (1796–1874). From his statistical studies Quételet drew the conclusion that the average or mean man is a fruitful concept; that moral and intellectual qualities are measurable; and that therefore a kind of "social physics" is possible. "The man that I consider here," wrote Quételet, "is analogous to the center of gravity; he is the mean about which oscillate the social elements."

Long after the scientist Quételet have come the priests and theologians who blew up his hypothesis into a faith, its prophet being the average man, its holy sign the bell-shaped curve. Among these wonder-workers are the makers of "personality" tests, industrial personnel psychologists, mass-communication geniuses, poll takers, media analysts, market researchers, adjustment counselors, many college presidents, and most successful politicians: those for whom the nonaverage man fulfills the functions of a personal devil.

As I would not quarrel with any doctrine grounded on pure faith, so I do not quarrel with this one. We might merely note in passing that whatever is cogent in it finds its source in the nonaverage brain of Monsieur Quételet. Even to think of a *dull* idea requires a superior mind.

Quételet's Average Man is commonly contrasted with the Great Man. But it is no less proper to contrast him with the Eccentric Man, who may have no more magnitude than the Average Man but is otherwise unlike him. Nowadays dwindling attention is paid the Eccentric. As an object of worship he is unrewarding: there exists no mass market of eccentrics. However, before the species dies out completely, like the whooping crane, let us pay the Eccentric the tribute of a few minutes' consideration. This is little to give him, for unlike the Average Man—a Moloch for sacrifice—the Eccentric usually asks only to be let alone. Indeed this is often his most marked eccentricity.

One might begin by arguing that it is the eccentric who is the truly normal man. That is, he dares to be himself, which is what Henry Jones would like to be, only the neighbors would talk. In a sense the eccentric is our surrogate, our vicar. He takes upon him the cross of whim which the rest of us shrewdly suppress. He is humanity's Punch or Jack-in-the-box, a type and a toy for which we feel a kind of derisive affection. But there is a Punch, a Jack-in-the-box in us all. The eighteenth-century English lords who kept an Ornamental Hermit on the estate and the payroll were, we are told, being modishly gothic. But perhaps they were also expressing the hermit hid deep in every man. Their level of taste being what it was, they did not know how to symbolize a love of withdrawal except by ostentation.

In one of his manifestations the eccentric is merely a man with an excess of good sense. Failing to use the checkrein of common irrationality, he permits reasonableness to get out of hand. Visit the Anatomical Museum of University College in London and you will come upon a cabinet containing the neatly wired skeleton of the philosopher Jeremy Bentham, dressed in the clothes he was wearing at his death in 1832. His will provided for this permanent window display. It also provided that his body be dissected. This was accordingly done, and an eyewitness of Bentham's posthumous devotion to the cause of science speaks of "the stern simplicity of that hour in which the principle of utility triumphed over the imagination and the heart." As a partial consequence of Bentham's will, the Anatomy Act was passed, removing legal barriers to dissection. Now—was Jeremy an eccentric? Or was he merely carrying out—to the final extremity—his idea, which has also been adopted by us, of the greatest good for the greatest number? I say he was so sane that he seems queer, whereas the rest of us, who look forward to encumbering with our remains a vast area of valuable real estate, are merely queer in such large numbers that we seem sane. Jeremy Bentham, peace to your ash—pardon, your skeleton.

What shall we say of the estimable sixteenth-century French humanist Guillaume Budé? Once, informed by his servant that the house was on fire, Budé replied, "Go tell your mistress. You know I leave all household matters in her hands." But, after you have laughed at Budé, recollect also that we probably owe to him the *Bibliothèque Nationale* and in part the revival of Greek learning in Europe. His achievements and his somewhat bizarre anticipation of the theory of the division of labor may very well be connected.

A notable contrast to Budé's bored attitude to conflagration is the impetuous nineteenth-century Englishman John Mytton who once set fire to his nightshirt in order to get rid of the hiccups. He succeeded, but I should make clear that he happened to be inside the nightshirt.

If all of us slept twenty-three hours a day, the man who persisted in staying awake for sixteen would seem eccentric. Yet the man of high intellect is rather in this position. His mind is always working. Mine is almost always asleep. To me he seems absent-minded because his mind is always present. But it is present in a country from which I am shut out.

Take the chemist and physicist Henry Cavendish (1731–1810), who was one of the richest men in England —a situation available to any fool who chooses the right ancestors—and also the first man to combine oxygen and hydrogen into water. Cavendish cared nothing for dress, social diversion, or, I regret to say, women. He had his meals delivered to him through a hole in his laboratory wall. He constructed a second staircase so that he might never encounter domestics or visitors. When he wanted a book from his own shelves he would go there as if to a public library and sign a formal receipt. He was something less than a normal man. But also something more. A memoir by one of his few friends sums him up brilliantly: "An intellectual head, thinking; a pair of wonderful acute eyes, observing; a pair of very skilful hands, experimenting or recording, are all that I realize in reading his memorials."

The eccentric as monomaniac is usually a pitiful case. But not always. Sir Edwin Chadwick (1800–1890) lived a long, useful life devoted almost entirely to the disposal of liquid manure. He was crazy about sewage, he lived for drains. His single-handed efforts created our modern disposal systems. We are proud of our bathrooms, and justly so; but, at the appropriate moment, give a thought to that eccentric, Sir Edwin Chadwick.

Just as eccentricity is sometimes merely an exuberance of good sense, so is it sometimes an exuberance of imagination. There was a man who walked to the horizon and touched the sky with his finger; who saw a tree filled with angels; who, with his wife, received, quite naked, a guest in their arbor, stating that they were Adam and Eve. This man nevertheless was one of the few who knew what he wanted: "not to gather gold, but to make glorious shapes expressing god-like sentiments." He was William Blake, poet, artist, and, if you will, lunatic.

But is the eidetic vision lunacy—or perhaps a gift marking the saint and the prophet, precisely as a gift for combinatorial arithmetic marks the great stock-market operator? It is a hard question. I will plump for Blake, who will be remembered when all we self-satisfied normals are dead. But I will not plump for one poor fellow I have read about who possessed eidetic vision to a degree that enabled him to see his own double in the chair opposite.

This other self got to arguing with him. Day after day he and him argued, with him, alas, too often winning the controversy. This mortified him—I mean he. The situation became more and more miserable until there was only one way left to settle the dispute. He put his affairs in order, paid all his bills, and, as the clock struck twelve on New Year's Eve, put a pistol inside his mouth and fired.

Up to our own time the rarest kind of eccentric was the man whose brain had a time warp; that is, one who literally lived in the future, at least in part. The thirteenth-century monk Roger Bacon was such a one, and, as I recall, he got into trouble. That is natural enough; a man who acts in accordance with things that are to come is bound to appear as odd as if he should act in accordance with the time of Julius Caesar or Sennacherib. When I first read the books of Georg Groddeck (1866–1934) I felt he might be such a man. Groddeck dubbed himself "The Wild Analyst." Count Keyserling calls him "eccentric through and through." (Incidentally, in less than a week, by a combination of psychotherapy and massage, Groddeck cured Keyserling of a relapsing phlebitis which other doctors had given up in despair.) Groddeck's hypothesis of the "It" (which is you as you are at conception and which continues to give you orders all your life); his notion that disease is *purposive;* his idea that, to cure my constipation, I must first find out what my motive is for being constipated; his fancy that people die of the disease they prefer and more or less when they wish: all this sounds almost like quackery. Almost, but not quite; for a good deal of it has crept into actual therapy since his death; and the rest of it has a curious, disturbing vibration, as if Groddeck had stumbled by intuition upon the psychology of the next century. Naturally he was put down by many as an eccentric, and I think he rather enjoyed the reputation. Groddeck, we are told, had incalculable charm. Many eccentrics do. They are not all crusty recluses like Cavendish, or the cynic Diogenes, who might be called the patron saint of eccentrics.

The Greek scholar Richard Porson is usually listed canonically among the eccentrics merely because he would drink anything, lamp alcohol, embrocation, even water; was so careless about his personal appearance that a single shirt constituted his entire luggage for a visit of several days; and was so rude and overbearing that Sam Johnson beside him seems like the product of a girls' finishing school. The only Porson anecdote that to my mind has the genuine eccentric ring is his abstracted reply when the banker-poet Samuel Rogers invited him to dinner: "Thank you, no, I dined yesterday."

A Bohemian like Porson may be an eccentric, but there is no necessary connection. A man who refuses to conform because he is naturally lazy, dirty, or averse to responsibility is merely a lazy, dirty, or irresponsible man. Similarly the miser is not an eccentric; he is a sick man. The Collyer brothers were not eccentrics; they were crazy. The true eccentric should not be interfered with but carefully preserved. He is in good health, only a different health than ours.

The full-flower eccentric is what his name implies. He is off-center. If he is too far off-center he belongs in a loony bin. If he is off-center, permanently, obstinately, but only on a single point, he is not an eccentric but a crank. Examples: circle-squarers, cube-duplicators, Baconians, gravity-removers (but beware! someone in the future may discover levity), racialists of all stripes and colors, saucer-seers. But a monomaniac about something sensible (remember Sir Edwin Chadwick) does not enter this category.

What is an eccentric? First, the eccentric at his best is a *little* off-center *generally*. That is, his view of the whole universe is colored and permeated with eccentricity. He sees everything through eccentric glasses, just as the true humorist sees everything through humorous glasses—because he cannot help it. Second, his eccentricity may be inconvenient socially, like that of Cavendish, but it must not be too disagreeable; and, if it be charming, all the better. Third, his eccentricity must be permitted full play: that is, he must be so placed that society either excuses or overlooks it. In effect, that means he is apt to be either quite rich or quite poor. There are middle-class eccentrics, but they operate against handicaps.

Fourth follows from third: the perfect eccentric, like the perfect dandy, is at once un-self-conscious and self-assured. Once put on the defensive by the normal, he begins to crumble. This combination of un-self-consciousness and self-assurance is found most frequently among members of the British upper classes; and any student of the subject knows if you want high-grade ore, that is the mine to work. It is in a class society (but it must not be too rigid) that eccentricity flourishes. It is in a democratic society stressing the liberty of the individual that eccentricity has a hard row to hoe.

The aristocratic outlook, which need have nothing to do with blue blood or solid bank balances, seems somehow linked with the eccentric outlook, at least sufficiently often to be noticeable. Years ago in my college days I had a friend who came of a distinguished Peruvian-French family. His father, a small, dapper gentleman of remote demeanor and exquisite manners, I knew very slightly. But I feel nonetheless that I knew him very well, and only from one anecdote. My friend and his father lived in a modest hotel suite. Day after day small objects, cufflinks and the like, kept disappearing from the old gentleman's chest of drawers. The sneak thief could not be traced. Finally the aristocrat from the Andes dealt with the matter once and for all. He left a note in the top drawer reading *Petty thief, I despise you!* There you have eccentricity at its most winning. It seems to involve the whole man. It stops just short of the unbalanced. Its noble quixotism has its own offbeat sanity.

As with my Peruvian acquaintance, a single sentence will sometimes seem to bring an entire character into focus. The Victorian mathematician, Augustus De Morgan, quotes an old and slightly deaf Cambridge don who in the course of an argument interjected: "I don't quite hear what you say, but I beg to differ entirely with you."

I should say that the most interesting eccentrics are aristocrats, either worldly or intellectual. A Churchill, visiting President Roosevelt, will not think twice about appearing in his host's bedroom for a conference, draped in a bath towel or less. An Einstein can pass an entire lifetime without bending his powerful mind to the problem of a haircut. Both are superior to convention—Churchill because men like himself *make* convention (which is but fossilized history); Einstein because in a world in which $E = mc^2$ a haircut $= 0$. When the two aristocratic types merge in a single eccentric individual, we get someone like the naturalist Charles Waterton.

As a scientist Waterton doesn't amount to much. Nor as a writer. His achievement—of which he seems to have been quite unconscious—centers in his creation of a character, himself. It is a work of art comparable to Sterne's Uncle Toby or Dickens' Old 'Un. He made out of eccentricity what I believe our current great statesmen, in their more heavily reflective moments, call a Way of Life. The full Watertonian flavor can be enjoyed only through a reading of his absurd, delightful book *Wanderings in South America* and of some of the many studies of his career.

Waterton (1782–1865) was a wealthy Yorkshire squire of a good though not noble family of the old faith. Among his direct ancestors he numbered Sir Thomas More. One of the kindest, most generous of men, he has the distinction of having been beloved not merely by mankind but by numerous species of the lower animals, including a sloth which for a time he kept in his bedroom. (Waterton would not have seen the point of Thurber's seal-in-the-bedroom cartoon. His natural reaction would have been, "Why not?") In South America his English sporting blood, which in noneccentrics manifests itself in the epically dull fox hunt, impelled him to ride on the back of a crocodile. He once, as part of a research experiment, slept with a fourteen-foot serpent, the coulacanara. Night after night he extended his big toe beyond the tent flap in the eager expectation that another of his friends, the vampire bat, would suck it; but he was rejected. Waterton put into real, if eccentric, practice Schweitzer's abstract doctrine of Reverence for Life: for him even the carrion crow had the redeeming feature of being a very early riser. Waterton himself in his eighties rose at 3 A.M. to spend an hour worshiping his God and several more in the most violent of exercises, including clambering among trees "like an adolescent gorilla" (Norman Douglas' phrase) as part of his bird-watching program.

Once, traveling down the St. Lawrence, he met a bug on his neck and struck up one of those short-lived shipboard acquaintances. He inquired of the ticketless stowaway whether it was bound from Canada to the United States or vice versa. Then, after a decent interval of conversation, he tenderly deposited the bug on some baggage, advising it to get ashore at the first opportunity. Waterton made friends everywhere. He had a special affection for those who rarely receive what the child psychologists now call T.L.C. (Tender Loving Care): toads, for example. On his estate, which resembled an exclusive animals' country club more than it did a zoo, he arranged the stables in such a manner as to make it convenient for the horses to conduct social conversation. In the evening he never failed to kiss his chimpanzee good night. I am happy, remembering the misogynist Cavendish, to state that the chimpanzee was female. It is the mark of the great eccentric that his oddities are often touched with the Good, the True, and the Beautiful—for instance, Waterton created the first bird sanctuary.

On the other hand, the eccentric does not err too dangerously in the direction of the normal. Waterton was the soul of hospitality, but one of his hostly gestures involved a semiannual dinner (in a grotto) for one hundred lunatics, drawn from a convenient asylum.

At seventy-seven Waterton could scratch the back of his head with his big toe and would do so for the gratification of his close friends. He was not above practical joking: in his eighties (probably his finest period) he received a guest by barking at him from underneath the table and inflicting a harmless flesh wound on his leg. He was brave: shortly before his death he invented a pair of wings and was only prevented by force from flying off the roof of an outhouse. Once, having been advised that dripping water would help his sprained ankle, he held it for a time under Niagara Falls.

The anthropologists tell us that a given region in the course of the centuries tends to develop a standard physical type. Waterton's animal friends, in obedience to this law, began to echo his own eccentricity: one of his favored cronies was a duck with a bill where her rump should have been, so that she fed paradoxically in a kind of eccentric circling.

Waterton, being a beautifully balanced eccentric rather than an eccentric eccentric, never went too far. He would not have been guilty of the excesses of, let us say, his contemporary, Lord Egerton, who dined daily with a dozen dogs, in armchairs and napkins, each attended by an obsequious servant. The student of Waterton ends in hearty agreement with his biographer, Father Wood: "The world would be much better than it is if such eccentricity were more common." But of course if it were more common it would not be eccentricity.

Is the practical joker an eccentric? He is often so deemed. But the title is too precious for such prodigal use. The ordinary practical joker is usually a man of exemplary normality, not to say distinguished dullness. The preceding sentence automatically brings to mind the name of Calvin Coolidge. The thirtieth President of the United States liked to hide in the shrubbery, then jump out and surprise his harried Secret Service guards. Jack Dempsey had a passion for hot-foots, if that is the proper plural of this otherwise singular amusement.* The young Charles Lindbergh drew deep satisfaction from such hilarities as stuffing a friend's pillowcase with a dead polecat. I admire Mr. Lindbergh greatly, but his mind hardly seems to me, any more than do the Coolidgean and Dempseyan minds, to speed in a true eccentric orbit.

The primitive practical joke, like the weird election bet, is a wistful attempt to discharge the faint eccentric impulse that lies buried in even a Coolidge. It usually takes an aggressive form. Aimed at humiliation, it is antisocial behavior of a type to which by common consent no penalties attach: it is tax-free. Not only does it require no imagination; imagination would act as a brake. Proof: the very bottom of the practical-joke ladder is occupied by the gleeful gooser; and the gooser, his mind unstained by intelligence, may most commonly be found in certain Hollywood circles.

There are at least two other kinds of practical jokers, however, who attain a rung not far below that on which

---

* Several of the examples directly following are lifted from H. Allen Smith's classic *Compleat Practical Joker*, dangerously available for 25 cents.

perch the pure eccentrics. The first is the Witty Practical Joker. For him the discomfiture of the jokee is a negligible by-product. He uses the joke essentially as a means of commenting satirically on human nature. It becomes satire in action, lived-out, dramatized.

Of this art the late Charles MacArthur was a master. The journalist Joseph McCarthy tells the story. One of MacArthur's tennis-court acquaintances was a young Englishman, innocent of talent, who held down a $65-a-week job with an oil company. MacArthur, irritated at Basil's habit of anxiously and overfrequently consulting his watch, decided to remove him to a sphere where he would have to worry about neither time nor money. He began to bring him along with him to Hollywood story conferences. When the producers grew curious about his companion, MacArthur explained that his friend was a brilliant young English dramatist, "the next Noel Coward . . . not interested in working for pictures. . . . I wouldn't make a move on a story line unless I asked his advice." Finally the studio head couldn't stand it any longer. "Could Basil be hired?" was his shrewd question. "No," said MacArthur flatly. But the studio head, more than a match for the situation, arranged a secret meeting with Basil. MacArthur had commanded his protégé to hold out for $2,000 per week, but the poor oil clerk gave in at $1,500. By following MacArthur's careful coaching he held down the job for over a year. After having refused every story sent him on the ground that it didn't suit his talent, which was certainly true, he was sent to northern Canada to research a picture about the Hudson's Bay Company. As it is difficult to be a wastrel among the Eskimos, Basil saved a fortune before returning to the great capital of illusion. That Basil was finally unmasked is beside the point. MacArthur had succeeded in what must have been his real aim: to dramatize his private opinion of the geniuses who run Hollywood.

Practical joking of this high order is miles away from the hot-foot and the goose. It is philosophical, noble, and a social benefaction.

Equally admirable, though for different reasons, is the pure Specialist, or Virtuoso of practical jokes. His interest lies neither in humiliation nor satire, but in the perfection of the thing itself. Art for art's sake is his credo, or perhaps oddness for oddness' sake.

Historically the two greatest masters in this not over-crowded field are the American Hugh Troy and the late Horace De Vere Cole, an Englishman. For an extended and scholarly treatment of Messrs. Cole and Troy I must refer you to the reflective pages of Dr. H. Allen Smith. It is perhaps enough to recall for you that it was Mr. Troy who carefully constructed the rhinoceros tracks in the snow of the Cornell campus. In a feat of the same general pattern as Mr. Troy's, Mr. Cole once arranged to fill nocturnally the Piazza di San Marco (which is almost entirely surrounded by canals) with baffling but incontrovertible evidence of the recent visitations of innumerable horses. To call such men practical jokers is to call Oistrakh a mere fiddler.

Yet, ungrudging as our admiration must be of both the Wit and the Virtuoso, I hesitate to call them simon-pure eccentrics. It is their self-consciousness, their professionalism that gives me pause. Their oddness, beautiful in itself, is none the less a kind of deliberate assault on the order of the universe. The true eccentric is an un-self-conscious amateur whose connection with the dull quotidian world is too tenuous even for opposition.

From our canon we must also exclude the following: those forced into weird lives by some uncontrollable circumstance—freaks of all sorts, misers, transvestites, sexual monsters like the Marquis de Sade, calculating prodigies, and in general the obsessed; those who, like the amiable publicity impresario Jim Moran, are impelled by practical considerations—you may remember that it was Mr. Moran who sold a certain refrigerator to an Eskimo and who helped to advance the dairymen's cause by confronting Gelett Burgess with a purple cow in a hotel lobby; regularly employed eccentrics like the career-zany Brusquet who served as court jester under Francis I, Henry II, and Francis II; publicity-seekers such as goldfish-swallowers, flagpole-sitters, or—plummeting to the lowest level—Elvis Presley; Peck's Bad Boy exhibitionists such as Jerry Lewis (on the other hand there do exist genuinely eccentric comics: consider the wonderful Bob and Ray); the cool-headed creators of elaborate hoaxes, such as Mr. Lozier who in 1824 sold several thousand worried New Yorkers on a proposal to saw off the lower, overcrowded end of Manhattan and attach it further uptown, in order to equalize the weight; those who have really abandoned our world entirely, like the French decadent who walked down the Champs Élysées trailing a live lobster at the end of a string because, as he said with understandable admiration, it knew the secrets of the sea. To all these there clings a flavor of the deliberate, the excessive, or the unbalanced.

Shall we admit the hobbyist? At what point does he elevate himself to the rank of eccentric? A nice point, not easily resolved. One thing is clear: the hobby should be statistically rare. The Sunday painter, the hi-fi fan, the basement-workshop troll—no matter how single-minded their devotion, they are but normals. There are too many of them.

Then where shall we draw the line? For example, campanologists form a numerous company—but not *very* numerous. Shortly before his death in 1799 William Elphich, yeoman of Sussex, calculated that he had pulled the treble bell at Chiddingly Church a total of 8,766 hours, or just over a solid year. Is the good Elphich to be assigned a place in the eccentric Heaven, free of all treble, out of chime into eternity? Or is he to be ignored, along with dun-colored hobbyists—trout fishermen, bird-watchers, and such small deer? I am unsure but inclined to give him the benefit of the doubt. Bell-ringing *—a mathematical exercise as well as an unusual sport—seems to have something of the smack of true eccentricity.

No question arises, however, in the case of the English sternutophile Margaret Thompson. Miss Thompson died in 1776 leaving a will whose more important provisions included the following: her coffined body to be covered with snuff; her bearers to be the six greatest snuff-takers in the parish; each to wear a snuff-colored hat; six maidens to accompany the bearers, each carrying a box of the best Scotch snuff with which to refresh themselves on the way; the minister to precede the corpse, inhaling snuff—not over

---

* The reader who wishes to read a first-rate detective story which is also a first-rate manual of campanology is directed to Dorothy Sayers' *The Nine Tailors.*

a pound; her servant to distribute a large handful of snuff on the ground every twenty yards. There you have, in Margaret Thompson who sneezed her way to Paradise, the genuine article. There you have the hobbyist whose ruling passion, strong in death, is surely shared by few.

Margaret Thompson was single-minded. But I suspect she was also strong-minded; and it is notable that the latter term is so frequently applied, with more respect than derision, to eccentric old ladies. Dickens' Betsy Trotwood was as odd as her colleague Mr. Dick. But her mind was as energetic as his was flaccid: they are polar to each other. I call to mind another ancient female eccentric, the admirable Sophia Banks, who died in 1818. A visitor happening to remark, "It is a fine day, ma'am," she replied, "I know nothing at all about it. You must speak to my brother upon that subject when you are at dinner." I know nothing at all about her brother, but it is hard to think him as interesting, or at least as mentally uncompromising, as his sister. The strong-minded eccentric old ladies of Boston have become proverbial. None pleases me more than the one who said, "There is no doubt about it, the modern thunderstorm no longer clears the air."

There was something Bostonian too about Lady Hester Stanhope. She was one of the three daughters of Charles Earl Stanhope by his first wife, who was a sister of the great William Pitt. (*All* the Pitts were a little odd.) For a time she lived like a female pasha, or perhaps an early Gertrude Stein, as a kind of object of pilgrimage in Syria. She was, though certainly a character, hardly a lovable one; yet is there not something endearing about her powerful emotional and intellectual attachment to her own pedal arch? A kitten could walk under it, she would declare proudly; and she was not afraid to state that her dislike of her countrymen was grounded, so to speak, on her conviction that their soles were disgracefully flat. When the French poet Lamartine, then not very famous, visited her she prophesied great things for him, but not till she had determined that water could flow under his arch without wetting it.

I intend no slur on the male sex. Massive masculine intellects are just as frequently associated with true eccentricity. Herbert Spencer, whose knowledge was almost as total as his unreadability, would stop London traffic while at frequent intervals he took his own pulse. During train rides he slung a hammock in his compartment, and always carried several pounds of manuscript by three trailing yards of cord tied around his waist. Such ingratiating habits mollify an otherwise rather rock-bound character.

Or take Sir Francis Galton, eminent in so many fields, renowned for his studies of inherited ability. In him we see mental superiority intimately linked with seeming eccentricity. I say "seeming," because upon close examination his oddity is seen to be both rational and fruitful—which is the case, though we shy away from admitting it, with much oddity. From James Newman's *The World of Mathematics* we learn that the great Victorian counted and measured everything, from the frequency of yawns to the number of fidgets per minute among a lecture audience. Compulsion? It might appear so; yet from these eccentric practices Galton drew conclusions that led to his famous concept of statistical correlation. What might in another be incipient lunacy was with him merely highly unorthodox curiosity. Mr. Newman writes: "His 'passionate desire to subjugate the body to the spirit' led him to subject himself to some strange experiments; the practice of slow self-suffocation had a strange fascination for him. Having invented an optical underwater device he amused himself by reading while submerged in his bath; on several occasions he almost drowned because he 'forgot that [he] was nearly suffocating.' He describes various adventures in auto-suggestion, such as pretending that a comic figure in *Punch* possessed divine attributes or that everyone he met while walking in Piccadilly was a spy." With men like Galton it is not so much oddness as energy of mind that generates eccentric behavior. From Socrates to Bertrand Russell, those whose mental lives are charged with a power possibly five hundred times greater than that of, let us say, the average Congressman, have betrayed their interior ebullition by behavior generally set down as irregular.

An observer named John Thomas Smith, writing in 1818, said, "It is scarcely possible . . . to pass through the streets of London without noticing what is generally denominated a *character*, either in dress, walk, pursuits, or propensities." Idealizing the past is a cheap and easy practice; yet I wonder whether in the London of today Mr. Smith would find so colorful a field of observation. The welfare state, whatever its virtues, is by its very nature bound to set a premium on conventionality: social security is its watchword in more than one sense. Whenever a government becomes certain that it knows what is good for its citizens, those citizens become more and more like citizens and less and less like "characters." The glorious ideal of life, liberty, and the pursuit of happiness loses some of its radiance once everybody has agreed on a definition of happiness. Perhaps we have there the reason why until recently England produced so many eccentrics. Formerly the Englishman would never have dreamed of defining the word happiness—except insofar as he was convinced that merely being English was itself happiness. But once you fix its content—whether it be eternal salvation or the continuous production of consumable goods—you run the risk of heading smack into Orwell's 1984.

I do not deny that eccentrics exist today. But the proof of their rarity is the eagerness with which they are sought out by biographers and journalists, as if they were an obsolescent race. You will find several examples in Joseph Mitchell's collection of odd fish, published under the title of *McSorley's Wonderful Saloon.* They are mostly men and women who lead obscure lives, on the edge of so-called civilized society. Perhaps the most genuine eccentric, by the standards we have been laying down, among Mr. Mitchell's discoveries is Joe Gould, the Greenwich Village Diogenes who, upon inheriting $1,000, bought a big radio, took it out on Sixth Avenue and kicked it to pieces. Mr. Gould lives by his own lights; he would not understand our modern admiration for "smoothness." But when we read about him we sense that he is a survival, not a true contemporary.

Something in our society, not necessarily entirely to be condemned, operates against the production of such characters as crowd the delightful pages of G. K. Chesterton's *Autobiography.* To show what I mean let me quote from that precious book:

I recall another quite Dickensian scene; a bland, round-faced little man in spectacles, the sort that is always chaffed anywhere; and a fellow-clerk named Carr, of more mysterious humors; both ghosts from my father's time of apprenticeship. At intervals the more sombre clerk would call out across the office, "Mr. Hannay!" The round face, bright with its smile and spectacles, would bob up with never-failing freshness and expectation: "Yes, Mr. Carr." Then Mr. Carr would fix him with a sphinxlike visage and say in hollow but resounding tones, "Boundless Space!" And then Mr. Carr would turn more briskly to the other clerks, shaking his head, and repeating in a hopeless tone, "He can't grasp it!"

Try to imagine that scene occurring ten stories above Madison Avenue.

Chesterton himself was a fine specimen. He may well be forgotten as a writer and remembered as a character, as with Dr. Johnson. I like to recall how, once, when he was making a living as a vagabond lecturer, he sent a wire to his wife: "Am in Market Harborough. Where ought I to be?" In our sensible view the eccentric is always in Market Harborough.

Anthony Eden is doubtless an admirable and useful person. His father, Sir William Eden, was less admirable and less useful. But Sir William could and would say things of which his distinguished son is quite incapable, such as the magnificently downright "The progress of civilization is the decay of taste." Can you picture Her Majesty's former First Minister shaking his fist at the pouring rain outside the window and ejaculating, "Just *like* you, God!"? Or tearing from the wall a barometer indicating "Fair" and hurling it through the window into that same rain, with the words, "There, you damned fool, see for yourself!" Or refusing to stay in a house because the crimson ramblers and calceolarias grew against red brick—"all of them framed in self-satisfaction." Gone are the Edens, gone the Father Days!

Perhaps I am being unduly unsentimental and ungrateful. I have had the good fortune to know in my own drab time a fair number of eccentrics. They have irradiated my life, as they have the lives of all they meet, for we need them badly. I think of Gjon Mili, the great *Life* photographer, whose speech is wild poetry. (In the course of three minutes I heard him refer scornfully to "a country pumpkin," to some proposal as "not worth a can of beans," and to a newly married friend as having "tied a milestone around his neck.") I think of Sinclair Lewis, of whom I have written elsewhere, of Robert Benchley, of James Thurber. . . . But most of all, when I reflect upon eccentricity at its most charming, I think of a distinguished mathematician who died in 1955, Professor Edward Kasner.

I cannot render him for you, that I know. It is part of the nature of eccentricity to be unable to leave behind a complete record of itself. Anecdotes, reminiscences do not suffice. True eccentricity, not freakishness or mere oddity but the capacity to see the whole world on a slant, is like a perfume. It is the permeating essence of a personality, and when that personality dies, the perfume disappears, and nothing can recapture it. Perhaps that is one of the secrets of Dickens' continued popularity—he supplies in imperishable form the eccentrics for which our souls thirst.

Edward Kasner (1878–1955) occupied until his death

the Adrain chair in mathematics at Columbia University. His specialty was the higher geometry, particularly topology. Topology is a branch of mathematics which has nothing to do with measurement, size, shape, numbers, or quantities. It deals with position, with the characteristics of nonrigid figures and bodies, with those properties that do not change under distortion. It is concerned with the geometrical qualities of doughnuts, pretzels, one-sided surfaces, rubber bands, knots, bottles with neither inside nor outside, the trade-mark of Ballantine's Ale, and the answer to the problem of how many colors are needed to color *any* map so as to distinguish countries that have a common boundary. In *The World of Mathematics* Dr. Newman describes this queer subject as starting from "the sound premise that there are no rigid objects, that everything in the world is a little askew, and is further deformed when its position is altered." Everything in the world is a little askew . . . topology was precisely the subject to engage a mind like Dr. Kasner's.

Like Thoreau, of whom he was a spiritual descendant, Dr. Kasner had early in his life drawn a line between what was essential and what was not. Unlike Thoreau, he did not make a doctrine of it. He made no noise in a world that he regarded with a benevolent but quizzical glance, as if the rest of us were somehow missing something. He achieved a transient fame, I seem to recollect, as one of "the twelve men who understood Einstein."

He was a small man, with a deceptively gentle voice, for hidden within it lay an overtone of tolerant irony. I never knew him to wear anything but a pepper-and-salt suit, winter and summer, and I do not believe he owned more than one. He had long ago discarded the belt as an unnecessary modern invention, and spent a good deal of his time holding up his trousers. At his lectures the students were often torn between conic sections and equally abstruse mathematical calculations as to whether or not Dr. Kasner's pants would fall down before the lecture period's elapsed time. His lectures were thoroughly unconventional and he was one of the greatest teachers I have ever known. Mr. Newman recalls: "He could make you see intricate mathematical relationships by his verbal images, by the graceful gestures of his delicate hands, and by the spidery, badly executed, but remarkably illuminating diagrams he liked so much to scrawl on the blackboard." Frequently he would wander into the classroom and put a few problems on the board. Then he would wander out and perhaps appear a half-hour later, glance at what the students at the board had been doing, and disappear. After all, he figured, it was the students, not he, who were concerned with the solution of the problem. He never hesitated to interrupt his more formal lectures by suddenly asking questions of the students. I have seen him do this (a difficult technique) with a class of ten and an audience of three thousand.

During the fall and winter he liked to live at the Half Moon Hotel in Coney Island, partly because in that season no one else would think of doing such a thing, and so he secured both privacy and special rates; partly because the sight of such quantities of sand set his mind working on problems of large numbers. He used to view trees in foliage with the same speculative glance. If you care to note this down, the number of grains of sand on the beach at Coney Island is 10^{20}, give or take a few grains.

Dr. Kasner had two main audiences: the great mathematicians of two continents, and children. I think he slightly preferred the children because they were more teachable. It was his theory that the way to interest children in mathematics was to begin with difficult concepts and only gradually work up to the multiplication table. It was a sound theory. His own nine-year-old nephew was so apt a student of higher mathematics that he invented a number. Asked to think up a name for an enormously large but still finite number, he suggested *googol*. As the spelling suggests, this has many zeros in it—to be exact it is the number 1 followed by a hundred zeros. The young genius went on to invent a still larger number, the *googolplex*, which is 1 followed by a *googol* of zeros. You may write it $10^{10^{100}}$. Kindergarteners took kindly to Dr. Kasner and his googols, and soon satisfied themselves that all the raindrops descending on New York in a century would fall far short of a googol.

Dr. Kasner had another way of teaching large numbers to small tots. He would ask them to guess the length of the Eastern coast line of the United States. After a "sensible" guess had been made—say 2,000 miles—he would proceed step by step to point out that this figure increased enormously if you measured the perimeter of each bay and inlet, then that of every projection and curve of each of these, then the distance separating every small particle of coast-line matter, each molecule, atom, etc. Obviously the coast line is as long as you want to make it. The children understood this at once; Kasner had more trouble with grownups.

He was very fond of solitary walks, particularly along the Palisades and, in anticipation of his needs, had a series of lunch boxes, filled with teapots and almost imperishable foods cached in secret places along the route. He carried his own tea and sugar. This foresighted system saved him time and trouble, and allowed him more opportunity for reflection.

Another goal of his Palisades walks was a certain worldly casino where games of chance were popular. He used to go there, not to gamble, but to study the laws of probability in action. He must have looked odd surrounded by the sharp, tough faces of the players, like Charlie Chaplin in a den of gentlemen thieves.

The Kasnerian humor is difficult to describe. Impish? Childlike? Offbeat? None of the words fits. He was fond of taking his summer vacations in Brussels, because there was a particular chair at a particular outdoor café that he had become attached to. He also liked Brussels because he said that from there he could easily organize a mountain-climbing expedition to the highest point in Belgium. He said he felt great satisfaction in attaining the peak of this eminence. I asked him how high it was. "Twelve feet above sea level," he replied.

Our encounters frequently had as their setting a midtown Automat. I frequented this Automat because I was poor, Kasner because, as he stoutly maintained, it had the best food in New York. I never quite perceived the force of this argument. It was not a product of ignorance either, because every once in a while, dressed in his drooping, pepper-and-salt suit and a cap (he never wore anything but a boy's cap that gave him the look of an elderly urchin) he would visit a first-class restaurant, solely for the purpose of reassuring himself that the Automat was superior.

Once at an informal evening attended by half a dozen

logicians and mathematicians, one of the latter ventured the opinion that to become a good mathematician you should *not* have good teachers, as they prevented you from learning by yourself. He then added, courteously, "I was lucky. I had only one great teacher—Dr. Kasner here." Kasner looked up, his eyes twinkled, he said mildly, "I had none."

Meditations of a
Mathematical Moron

Lucy, dear child, mind your arithmetic. You know, in the first sum of yours I ever saw, there was a mistake. You had carried two (as a cab is licensed to do) and you ought, dear Lucy, to have carried but one. Is this a trifle? What would life be without arithmetic but a scene of horrors?

SYDNEY SMITH

My friend G. H. Hardy, who was professor of pure mathematics, . . . told me once that if he could find a proof that I was going to die in five minutes he would of course be sorry to lose me, but this sorrow would be quite outweighed by pleasure in the proof. I entirely sympathized with him and was not at all offended.

BERTRAND RUSSELL

SOME OF MY READERS may recall that Marx Brothers comedy in which quantities of people are crowded one by one into a tiny stateroom until at last forced to come catapulting out. On witnessing this scene you doubtless ticked it off as an interesting case of the law of continuity of an incompressible fluid.

Hanging on my office wall is a treasured Abner Dean original. It portrays Mr. Dean's famous little man sitting all naked and complacent in an armchair in a corner of a room whose walls are covered with mathematical formulas. Caption: No One Can Touch Me. The ancient Egyptians when banqueting would pass a mummy around to remind them of death. So do I keep this drawing at eye level and mind level to warn me of the limitations of abstract thought.

Yet I cannot help asking myself whether these equations are wholly delusive. Mr. Dean's little man, like the people in the Marx Brothers picture, is a collection of particles as well as an immortal soul. He is restricted and therefore in a way protected by certain formulas no less surely than are Newton's planets. In the mysterious metaphors we have agreed to call mathematics all creation is involved, from the symbol-happy logician down to those cunning geometers, the bees. When I trust myself to a ladder I lean upon an equation. Every baby is a formula-baby, for when we say that its growth is a function of its nourishment, what are we citing but a case of the calculus?

These equations do not rule us like tyrants. They seem rather to be part of the structure of our minds, more akin to memory than to a learnable discipline. The toddler, gratified to discover a correspondence between the toes of his right foot and those of his left, has taken his first steps in number theory. The amateur paper hanger who has forgotten all his high-school geometry but somehow manages the job of papering his wall with a minimum of waste is a whistle-stop Euclid. Ralph Greenleaf's built-in space sense makes him a poor relation of the great natural geometers, like the self-taught nineteenth-century genius Steiner.

Just as there are no unseducible women but only inept men (an article of faith with all men and no women) so we may say that there are no nonmathematical minds but only nonmathematical teachers. The mass of us who quail before the word "mathematics" are often merely suffering from a bad persistent case of early pedagogy. We were poisoned in our youth by the notion that mathematics is identical with problem-solving. But in truth it is no more equivalent to problem-solving than music is to counterpoint. As Scott Buchanan puts it in his wonderful little book *Poetry and Mathematics:* "The structures with which mathematics deals are more like lace, the leaves of trees, and the play of light and shadow on a meadow or a human face." The fact is (I quote here from G. H. Hardy's *A Mathematician's Apology*) "most people have some appreciation of mathematics just as most people can enjoy a pleasant tune."

Such enjoyment has nothing to do with being "good" at mathematics. Particularly has it nothing to do with being "quick at figures." As mathematics freed itself from its practical origins, calculation became less and less important. Soon the geniuses of I.B.M. will see to it that no mathematical mind is compelled to waste valuable time laboring in the swamp of mere reckoning.

Even more encouraging, you need not, in order to derive a certain pleasure from the subject, be able to decipher a single page of real mathematics. Mathematics is one of the

few sciences that yields dividends to the perimeter-reader.
I, to take a handy example, am a mathematical moron. I
stopped at the calculus, which I understand but cannot
really handle. Yet for some twenty years I have found it a
rewarding hobby to read *about* mathematics and mathematicians, cheerfully vaulting every equation that looked
at me too sternly. In consequence I do not feel ill at ease
when I visit this vast and beautiful mansion, even though
I know I can never dwell within its walls.

It has taken me, as I say, some two decades to collect a
small library of books about mathematics suitable to one
as unlearned as I am. Now a short cut is available. James
Newman has edited a four-volume collection of mathematical writings called *The World of Mathematics*. His title
is just: mathematics is not a subject, it is a world. Within
his 2,500 pages you will, it is true, encounter a few Greek
letters and a few eccentric symbols. But you will also meet
soap bubbles, calculating prodigies, chess-playing machines, the mathematics of golf, the astonishing mind of a
superman named Gauss, birds who count, the laws that
govern poker, a professional teataster, Bernard Shaw on
the vice of gambling and the virtue of insurance, assorted
infinities, a one-sided strip of paper, and even some fiction,
odd or brilliant, involving mathematics. Most anthologies
are merely the sum of their parts, but this one is truly
creative, the product of fifteen years of research by a
superlative editor. *The World of Mathematics* is not a
book. It is an education.

The reflections that follow are not a review of the book,
which has already been considered and praised by authori-

ties. Nor can they be of any conceivable interest to even a barely competent mathematician. They are addressed to my illiterate peers, to those who, without being aware of it, are as capable of drawing delight from reading about mathematics (whether in Newman or elsewhere) as they are capable of drawing delight from listening to music. Throw out the window your antimathematical prejudices born of ill-conducted classrooms, of discouraged teachers, of dust-heaped textbooks, of the delusion that mathematics is a tool for specialists, its dull emblem a meter stick.

Let's start with a few questions. Never mind the answers: interest starts with curiosity, not solutions.

Would anyone here care to push a piano through a piece of paper eight inches by ten inches? Do you think the total number of words printed since the Gutenberg Bible is more or less than 10^{16}? Release the book you now hold in your hand; it will fall; will it *ever* rise? How many possible moves are there in a game of chess? Is the whole always greater than any of its parts? What connection exists between the number of people who will be alive at the end of a given period—and the length of the diameter of a circle relative to its circumference?

Is the geometry you learned at school suitable for drawing a map of the United States? Starting from the beginning of the Christian Era, how many ancestors do you have? Can two men, unrelated, have the same sister? Does *all* of a railway train move in the direction the engine is traveling? How would you proceed to reduce the sun to the dimensions of a pea? If the barber shaves everyone in the village who does not shave himself—does he shave himself? After you have tossed a penny ninety-nine times and it has come up heads every time, what are the chances that on the hundredth toss it will come up tails? Did you ever hear of a closed surface with no outside and no inside? Can you remove your vest without removing your coat? Can you draw an infinitely long curve on a postage stamp? Do human beings exist who cannot count beyond two? What links the shape of a bellying sail to this decimal: 2.7182818. . . . ? Could you afford to join a Christmas Club savings plan whereby you deposited one cent the first week, two cents the second, four cents the third, eight cents the fourth, and so on for fifty-two weeks? How probable is it that of twenty-four random people gathered in a room a pair will have identical birthdays? How many different shapes of tile can you use on your bathroom floor? How many protons and electrons are there in the universe?

It is with such questions as these (among other really profound ones) that much of mathematics deals. That the answers would be comprehensible to my readers I am perfectly sure, inasmuch as they are comprehensible to me.

Being incapable, I cannot talk about mathematics itself. But I can talk about the charm of reading about and around mathematics, for I have sensed that charm, as vividly as one may sense the charm, without ever being quite able to define it, of a lovely face or voice or piece of architecture.

Mathematicians (not necessarily the greatest ones) are fond of citing the rigor and precision of their subject. But it is not at all clear what they are being rigorous and precise *about*. It is the many-meaningedness of mathematics that lends it a curious seduction. Like music, which is also all things to all men, it resists definition, as Proteus resisted capture. Bertrand Russell's is here the classic comment: "Mathematics may be defined as the subject in which we never know what we are talking about, nor whether what we are saying is true." This very uncertainty has its charm, especially in a world like ours, thick with mass-communicators' dogmas. Einstein, with his customary crushing mildness, tells us that "so far as the theorems of mathematics are about reality, they are not certain; so far as they are certain, they are not about reality." I find this comforting rather than appalling.

Aristotle, who was as sure of everything as anyone can be of anything, thought mathematics the study of quantity; whereas Russell, in a less playful mood, thinks of it as the "class of all propositions of the type 'p implies q'," which seems to have little to do with quantity—or indeed (that is the point) with *any* special thing. Willard Gibbs thought of mathematics as a language. Hilbert thought of it as a meaningless game. For Benjamin Peirce it was "the science that draws necessary conclusions." G. H. Hardy joyfully stresses its uselessness; Lancelot Hogben joylessly stresses its practicality. J. S. Mill thought it an empirical science, like chemistry, only more general and more certain, whereas to J. W. N. Sullivan it was an art, and to the wonderful J. J. Sylvester it was "the music of reason." Finally, Spengler is sure that there is no such thing as mathematics, but only mathematicses, differing absolutely with each culture.

I find this ambiguity consoling. It suggests that mathematics has so many mansions that there is room for all of us; it does not appeal merely to one type of mind.

Many of us like to read history and biography. Few suspect that mathematical history and biography are as fascinating as any other kind, and in certain respects more so. In the last analysis what makes biography interesting? I would say it is a matter of dimension. In one way or another, even if it be in the domain of evil, the subject of a good biography is larger than we are. Biography is the literature of superiority, just as surely as journalism is the literature of mediocrity.

Now of all forms of superiority the most interesting is that of genius. And of all forms of genius I would assert that the mathematical is the most unqualified and most undebatable. Even a supreme literary figure—think of Shakespeare—is in perpetuity condemned to defend his reputation against often quite cogent detractions, Shaw's, for example. Even a towering conqueror such as Napoleon can be whittled down by the polemical cutlery of a Tolstoy or an H. G. Wells. And a man—Lincoln—may be universally admired without being able to give us that almost frightening sensation of *absolute* superiority.

But one cannot read a really knowledgeable account—Keynes', let us say, or Sullivan's, or Andrade's—of Isaac Newton without trembling to this eerie thrill. One cannot of course get inside such a mind but one can vibrate to its effects. These effects are shattering in two ways: in scope and in timelessness. To study the career of Newton or Gauss or Archimedes or Poincaré, to emerge from that study with some sense, however vague, of what they did *for all mankind forever* is to feel exalted, knowing that one actually belongs to the same species as these titans. One voyages with them as far as the mind can reach, at least in our present state of human evolution. The great historian of science, the late George Sarton, put it in another way: "In mathematics, as in music, genius can be contemplated in a greater state of purity, and hence the history of mathematics is perhaps more interesting to the psychologist than that of any other science." I would add only that one need not be a psychologist. Einstein was not a supreme mathematician but a supreme theoretical physicist; yet it was mathematical reasoning that led him to the epochal equation $E = mc^2$, of which the universally paralyzing Bomb is one of the *lesser* consequences.

This is the great charm of reading mathematical history, to sense the operation of genius at its absolute. Let me speak of lesser charms. There is a word for the accidental and happy discovery of something one was not looking for. It is serendipity: Columbus' finding of America was serendipitous. The history of mathematics is full of such serendipitous delights. The calculus, upon which a large part of our technical culture rests, sprang from the problems involved in measuring kegs. One of its seemingly most abstract forms—the absolute differential calculus—was, oddly enough, found vital to the construction of that theory of relativity which will form the basic world picture of all our descendants. A seemingly absurd—indeed it is called "imaginary"—magnitude, the square root of minus one, turns out useful to an analysis of alternating currents. And, as Tobias Dantzig reminds us in his fine book *Number: The Language of Science,* the conic sections, invented by the ancient Greeks in an attempt to solve the problem of doubling the size of the altar of an oracle, have so far climaxed their career, to everyone's blank astonishment, by becoming the orbits traced by the planets in their furious races about the sun.

One might suppose, prior to investigation, that mathematicians lead closeted lives, not subject to the dramatic changes and chances of supposedly more adventurous humans. But a little research—try E. T. Bell's *Men of Mathematics*—reveals how wrong is such a judgment. In the first place, there is nothing more perilous, quicker with tension, than a really hand-to-hand encounter with a large idea. (Which is why the story of the Constitutional Convention is far more thrilling than the story of the Revolutionary War that preceded it.) Mathematicians war with ideas incessantly, often tragically.

But, beyond this, mathematicians have often led lives of the most colorful and even bizarre nature. One thinks at once of Galois, far more truly than Chatterton

> *the marvellous boy,*
> *The sleepless soul that perished in his pride,*

spending the night creating his immortal memoir on the theory of groups, and next day, at the age of twenty, perishing in a senseless duel. One thinks of the arithmetician Cardan, half-charlatan, half-genius, who is supposed to have committed suicide on a certain date in order to maintain his reputation as an astrologer. Of the amazing Bernoullis, the Bachs of science. Of Gauss, a supreme combination of mental power and mental versatility. Of Napier who invented not only the logarithm but also artillery capable of killing all cattle within a one-mile radius—and then, possessing wisdom as well as intellect, refused to exploit his device. Of the haberdasher who founded statistics. Of Descartes who created analytic geometry while lying in bed. Of John Harrison, the Yorkshire carpenter who devised the chronometer that finally settled the problem of the longitude. Of John Couch Adams and the discovery of Neptune. Of Omar Khayyám, far more notable as mathematician than as poet. Of the marvellous Indian Ramanujan, of whom it has been said that every positive integer was one of his personal friends; of whom his teacher, Hardy, worried over his disciple's imperfect education, remarked, in a delicious sentence, "It was impossible to allow him to go through life supposing that all the zeros of the Zeta-function were real"; of whom another mathematical colleague, Littlewood, tells this wonderful anecdote: "I remember once going to see him when he was lying ill at Putney. I had ridden in taxicab number 1729, and remarked that the number seemed to me rather a dull one, and that I hoped it was not an unfavorable omen. 'No,' he replied, 'it is a very interesting number; it is the smallest number expressible as a sum of two cubes in two different ways.' "

Indeed my enthusiasm for mathematical biography is so unfettered that I make bold to say that in a few hundred years President Garfield may achieve the immortality of an obscure footnote, not because he was assassinated but because he once contributed an original proof of the Pythagorean theorem.

It is a curious circumstance that, though mathematics is but a set of marks on paper, it should have such numberless connections with what is called the real world. This airy structure, shimmering like a heat haze in the minds of a few men, is also a kind of hub of the universe from which radiate the spokes of a hundred arts and sciences. Or it is like a circular window opening on 360° of thought. It points toward everything else, from a Bach fugue to the propulsion of a spitball, from soap films to diplomacy. Study the myriad spirals of nature and at once you meet the logarithm. Look into D'Arcy Thompson's endlessly fascinating *On Growth and Form,* and see how mathematics enters into the growth of the wild goat's horns, the architecture of the snowflake, the shapes of eggs. The mathematical concept of symmetry is tied up not alone with music, but with women's veils, flower petals, and the activities of bees. Mathematics is part and parcel of modern war, not merely in the gross concerns of ballistics but in the subtler ones of strategy and tactics. There are few human concerns on which it does not throw some light: it can supply you with a formula for the trade-in value of your car, and a pitiless mathematician named Turing (who committed suicide) will demonstrate to you that if you have a mind, so has the latest supercomputer. It is this marvellous connectivity of mathematics, its bewildering universal-jointedness that leads the shallowest student to echo Einstein's wonderment: "How can it be that mathematics, being after all a product of human thought independent of experience, is so admirably adapted to the objects of reality?"

Yet we must not overstress the value or the interest of this adaptability; or, stressing them, we must keep in mind that this adaptability is not that of a tool but that of an idea. A tool retains its utility but not its power to stimulate the imagination: the airplane is already beginning to become a necessary bore. Faraday tells us that there is nothing so prolific in utility as abstractions—and abstractions is here the operative word. Whitehead puts it even more pointedly: "The utmost abstractions are the true weapons with which to control our thought of concrete fact."

These abstractions, these refuges "from the goading urgency of contingent happenings," have a still, powerful charm, like the remoteness and inviolability of virgins. There is something in us that cries shrilly for the concrete, the applicable. But there is something in us also, far deeper, far more avid of satisfaction, that raises its still, small voice, calling for the abstract and the useless. Lord Melbourne approved the Order of the Garter because there was no damned merit in it. So, in its more rarefied domains, mathematics pleases because there is no damned utility in it.

It gratifies that part of the mind which thirsts for generality. Bertrand Russell expresses a familiar insight when he reminds us that "it must have taken many ages to discover that a brace of pheasants and a couple of days are both instances of the number two." How radiant a discovery it must have been! How the mind swells with pride when it is able to state a proposition that is demonstrable not for a particular thing, but for a large class of things—or even for *anything*. There is something wildly admirable as well as wildly funny about George Polya's imagined eccentric mathematics professor when he remarks: "This principle is so perfectly general that no particular application of it is possible."

The final enchantment of mathematics lies in its appeal to the imagination. (Voltaire, who lived, like ourselves, in a great mathematical age, considered that there was far more imagination in the head of Archimedes than in the head of Homer.) It is not the certainty of mathematics that produces this appeal, but the endless vistas of interpretation, even of emotion, that are opened by this certainty. There is a certain equation, De Moivre's, always cited by mathematicians as a perfect example of elegance and economy. This equation combines in one terse statement the two chief mathematical relations ($+$ and $=$), the two most significant whole numbers (1 and 0), the base of Napier's logarithms, the ratio of the diameter to the circle's circumference, and the mysterious, omnipervasive sign for the square root of minus one. The American mathematician Benjamin Peirce would write this formula on the blackboard, turn to his students and say: "Gentlemen, that is surely true, it is absolutely paradoxical; we cannot understand it, and we don't know what it means, but we have proved it, and therefore, we know it must be the truth."

One has a kindred feeling when listening to the last quartets of Beethoven or repeating the most highly charged passages of *King Lear*.

It's a Small World—and
a Better One

"CHILDREN," once remarked Desmond MacCarthy, "are a subject on which I can speak with some authority as I have been a child myself." Let us shake hands: we are all authorities. All of us once dwelt, half lost in a forest of Legs and Don'ts, in the same strange land. To repossess its strangeness you have but to gaze down at that sleeping child who gave to Emerson the impression of a traveler in a very far country.

But what sort of traveler? To the Calvinist the small child is a vessel of original sin—as indeed, with a change of metaphor, he is to the Freudian. To the modish parent he is the object of indulgent irony. To the earnest PTA-er he is a kind of animal maze through which the hapless mother and father, Spock in hand, thread their way, solving puzzles. How remote they all are from Wordsworth, in whose vision the child came trailing clouds of glory.

I have three children. The two younger ones, a small boy

157

and a smaller girl, are for the moment apathetic to maturity and adjustment. Do they trail clouds of glory? Not noticeably. Yet they seem to my old-fashioned eyes rather more like little angels than like little monsters. And so, even though it makes only two of us, I'll string along with Wordsworth.

I begin my praise of these exquisite creatures with a question. Why do we all love babies? When someone asked Franklin what was the good of the balloon, he retorted, "What good is a baby?" Fair enough as repartee but little more. The goodness of a baby does not reside in its future, a mere question mark, but in its present, the most unqualified of affirmations. A baby is no acorn. He is good precisely because he is a baby, not because he will become a man. It is our nature to grow larger—but not necessarily in every way. Who has not had the uneasy sense, as Wordsworth did, that to develop is also in some odd manner to diminish? "If children," says Goethe, "grew up according to early indications, we should have nothing but geniuses."

Indeed it is a queer thing that in babies and small children we welcome joyfully every sign of that intelligence we so much distrust in adults. An intellectual baby, whose very gurgles prove to its judicial parents its strong powers of perception, is the pride of the family. But an intellectual candidate for the Presidency arouses serious doubts. It is as though infancy alone could call into play our capacity to admire intelligence.

The baby, the small child has not yet learned how to be stupid. It requires considerable training before we can modify our natural infantile good taste to the point at which we can enjoy Mr. Jerry Lewis. The baby who laughs as he is dandled on your knee is responding to amusement on a much higher and purer level than we are when we applaud Elvis Presley. The baby has not yet descended to this plane of appreciation. To achieve it he must first go through the course of adjustment we have so satisfactorily substituted for education.

I am not, however, suggesting that we love babies because their aesthetic taste is superior to ours. Nor do I think it is their helplessness that wins our affection. The baby's value lies not in what we do for him but in what he does for us. He confers on us, by the very circumstance of his babyhood, a priceless boon. He forces us to be ourselves, or rather the best of ourselves. Except pet animals, babies are the only creatures we don't have to be *wary* with. We cannot impress them, cajole them, charm them, win them over, or lie to them. Masks mean nothing to them, achievement means nothing, dignity nothing, high-bracket income nothing. Stubborn, unbluffable, they respond only to love. If you are not good enough to love them, you are just not good enough. Hence they draw out whatever rock-bottom sweetness and naturalness we possess. It is not *their* lack of self-consciousness that gratifies us. It is the sudden pleased sense of our own. A baby restores to us our lost innocence. He can make an honest man or woman out of a grownup.

A baby is fascinating also because he is incapable of using language to obscure his personality. Most conversation, after all, is a bridge connecting two uninteresting points. A good talker or writer is one who has learned to use words in such a way as to reveal himself in a light almost as clear and illuminating as that which glowed about him when he was an infantile illiterate. All children talk with integrity up to about the age of five, when they fall victim to the influences of the adult world and mass entertainment. It is then that they begin, all unconsciously, to become plausible actors. The product of this process is known as maturity, or you and me.

Before the child has learned that the main use of language is to conceal either thought or the absence of thought, he speaks with a force, a conciseness, and a cleanliness of diction worthy of Ernest Hemingway. When our son Kim was less than three, he had already begun to look with a somewhat jaundiced eye on the competitive charms of his baby sister, Anne. It was at that time that we moved to the country and were compelled to leave behind us our Japanese cook. We asked Kim what he thought would be a nice good-by present for Kami. He reflected for no more than a few seconds. Then his face cleared. "Give him Anne," he said. I have read novels that conveyed no more than these three words.

A child will of course play with sounds as he would with blocks, that is, he will talk nonsense. But it is his own nonsense that he relishes, because he has made it, and not yours, which he rightly suspects of being a fake. A child cannot recognize the excellent, but he can recognize the spurious. Grownups who talk nonsense to children are generally of one of two classes. The first class talks nonsense out of a kind of complacency. "Look how clever I am—I can put myself on a level with this strange being." The second class, more numerous, talks nonsense because, quite literally, it does not know how to talk sense, that is, to use simple but proper language of a kind that really engages the child's interest.

High-order intellects are frequently susceptible to the baby-talk fallacy. A dear friend of mine owns perhaps one of the dozen finest intellects still at large in our country. When his children were young, he spoke to them in a kind of grotesque gibberish, under the impression that only jungle gobbledygook could possibly penetrate to the untutored minds of childhood. His children received his imbecile barks and grunts with studied apathy, beneath which lay real fear—a fear that something was not quite right with Daddy's brain.

It is told of the great biologist T. H. Huxley that he once tried to charm his granddaughter with a torrent of nonsense. She listened and finally remarked, "Well, you are the curious'test old man I ever seen." Baby talk is a confession of our weakness, not a concession to theirs. The only spectacle more pitiful than an adult using baby talk is a father trying to be a pal.

I would suggest that, far from using baby talk, we should make an effort, when talking to children and even to babies, to employ the purest speech of which we are capable. It is a piece of luck that the child is imitative: if, to suggest the improbable, he should hear nothing but the King James Bible he would command an English which, though too rich and beautiful for our modern ears, would be none the less magnificent. It is too late for us to bother to speak properly to each other—slovenly English has of late become virtually a badge of respectability among us American grownups. But it is not too late for us to speak properly, even carefully, to our children, in the hope that when they are older they will be immune to the street-corner slur-and-gabble that is our own linguistic hallmark.

Another curious notion is that when speaking to children we must become ventriloquists. Some of us speak extra loudly, as if the child were an imbecile—which, of course, is what he is thinking *we* are. Others break into falsetto, as if there were some natural kinship between children and *castrati*. Children do not care to watch grownups assuming such masks. It makes them either uneasy or contemptuous. As they do not feel like fools themselves, they are unable to conceive why others should want to feel like fools.

Said Gauguin: "I'm two things that can never be ridiculous—a child and a savage." A profound remark. The dignity of the civilized adult, when he has any, is learned, and shows the telltale marks of the process. That of the child and the savage is native. Thus, when we laugh indulgently at the child, it is not the child we are really laughing at. We are laughing at what we assume to be the ludicrous distance that separates him from us. But our laughter is at bottom an unconscious means of reassuring ourselves of something we are not quite certain about—our own superiority.

The dignity of the grownup springs from his remembrance of who he is. The dignity of the child and especially the baby proceeds from his forgetfulness of who he is. He is fascinated by himself, of course, but his is a pure emotion, he has no *object* in knowing himself, it is a gratuitous act, akin to the emotion of the theoretical scientist. It is this which accounts for the fact that the pleasures of childhood are those of absorption, which is unconscious, rather than those of gaiety, which involves a conscious sense of being amused or happy. Indeed it is doubtful that small children ever are really happy. Aristotle thought they could not be, for they are "not old enough to be capable of noble acts." To the Greek mind happiness could proceed only out of a moral equilibrium involving the rational choice of good over evil. The child is not *beyond* good and evil; he has not reached either.

In James Agate's *The Later Ego* (a book brilliantly edited and introduced by Jacques Barzun and herewith strongly recommended) he quotes a sentence from a friend's letter: "Have you ever seen a child reading *Alice?* Intense *interest*, but not a smile, it being of course his or her world." It is this same absorption, the same lack of split between himself and the universe, that makes all the gestures of children, as Joshua Reynolds noted, invariably graceful.

On the whole it is difficult to be allowed the privilege of living with small children without concluding that in many respects they are a superior race, possibly Martian invaders who under our influence are gradually induced to lose the memory of their native land. It requires considerable talent to be a child. Anyone can be a grownup. If you doubt it, look about you.

Life's Minor Pleasures

THE HAPPINESS that floods you when for an instant you glimpse your children, not as parts of a domestic frieze but as free-standing beings. The absolute sense of completion that follows an important task well done. The external world transiently seen, as the poet more constantly sees it, in all its beauty and strangeness. The conviction that your mind or body is working at optimum speed or capacity. The utterly successful moment of love. Of such stuff are the great moments of pleasure made.

But because such experiences are common to us all, they do not singularize human beings. They come to us in that we are men and women rather than a particular man or woman. It is our minor pleasures that differentiate us. It is in them that the delicate lines of separation are drawn. The man who tells us that he is fond of eating exposes little of himself that we do not already know by reference to our own appetites. But the man with a master passion for rare steak is at once sharply if minutely distinguishable from such a one as Sydney Smith, who thought Heaven a place where *pâté de foie gras* is eaten to the sound of trumpets. We have but to recollect that this same witty parson (incidentally, why are there no longer witty parsons?) once said, "Madam, I have been looking for a person who disliked gravy all my life; let us swear eternal friendship," and the unique profile of the man begins to trace itself in our understandings.

It is of course only the life, not the biography, that is truthful and complete; yet you might compose a more accurate biography by recording the biographee's minor pleasures than by recording his major experiences. One's ruling passion may be less a passion than a mere habit, and what we think of as the Grand Design of our lives be little more than the pattern drawn by inertia's flaccid finger. But the nonsovereign passions, the wayward inclinations, the secret whims may when totaled sum up a large part of what we are.

Just as a petty vice may be more revealing than a large, unavoidably public weakness, so some trivial enjoyment, particularly if it be confessed only to oneself, may prove the Ariadne's thread leading to a man's center. When Charles Lamb remarked that the greatest pleasure he knew was to do a good action by stealth and have it found out by accident, how much of himself was declared! When Rochefoucauld noted that if we were without faults we should not take so much pleasure in remarking them in others, how much of himself was declared! And what vividly opposite selves are revealed in the two brief sentences. By their fruits ye shall know them, but also by their small pleasures: he who loves to tickle lives in a different world from him who loves to be tickled.

Minor pleasures may be divided into the groovy and the antigroovy. A groovy pleasure is one that is both repeatable and confirmatory of one's own established personality. An antigroovy pleasure is a one-shot that reveals to you something hitherto unsuspected about yourself. The essence of the first is complacence; of the second, surprise.

I have been balancing my checkbook monthly for thirty years and have never once failed to receive a small satisfaction from an accurate reconciliation (to discover the bank in an error is something *hors concours*, a hole in one). This is a groovy pleasure. It reveals a number of things about me: that I am a bit of a fuss-budget, rather simple-minded with regard to practical affairs, and, as I am still struck with a certain wonder that I can add and subtract, a dubious arithmetician.

On April 8, 1956, four inches of snow fell upon us in Connecticut. The pleasure of surveying the suddenly magical landscape was common to us all. But there was also the more subtle pleasure, rooted in philosophy, springing from the sudden realization that Nature was capable at almost any time of confounding with its impudent, outrageous irregularity the dailiness, the habitualness of man. This was an antigroovy minor pleasure. It comes of being shaken out of rather than into a rut.

A certain rare minor pleasure seems to combine the groovy and the antigroovy. It is the consequence of being jolted out of one rut into another, out of the rut of Now into the rut of Then—a Then one had imagined clean forgotten. This is a specialized form of the pleasure of memory. The other day, to amuse my young son, I began almost in a trance to make a ball out of rubber bands. On a

small spindle of folded cardboard or crumpled paper you
stretch and wind your rubber bands. As you twist and wind
and stretch, these bands round gradually into a near-sphere.
The more bands you use the more nearly you approach a
perfect globe. A careful winder can make one as large as
a croquet ball, possessing an almost dangerous bounce-
ability.

Now I had not performed this simple feat since I was
ten years old. How pleasant and interesting was the revival of the childhood art; to note that my fingers were
charged and packed with recollections; to feel again that
same solid, satisfactory elastic mass unchanged, as it were,
in the course of over forty years; to hear again in memory
the curious sound, a kind of dull click, the ball made as
you threw it against a brick wall in the game known, I
think, as "stoop ball." . . . The trivial bit of rubber, as
useful for me as Proust's madeleine was for him, had,
freely, effortlessly, made me a gift of extra life, for memory
is no less life than is experience. Perhaps we should almost
consciously devote a few minutes of each day to such
exercises of evocation. They can be among the most warm-
ing of life's minor pleasures; and the determinedly present-minded miss them completely. I feel sorrow for these
poor folk. They possess large bank accounts whose existence they have forgotten, bank accounts of memory; and
so in their obliviousness they pass up riches.

The minor pleasures of many of us are linked to the play
of the body, to sport, to organized competition. I have no
quarrel with such diversions but merely suggest that play
and competition are equally possible for the mind. The
mind has one slight advantage: it needs no equipment, no

playing field, and it is its own ever-present adversary. For example, there is the simple but never monotonous game of image-making. Children, wiser in their play than their elders, know how to close their eyes and see things. It is curious how few grownups ever avail themselves of the delights of the imagination. We will go to some trouble to visit a picture gallery when behind the thin walls of our eyelids lie ten thousand Prados and Corcorans and Louvres. The child is overjoyed to discover that "he can see anything he wants to." We renounce that joy, saying it is "childish" or "a waste of time" or "daydreaming" or some other pitiful phrase that points merely to the withering of the interior life. In his memoirs of his childhood Tolstoy tells us that he and his brothers and sisters used to play games of this sort: try *not* to think of a white bear. It is surprising, if you face your mind with such odd challenges, what curious nooks and crannies you can discover in it.

It is a great pleasure to do something you are good at. It is a small but unarguable one to do something you are bad at. Last summer I cleaned an outdoor catch basin, removing from it the conglomerate evidence of a violent winter and spring. I did it awkwardly, slowly, doubtless stupidly, but with a peculiar satisfaction, richer in certain ways than the satisfaction I get in writing this essay, which is a job I know I can handle with passable competence.

One of the deepest of minor pleasures is the common one of collecting. I say deep because it is rooted in the soil of the primitive. It is akin to the pleasure we take in being snug and warm when outside the elements are raging. It must respond to the caveman within. The philatelist will tell you that stamps are educational, that they are valuable, that they are beautiful. All this is quite true but only part of the truth. Such reasoning can hardly account for the fact that collecting can be and often is a passion, saturated with the irrational. My notion is that collecting is a symbolic gesture. The collection is a hedge, a comfort, a shelter into which the sorely beset mind can withdraw. It is orderly, it grows toward completion, it is something, as we say, that can't be taken away from us. The miser is merely a collector gone mad; but all collectors are a little mad in that they can draw from an assemblage of inanimate objects a pleasure that is profoundly emotional and tied to the core of their being.

I am not much of a collector, and my hobbies are hardly startling. I collect books—just good ones, not rare or beautiful ones—and bottles of wine. I know I will never read all the books on my shelves (I have about one-eighth of a mile of shelves). I know that not I but my children, and I hope their children, will enjoy a goodly portion of the cellar. But the objects themselves give me an unreasonable pleasure: the knowledge that they are *there,* neatly arranged, ready for use. Merely to shelve a new book properly is pleasurable, as filling a vacant space is. Similarly, to bin a case of wine—always alone, this is not a social pleasure—never fails to induce in me a succession of pleasurable thoughts, daydreams, images. A wine cellar, even one as small as mine, has a monastic quality; the fever and fret of the outside world can never penetrate to these tranquil life essences, living their careers of growing perfection behind translucent glass. Collection is protection.

One of my unfailing minor pleasures may seem dull to

more energetic souls: opening the mail. Living in an advanced industrial civilization is a kind of near-conquest over the unexpected. We are so clever that at last we have arranged things so that we know pretty much what's going to happen. We have even arranged to destroy ourselves, and have worked out and publicized the details of the process so carefully that when it occurs it will hardly come as a surprise. Such organization, in which the chancy and the fortuitous have been virtually eliminated, where the proper button is always there to be pressed—such efficiency is of course admirable. It does not, however, by its very nature afford scope to that perverse human trait, still not quite eliminated, which is pleased by the accidental.

Thus to many tame citizens like me the morning mail functions as the voice of the unpredictable and keeps alive for a few minutes a day the keen sense of the unplanned and the unplannable. The letter opener is an instrument that has persisted from some antique land of chance and adventure into our ordered world of the perfectly calculated.

There are certain minor pleasures whose particular note is that of relief, such as the pleasure that comes of surviving a children's party for five-year-olds; or of indulgence after denial, such as the late-afternoon Martini which would be repulsive in the morning; or of the mildly illegitimate, such as the midnight raid on the refrigerator for the purpose of eating all the things that are bad for you; or of re-education—recently I discovered that I have been wrong for years in thinking that I disliked sherry; or of the unexpectedly comforting, such as awakening on a cold morning, consulting the clock and finding that you still have two hours of sleep; or of delay, such as the pleasure a writer feels in rearranging his desk, sharpening his pencils, and lengthily informing each and every member of the family that, being about to set to work, he is not to be disturbed.

Whatever our pleasures may be, the important thing is never to fake them, never to attend a ball game because that is the right thing to do or read a book because it is fashionable. "Thank heavens," said Logan Pearsall Smith, "the sun has gone in and I don't have to go out to enjoy it." The discovery of what one really likes is not as easy as it sounds. It involves the discovery of oneself, a laborious and frequently painful business. It means having the courage not to imitate, not to conform. It often means forgoing the pleasure of telling others about your pleasure, if it should happen to be eccentric or otherwise socially inadmissible.

In our time mass enjoyments are so effectively, so seductively promoted that at times they seem to be the only kind available. All the more reason for us to keep delving into the mysterious inner world of our selves, to isolate and develop our special pleasure skills, often unsharable, often even inexplicable.

In Praise of Quotation

ONCE, in the course of one of his magnificent wartime broadcasts, Winston Churchill introduced certain lines from *Say Not the Struggle Nought Availeth,* by the English poet Arthur Hugh Clough. The reader may remember them. They ended: *But westward, look, the land is bright.* The speech was of momentous, the quotation of momentary, interest. Yet, oddly enough, considerable attention was paid to Sir Winston's eight lines of quotation. What caught our fancy was the novelty of a practical twentieth-century statesman daring to embellish his argument by invoking the words of a dead minor poet. We had forgotten that among the public figures of an earlier day happy quotation was common practice. We were startled and in an almost childish way pleased to see how effective it could still be in our own time—just as we are startled and sometimes pleased when any of our Chief Executives, risking his political life, uses a word beyond the ken of the eighth grade.

But to get by with this sort of thing one must be a

Churchill. In general we object to the man who quotes, as we object to the man who speaks perfect English, on the ground that he is being "superior." He who flashes a new Cadillac is enviable. He who flashes an old classical tag is pedantic. The job aspirant with good references is welcome as long as they are not from Shakespeare.

Yet what are the young account executive's crew cut, his J. Press suit, his button-down white shirt, his conservative, diagonally striped tie—what are they but a series of neat quotations? Indeed the man himself may be but a quotation, or a quotation of a quotation. None the less we will wear him in our heart's core, ay, in our heart of heart (*Hamlet*, Act III, Scene ii). But let this same walking allusion to the Ivy League let fall a passing allusion to the *Aeneid*—and how properly and quickly are our suspicions aroused!

We prefer to believe that the absence of inverted commas guarantees the originality of a thought, whereas it may be merely that the utterer has forgotten its source. "It is the little writer," says Havelock Ellis (and I quote), "rather than the great writer who seems never to quote, and the reason is that he is never really doing anything else."

I have probably already exceeded my quota of quotes. But I will venture another, to give the antiquoter a fair shake. The most amusing attack on the quotation habit that I can recall was made about forty years ago by the superb American essayist Frank Moore Colby. I offer a few sentences from his essay on *Quotation and Allusion:*

When young and helpless I once fell into a family that made it a daily duty to study up things to quote, and every

Sunday morning at breakfast each would recite a passage memorized during the week. The steam from the coffee vanished into literary air, and the muffins, by the time we got to them, seemed to be bound in calf. . . . Large blocks of poetry would suddenly fall athwart the conversation, no one knew whence, while with bowed head the startled Philistine would wait for the seizure to pass. . . . One learns little more about a man from the feats of his literary memory than from the feats of his alimentary canal.

The kind of quoter Colby is talking about is practically nonexistent these days. Even professors of literature, blushing to be thought either professorial or literary, have stripped themselves of their allusions and use a prose as single-gallused as that of any congressman up for re-election. We live in a time in which men will take great pains to conceal their knowledge. I know ambitious politicians who would give much to have received a poor education. A lot of learning is a dangerous thing. (See Pope, *Essay on Criticism*, Part II, l. 15.)

We are nervous about quoting, not because we think the quotation may fail of effect but because we fear its effect may be bad. A man is known by the company he keeps (cf. Euripides, *The Phoenissae*), and few can bear the accusation of consorting with dead poets and sages. Why stand on the shoulders of titans when we have two fine clay feet of our own?

One confusing thing about the quotation controversy is that the most memorable statements on both sides have been made by the same man. Even more baffling is the fact that to make this point I am forced to quote him. The man is Emerson. In his *Journal* for May, 1849, he says sharply, "I hate quotations. Tell me what you know." In his essay *Quotation and Originality* he notes warmly, "Next to the originator of a good sentence is the first quoter of it." You pays your money and you takes your choice (source unknown).

For all its unfashionableness and its suspicious smell of subversion, I choose quotation.

In one sense we are quoting all the time. To whistle Tin Pan Alley's latest inanity is to quote. To repeat the morning's opinions of our pet editorial writer is to quote. To transmit the tired gag of a television comic is to quote. To pass on the gossip columnist's modish anecdote is to quote. To agree with the boss is to repay him with automatic oral flattery—a kind of quote *pro quid*. Much of our conversation is but a series of dittos, often typed on fifth carbons.

This kind of quotation is socially acceptable, indeed in some circles mandatory. I do not quarrel with it. I merely urge the claims of a different *kind* of quotation, drawn not from the trivial and the transitory but from the excellent and the traditional. I suggest that we raise our sights and our citations, that we stop feeling inferior because by chance we possess superior knowledge. The man who leans upon John Milton is no more infirm than the man who leans upon Bob Hope.

"Only the past is immortal" (Delmore Schwartz). But its immortality is not unconditional. It cannot be kept alive solely by scholars and professional intellectuals. It must be kept alive by you and me. All mankind is but a carrier, and part of our precious burden consists of things that have been said perfectly. To repeat them, appositely and not too frequently, is to add to the general stock of knowledge and pleasure. Indeed it is a kind of good citizenship, for we are all citizens of History, a country whose continually threatened borders we must be at any time prepared to defend. To still in ourselves the golden voices of the past is to regress toward the voiceless condition of the fishes.

Our American speech is not so rich that we can afford to quote only each other. Current income cannot maintain our linguistic economy—at least not in the style to which she is accustomed. We must levy a tax upon the dead, a tax they will pay cheerfully, for, having passed beyond the worries of the fiscal year, they post no guards at the gates of their Fort Knox.

Quotation—not the kind Colby was laughing at, but quotation used to make our own speech gayer, our thought clearer—does not constrict or paralyze the language. On the contrary it enlarges it, gives it more scope and freedom. At the same time it surreptitiously infuses into our speech—now in peril of subsiding to a prairie flatness relieved only by the tumescences of current slang—a needed elegance, even splendor. Just because we can no longer talk like the Elizabethans is no reason for rejecting an occasional loan from the treasury of their wit and the vaults of their vigor. Isaac Disraeli has said the final word on this head: "Whatever is felicitously expressed risks being worse expressed; it is a wretched taste to be gratified with mediocrity when the excellent lies before us." I bid the reader note how "felicitously expressed" is Disraeli's thought; I am forced to quote him simply because I cannot make the point so well myself.

Our language, both written and spoken, seems to me to be undergoing an evolution analogous to that of our architecture. Miës van der Rohe's functional box, stripped so as to remove all friction from living, risks also removing all living from living. Our picture windows open on a void or on another picture window—a kind of architectural mirroring of clichés. Our industrial architecture is so clean-lined that it no longer arrests the eye, nor rests it either. So with our language, even among our most admired stylists. I plead for decoration; man is an ornamenting animal. I plead for a little "unnecessary" mental furniture, transferred from the storehouses of great or merely interesting persons. Quotation *is* embellishment and rarely more than that. But embellishment has its value. Purely purposive prose can become so dull as to fail of its purpose, which first of all presupposes the engagement of the attention.

We are quite ready to quote platitudes, for we feel at ease among ideas that have been so often expressed that they no longer stand in peril of examination. It is the slightly unfamiliar quotation that bids us pause. Do not pause. Use it or listen to it. It too, consoling thought, will soon lose its unfamiliarity. Today's quotation is tomorrow's cliché: Thoreau's "The mass of men lead lives of quiet desperation" has in the past twenty years been murmured by thousands of uneasy human beings.

If you quote, do not be too nice in your quotation, or correct a man if he misquotes slightly. It is not pedantry to mention *fresh fields and pastures new*. It *is* pedantry to remind the speaker that Milton wrote *fresh woods*. Actually *fresh fields* is a slight improvement, at least for mnemonic purposes. Shakespeare wrote *An ill-favoured thing, sir, but mine own.* We generally say *A poor thing but my own,* and our slight updating of the phrasing rescues it for our time: *a good thing, sir, and our own.* To quote with aptness and with pleasure is more important than to quote with prissy correctness.

The nub of the problem has been touched by Fowler in his *Modern English Usage.* With his usual good sense he warns us:

> . . . to each reader those quotations are agreeable that neither strike him as hackneyed nor rebuke his ignorance by their complete novelty, but rouse dormant memories; quotation, then, should be adapted to the probable reader's degree of cultivation; which presents a very pretty problem to those who have a mixed audience to face; the less mixed the audience, the safer is it to quote for association.

Our difficulty is that almost all our audiences *are* mixed. We no longer possess what large segments of the citizenry of the nineteenth century possessed—a common body of knowledge, a common world of associations. No senator today would dare, as Gladstone as a matter of course did, to interlard his speeches with long (and beautifully apt) passages from Lucretius or Horace. He would not wish to insult his colleagues by presuming that they knew Latin.

In these circumstances I think we must take the bull by the horns (popular saying, c.1880) and, making due allowances, quote whenever we feel that the allusion is interesting or helpful or amusing. If the audience is completely unfamiliar with it, they will be less so after they have had it quoted to them. You must run the risk of their thinking you snobbish. If the rest of what you say is not "superior" or patronizing, they will revise their opinion. And if you really are patronizing, refraining from quotation will not fool them.

Finally, in defense of a habit that it is too late for me to change and that is part of my equipment as a writer, may I call again upon Isaac Disraeli? "Those who never quote," he says in his *Curiosities of Literature*, "in return are seldom quoted."

I Shook Hands with Shakespeare

Insomnia is a gross feeder. It will nourish itself on any kind of thinking, including thinking about not thinking. As for so-called soothing thoughts, fewer people have been kept awake by innumerable worries than by numerable sheep. Dull books are equally dormicidal. A bed full of animal crackers is far more lulling.

One night I devoted two sleepless hours to establishing the above to my satisfaction. This accomplished, I went on to play a familiar mental game. The game is called Shaking Hands with Shakespeare, or Palmy Nights. It goes thus—or did that night until dawn.

One of my valued friends is the distinguished actress Cornelia Otis Skinner. On occasion I have shaken her hand. Now *she* in turn surely at sometime or other shook hands with her father Otis Skinner. *He* must have shaken the hand of Edwin Booth, with whom he worked as a young actor. Edwin Booth's father was Junius Brutus

Booth, who knew Edmund Kean. I got into a little trouble
forging manual links between Kean, who was born in 1787,
and Garrick, who died in 1779. (It's easier, of course, if
you admit categories other than actors, but that's for
beginners or people who want to sleep.)

Once past Garrick, however, it was all smooth hand-
clasping. With way stops at Thomas Betterton, Sir William D'Avenant (D'Avenant, as manager of Drury Lane
Theatre, was *almost* an actor), and Richard Burbage, I
finally managed to shake hands with Shakespeare. The
Bard, by the way, was completely indifferent. I suppose
he had something else on his mind.

It was some time before I realized—this is not a conclusion I jump to—that I was a lunatic. At about 5 A.M. it
occurred to me that in the course of her crowded career
Miss Skinner had doubtless shaken hands with perhaps
10,000 people in addition to myself. Each of these 10,000
must have shaken hands with many other thousands, and
these in turn with others. In fact, the more I thought about
it the more probable it seemed that virtually every living
American could claim that he had shaken hands with
Shakespeare. After this became clear to me, I fell into a
refreshing, thirty-seven-minute night's sleep.

Why do I tell you this phenomenally dull story? In order
to single out the one interesting circumstance connected
with it. That circumstance is a confession. I confess that
when I finally succeeded in setting up this imbecile bucket-
brigade contact with a Great Name I felt a passing quiver
of pride.

Now the impulse that drove me to wring Shakespeare's
hand is the same as that which drives the bobby soxer to

tear the clothing off the latest interpreter of rock and roll. True, the objects of worship stand on different levels. But the motives of worship do not. In both cases the motive springs from a belief in sympathetic magic. The bobby soxer and I are equally hairy primitives, mumbling over our bones and fetishes, believing that if we can only name the right names we can become larger than we are.

We are all name-droppers. The double-dome who studs his conversation with Sartre and Kierkegaard, and the schoolgirl who studs hers with Grace and Rock. The autograph collector proud of his Button Gwinnett, and the autograph collector proud of his Eddie Fisher. The drill-press operator who calls the big boss Tom, and the big boss who calls the drill-press operator Mike. The jargoneer with his "sense of insecurity," his "super-ego," his "extrapolation." The Broadway columnist who flicks off café-society allusions like cigarette ash. The Indian peasant who trudges two hundred miles to receive "darshana" from the sight of Gandhi, and the good American who waits in line to shake the President's hand. The Madison Avenue man of the world who preens himself on his head-waiter acquaintanceship. Even the man of the cloth who too frequently, too familiarly drops the greatest of all Names.

We may name-drop by not dropping names. Suppose I slightly alter a well-known passage and, waiving quotation marks, write: No man is an island, entire of itself . . . Any man's name increases me because I am involved in mankind . . . I expect you to murmur "John Donne." More to the point I expect you to recognize that *I* have read John Donne (or at any rate Ernest Hemingway) and to salute

me as quite a learned fellow. Writers are much given to
this form of name-dropping by omission, in which, though
the sign is changed from plus to minus, the value of the
linguistic expression is presumed to be increased.

My Shakespearean handshake was a gesture of alliance
with the past and is a kind of dead-name-dropping, a
verbal tic to which habitual readers are particularly subject. Much commoner however is the desire to ally oneself with the future. In a recent ingenious essay called *The
Anatomy of Snobbery* Arthur Koestler instances the case
of a young woman he once knew. She worked for a publishing firm and was generally supposed to have granted
the ultimate favor to every male author on the list who had
sold over 20,000 copies. Mr. Koestler quotes her defense:
"Having an affair with a famous man is not frivolous—it is
like going to bed with History. Who would blame Marie
Walewska for surrendering to Napoleon? Everything you
do with a famous man is redeemed from its sinfulness by
becoming a Historical Anecdote."

I do not think the young lady was trying to find an excuse for an unduly pliant disposition. I think, like all of us,
she panted for immortality, at least the immortality of
being recorded. The boudoir may seem to some an odd
embalming parlor, but it is no odder than standing in line
to be the first to cross a newly opened bridge.

Only the amoeba is immortal; the rest of us little may-
fly bugs attach ourselves to bigger bugs with greater survival value. The man who casually mentions his acquaintance with Mr. Big may never be emblazoned on the pages
of history, but—who knows?—he may turn into a footnote.
There is a certain pathetic nobility about these name-drop-

pings. They are honorable mentions. At least they point to an awareness on the name-dropper's part of something genuinely greater than himself. Such snobbery is impure in a good sense: conceit partially redeemed by imagination.

Its bluer-blooded cousin is family pride, for which there is something to be said. Much has been urged against it by those who, like most of us, have progenitors but no ancestors. The self-made man can be and often is an admirable fellow. He is less admirable however when he boasts of it, in which case he appears to be a highly specialized name-dropper, the name being his own. As a matter of fact there is a certain danger in owing nothing to those who have gone before you, a slight tendency to strut. An Aldous Huxley cannot strut; grandpa would disapprove. Nor can a Churchill; he cannot afford to let Marlborough down. These are men of the highest achievement in their own right. Yet I think a part of that achievement may well be rooted in a worthy desire to live up to glittering ancestry, an impulse probably more powerful than the impulse to live down sordid ancestry. It is true that an Adams or a Cecil, humanly proud of his genealogy, may lean from time to time against some luxuriant branch of the family tree. But precisely because he feels himself so comfortably backed up he is less inclined to general name-dropping than is the traditionless self-starter.

It is this circumstance, I think, that accounts for the fact that the most inveterate name-droppers I know are to be found in and around the entertainment industry. Most of those in its lower reaches, such as television, are Johnny-come-latelies. The young man whose father and grandfather have built up a dignified banking business *may* insist on becoming a gagman. But he is more apt to follow the family tradition. Thus show business is full of people who are given praise, money, and publicity at best and excitement at the least, and who are none the less never quite certain of their social status. A movie star may receive crowd adulation. But when the chips are down he must feel that there is something faintly ridiculous about a trade based on making faces and mouthing other people's words.

In show business we still vaguely feel an uneasy kinship with the mimes of not so long ago who were denied Christian burial. We may be given knighthoods, we may be buried in Westminster Abbey, we may marry princes, we may tutor Presidents—but we're still not quite respectable. That is why there is so much name-dropping in show business, so much first-naming (which gives one the illusion of being part of a mutual-aid society), so much marrying into the Social Register, so great a desire to consort with politicos and men of large affairs, so many touching attempts (as with Miss Monroe and Mr. Brando) to demonstrate one's ability to be at ease in a world other than that of entertainment. We name-drop in order to establish some contact with a tradition more acceptable than our own, for our own, after all, has its origins in the clown, the traveling mountebank, the juggler, and the court fool.

It is true that name-dropping, being at bottom a consequence of the human condition (for all their hierarchy one doubts its existence among the angels), is to be found in all times and climes. But it is probably most marked in fluid, unjelled societies like our own where, though lineage and personal distinction are prized, they are less prized than prominence and possessions. The ability to drop a sounding name with elaborate casualness is among us a definite asset, like a Cadillac or a sound commercial rating; and it would be unrealistic to deny it. "It's not what you are, it's who you know" goes an old saying; and some truth still remains if we change it to "It's not who you know, it's who you say you know." The really artistic name-dropper who never overdoes it, who chooses his openings well, begins to sound like a good credit risk. We have a feeling that we can rely on him, as the primitive feels he can rely on his medicine man. Both are somehow "in touch" with a bigger, better, more powerful universe.

One of the curious features of name-dropping is that the prestige always seems to grow greener in the other fellow's meadow. I once knew a great musical executant who was also a great name-dropper. But the names he dropped were rarely musical names. They were titled names or socially prominent ones. This wasn't simple snobbery. Rather was it simple innocence, the perfectly human feeling that people we know well and who can do the same thing we can do are somehow not as interesting, have less magic, less mana, than those who exert their powers in an area alien to us. Thus advertising men like to drop the names of writers. Writers often like to drop the names of men of action. I am acquainted with industrialists who actually name-drop philosophers. Philosophers however are different. Convinced, with some reason, that their field of endeavor is the supreme one, they will name-drop nothing less than abstract ideas. From this they draw a sense of personal enhancement that I get by shaking hands with Shakespeare.

Nevertheless there are fashions in name-dropping, tidal waves of name-dropping that influence us irrespective of our calling or status. These change from decade to decade. Only a few years ago café celebrities were In. Today they are on the way Out. There are too many of them, they have been too systematically publicized, not so much magic rubs off them. At the moment they have been replaced by industrialists. Men of affairs are In. The lucky fellow who knows Henry Ford II has the name-drop on the poor chap who only knows Picasso.

In my youth the word "executive" made people chortle. Humorists, such as Lardner and Donald Ogden Stewart, made a good thing out of kidding executives. Today the word has become the most honorific adjective in the ad-writers' lexicon. An Executive car or house or suit of clothes has somehow become better than any other kind; and accordingly the national character of name-dropping has changed. In the event of a Depression, Men of Distinction may go out, lyric poets come in.

In the meantime, hoping to escape the vast intimidating anonymity which is our general lot, like prisoners tapping out foolish but somehow comforting messages to their fellow prisoners in the adjoining cells, we drop what names we can and shake hands in the sleepless dark, each with his own Shakespeare.

Brief History of a Love Affair

Dead Lucre: burnt Ambition: Wine is best.
HILAIRE BELLOC, *Heroic Poem in*
Praise of Wine

LIKE MOST LOVE STORIES mine will mean something to lovers; rather less to those merely capable of love; to the incapable, nothing. And, since no love affair's wild heart lets itself be netted in words, this chronicle of a passion may likewise fail of effect. Yet what lover, telling his tale, has ever been put off by the thought of failure? For he speaks not to persuade but to dress his delight in another guise, and, if he cannot command attention, will settle for being overheard. If his defective audience-sense often makes him a bore, it is a risk he runs cheerfully enough.

When I was about eleven I chanced to be left alone of a summer afternoon in the house of a family friend. Researching, I came across a cabinet enclosing many interesting bottles, clearly drinkables. One dwarfish flagon, looking as though it had escaped from a woodcut in a Grimm's fairy tale, was labeled, most gothically, *kümmel*. The bottle, perhaps half-full, played apple to my Eve. Sampling

189

it, I found it good. There was no one to tell me that an ounce of *kümmel* is a better thing than two ounces, and a far, far better thing than twelve ounces. So, in the course of the long, drowsy, solitary afternoon, in sips that grew more and more abstracted, I absorbed the *kümmel*. Perhaps I am the only man alive who at the age of eleven survived a lost weekend based on a flavoring of caraway seeds. I was not even reprimanded. For one thing I was for some time in no state to grasp the moral force of any reprimand. For another, any impulse my host may have felt to warn me against solitary tippling was lost in awe of my capacity.

Prohibition and my college career, neither of them a successful experiment, partly coincided. A lean purse hindered me from becoming even a modest representative of the Fitzgerald era. But from time to time a more worldly companion and I would pay a furtive visit to a speakeasy. There, as a gesture of decadence, we imbibed a pousse-café. Sometimes two. Speakeasy illumination being what it was, I do not believe I ever actually made out the colors of the seven traditional liqueurs that compose this sybaritic concoction. But I had full confidence that, together with the reciting of Swinburne, they made up the iridescent symbol of abandonment.

This brace of anemic encounters with the Demon would seem to have little to do with my love affair. I fish up these memories only to emphasize the fact that I came to wine an oenological virgin. For, though I concede the gross chemical kinship binding all alcoholic liquids, the worlds of wine and nonvinous spirituous beverages remain distinct. Thus I was all of twenty-three before being introduced to my first real bottle.

In successful love affairs the most radiant moment often occurs at the outset. Consummation, repetition, recollection: each diffuses its appropriate delight. Incomparable, however, is the moment when, all innocent of experience, knowledge, and judgment, one for the first time meets the object of a future passion and feels chosen, marked, almost *fated*. The narrator in Conrad's *Youth*, sailing at dawn, in stillness and exaltation, through the gateway of the fabled East; the boy Napoleon leading his troops in play battle on the Corsican uplands, feeling in his bones the electric shock: "I am a soldier!"; the awkward beginning angler or duck shooter with his very first cast or shot sensing, amazed, his future vocation—all, long before achieving success or even skill, vibrate to their joyful destiny. Any knowledge is good. But the most exquisite knowledge flows from the sudden insight that you are by a quirk of nature fashioned to acquire still greater knowledge.

Paris in 1927: of all places on the round earth's varied crust the best place in which to try one's first bottle. My wife had by a few weeks preceded me there so that when I arrived she was already wearing the city like a glove. We met at noon of a brilliant August day, a day like a pearl. We had little money but much youth. For our lunch my wife, shrewdly deciding to start me off modestly, chose the Bon Marché, the Macy's of the Left Bank. She could have saved her pains: I was in Paris: a department store was Aladdin's palace. Was the lunchroom on the fourth floor? Or in Heaven? I have forgotten.

With our lunch my wife, already to me formidably learned in these matters, ordered a cheap white Graves. Its deep straw color was pleasing to the eye. Even in this busy department store it was served with just a graceful allusion to a flourish. It was properly chilled against the midsummer heat. For the first time I tasted *wine*. It must have sent me into a mild catatonia for it was not until perhaps sixty seconds later that I seemed to hear my wife's voice say from far away, "You have the most peculiar, *foolish* smile on your face." "Do I?" was all I could reply. We may know we are happy when we do not know we are smiling.

And so the die was cast. I felt not so much that here was a new experience as that here was an old experience that had been waiting all my life for me to catch up with it. It was almost enough to make one credit Plato's crazy doctrine of reminiscence.

When one is young and has little money it is prudent to spend that little on the unnecessary, the emotional dividends being higher. We stayed six weeks in Paris and a large part of our budget went on wine that, I am proud to say, we could not afford.

By the time I had finished my tenth bottle in Paris and could tell claret from Burgundy without glancing at the bottle's shoulder slope, I had grasped a fundamental fact: that the pleasures of wine, being both sensory and intellectual, are profound. There are few pleasures of which this can be said.

The appeal to the senses may be simple; one can toss off a glass of a *vin de carafe* with mild pleasure, and so an end. But it *need* not be: there is wine available (nor should one drink too much of it) proffering a whole world of complex stimuli involving taste, color, and fragrance. Add to this the fact that one tastes a wine in several different ways, all involved in a single swallow, for this swallow leads a triple life: one in the mouth, another in the course of slipping down the gullet, still another, a beautiful ghost, the moment afterward.

This much I learned quickly. Nor have I ever tired of learning it again and again. The sensory satisfactions of wine, varying with each sip, each bottle, each occasion, are so ramified that boredom is impossible. I know that T. E. Lawrence, hardly a well-balanced type, despised wine because he felt its gratifications were too simple. He preferred to discriminate, he declared, among varieties of water. For such refinements I lack the necessary sophistication, or perhaps merely the necessary puritanism. Water and milk may be excellent drinks, but their charms are repetitive. God granted them swallowability, and rested.

The intellectual attractions of wine are less quickly understood than the sensory ones. At twenty-three I did not grasp them at all, and thirty years later am still but a grade school student. The fact is that, like philosophy or law or mathematics, wine is a *subject*, or what Arnold Toynbee would call an intelligible field of study. The easiest way to comprehend this idea is to realize that one can *talk* about wine, and on a dozen planes, from the simple one of an exchange of likes and dislikes, to more complex ones involving the careful analysis of sensations together with such fields of inquiry as history, geography, topography, physics, chemistry, law, and commerce. Name me any liquid—except our own blood—that flows more intimately and incessantly through the labyrinth of symbols we have conceived to mark our status as human beings, from the rudest peasant festival to the mystery of the

Eucharist. To take wine into our mouths is to savor a droplet of the river of human history.

The old-fashioned phrase, at once noble and jocular, "to discuss one's wine" glows with meaning, just as no meaning would attach to a "discussion" of ice-cream soda or Coca-Cola, or any of those children's beverages which we grown-up Americans actually *drink*, giving the unsympathetic observer the same queasy feeling one gets from watching an adult playing with a rattle in a lunatic asylum.

Similarly, it is no accident that the subject of wine should have stimulated the thought of so many serious writers, from the greatest, such as Plato and Euripides, down through Peacock, Thackeray, Meredith to such rare spirits of our own day as Samuel Eliot Morison (who has written beautifully on port) and the late Hilaire Belloc.

These writers have done much for wine; but so powerful is wine that it can do as much for writers. Interesting, for example, is the case of George Saintsbury (1845–1933). By general consent his *Notes on a Cellarbook* ranks as the nearest thing in English to a wine classic. Saintsbury was by trade a historian and professor of literature, the author of perhaps half a hundred fat tomes of solid though often crotchety scholarship. He had apparently read everything in half a dozen languages. Yet nothing he wrote will last except a tiny volume that you may read in half an hour and savor for a lifetime. He put together *Notes on a Cellarbook* when he was 75, many years after he had been compelled to abandon serious wine-drinking. The wines he discusses are virtually all from the nineteenth century, and you and I will never drink them. Yet, so vast is his knowledge, so accurate his memory, and so delightful his Tory wit, that this little collection of casual notes will be read when all his scholarship is dust. His character was as crusted as the port he prized, and character impinging on a miracle (wine is a miracle) may be one of the keys to the secret of literary survival.

I can think of another piece of wine-writing that may, along with Saintsbury's, pass this final test. That is Hilaire Belloc's *Heroic Poem in Praise of Wine*, conceived at a Miltonic elevation. The seven words quoted from it that head this essay enclose more of life's heartbreak than will all this year's novels.

Civilized minds, such as Saintsbury's and Belloc's, turn to wine precisely because they *are* civilized; because wine is a civilizing agent, one of the few dependable ones, one that again and again has proved its life-enhancing properties. When you find a first-rate brain, like Shaw's, rejecting wine, you have probably also found the key to certain weaknesses flawing that first-rate brain. The Founding Fathers, if recollection serves, were all wine drinkers; some subtle coarsening, a slight lowering of the national tone, made its entrance with Andrew Jackson and his gang of corn liquor devotees. H. Warner Allen's claim may seem a trifle expansive, but surely not absurd: "Main Street would vanish if all its inhabitants drank half a bottle of wine with each meal."

As a subject one can as easily finish with wine as with Shakespeare. There is always more to be learned and therefore more to be communicated, for wine does not isolate but binds men together. As one drinks more and better bottles many mental processes are called into play—memory, imagination, judgment, comparison are but a few. Even volition is involved, as when one summons the will power not to aquiesce in the opinions of other wine drinkers, or refuses to be bluffed by the prestige of a year or label. At such moments one may even claim to be performing a moral act.

I believe these things deeply, just as, like any sensible person, I discount the abracadabra of wine: the excesses of connoisseurship, the absurdities of finicky service, the ceremonial of a hierarchy of glasses, the supposed ability of the expert to determine from a few sips which side of the hill the original grapes were grown on. One can make excellent love in a meager hall bedroom, the requisite elements being three: two lovers and a means of support. So with wine, the requisite elements being likewise three: a bottle, which may be a country-wench Rhône, surrendering at once its all, or a magisterial Romanée Conti, calling for involved investigation; a glass, preferably thin, clear, and holding at least half a pint; and a lover. (Perhaps I should add a corkscrew.)

But, because wine may be enjoyed without hoopla, that does not mean that care should not be taken in its consideration. Wine is elemental, not elementary.

This said, the time would seem to have come for a short, testy digression on those two opposed figures, the wine-snob and the wine *sans-culotte*.

It is easy to make fun of the wine-snob. It is also often good fun. Everyone recalls James Thurber's caption to his drawing showing one would-be connoisseur offering his dinner guests a glass of wine: "It's a naïve domestic Burgundy without any breeding, but I think you'll be amused by its presumption." Such silliness exists, and should be laughed out of court. On the other hand a "wine-snob" may simply be someone who knows more about wine than I do—I meet him frequently—and has not yet learned to convey his information tactfully or clothe his enthusiasm in quiet English. But we must qualify further. Thurber's popinjay *is* a popinjay—and yet the word "breeding," which may seem affectation, has a fairly definite meaning. It is part of the slang of wine lore. A good Châteauneuf-du-Pape may boast a dozen excellent qualities, including its moderate price. Taste it, however, after a first-rate Latour and it is not difficult to sense that the claret is clothed in a certain unaggressive elegance to which the forthright Rhône makes no claim. The plain fact is that wine has personality. It is not dead matter, like a motorcar, but a live thing, like a human being or a page of fine prose. One must be wary of snob-calling: the inferior man is often known by the number of snobs he complains of meeting. The man who drools his comparative history of the major-league shortstops of the past twenty years is hailed as a fan. But he who knows something about "one of God's greatest gifts to man," in André Simon's phrase, is called a wine-snob. A man who tells you in detail about his special-body motorcar is listened to with rapt attention. But one who writes with love about his magnum of Mouton-Rothschild '69 is a suspicious character, even though the car's body cannot compare with the claret's, even though obsolescence is built into one as longevity is built into the other.

The wine-snob at his worst is a bit of a bore and a bit of a fool. But at least he is a learned bore and a learned fool. The wine *sans-culotte* is a complete bore and a complete fool. He is opposed to a hierarchy of taste (even when it is patiently explained to him that this is not a fixed hierarchy) as his kin spirit is opposed to a hierarchy of political competence. So widespread among us is the notion that the only way to discover the right standard is to count the noses of those adhering to it, that even wine dealers, who know better, and writers on wine, who know much better, give lip service to such dogmas as "A wine is good if it tastes good" or "A good wine is the wine you like." Back of these statements probably lies the idea that they will make converts to wine by making wine seem as accessible, as "democratic" as orange pop.

Yet the very wineman who, for what he thinks sound commercial reasons, expounds this nonsense, will spend a great deal of his time contradicting it by his actions. For he is constantly offering his friends, not the wine they will "like" or that he thinks they will "like," but simply the best wine he has, in the conviction that the palate is as educable as the mind or the body.

That the mind is educable may be questioned by those leaders of American education who, having made the profound observation that the majority of children prefer play to study, are led by the iron logic of the count-noses theory to rebuild the curriculum around play. Such play is frequently disguised as "study": visiting pickle factories or learning how to answer the telephone. (In one school of my acquaintance this latter scholarly activity is part of a course known as Communication Skills.) That the body is educable, however, no good American denies. The duffer doesn't boast of his dufferdom. He doesn't say,

"Well, I enjoy shooting over 100, therefore shooting over 100 is good golf." He does his best to reduce his score, because he *knows* there is such a thing as better playing than his own.

Perhaps I can make my point clearer by instancing a certain beverage that advertises itself on the car cards and subway posters of New York City as "the wine you can cut with a knife." Now it is highly probable that a great many people (who do not really want to drink wine, but *do* want to drink sugar) actually buy and like this bottled emetic. No one objects to this: the palate is a free agent. But it is not fair to say that because this peculiar concoction "tastes good" it *is* good. It may be a good *drink* (though on what grounds I cannot conceive) but it cannot be a good *wine*. And it cannot be a good wine because the capacity to be "cut with a knife" is simply not one of the qualities of wine. Such a quality is proper for honey or Turkish coffee or for other preparations whose characteristic charm lies in their syrupiness. But it is not proper for wine. You may object that a great sauternes is sweet, or a fine port. I ask you to taste them and to note how perfectly balanced is the sugar, how lightly it lies on the tongue, to what *other* qualities it is married. I ask you also to remember that "the wine you can cut with a knife" is sold as a table wine, presumably for hearty consumption, whereas no one in his right senses would think of drinking over three ounces of a Château Yquem at a single meal.

The childish palate will *always* at first prefer the excessive or the unbalanced taste. Upon certain primitive African or Melanesian tribes you cannot confer a greater gift than a can of peaches. This does not make canned peaches a delectable food; canned peaches remain exactly what they are, no matter how many savages tell you they are superior to a *soufflé Grand Marnier*.

Few men can afford to drink only the best; and indeed no man should want to, for there is a certain monotony in excellence, as there is in mediocrity. But that need not hinder a man, even as he sips his sound, cheap wine, from knowing that there are other wines capable of giving him, if he has paid any attention to his palate, rarer and finer pleasures. A wine is not good merely because I like it. It is perfectly possible however that I may like it because it is not good; in which case it is pointless for me to change the wine before changing myself.

These intemperate remarks off my chest, I return to the narrative of my small *affaire*. This narrative, as you must already have noticed, will not teach you anything. To learn about wine you must consult the manuals of the learned. I record here, not information, but merely the birth and growth of an emotion. The small store of knowledge I possess I did not begin to accumulate until about seven years after my return from Paris. During those seven lean years Prohibition played out its dismal tragicomedy. In 1933 I made the helpful acquaintance of Frank Schoonmaker, then a youthful amateur, now one of the greatest living experts, particularly in the subtle field of German wines. In a small way I helped to launch *The Complete Wine Book*, by Mr. Schoonmaker and Tom Marvel, one— and by far the best—of the flood of manuals released by Repeal. I even invested the sum of five hundred dollars in a wine-importing concern, lost every cent of it, and have no regrets. A visit to the beautiful Widmer winery at Naples, New York (where the hospitable Mr. Widmer laid out for us twenty-three wines on a broad open-air trestle table), made me aware of the treasures of my own country.

I learned that most of the few simple rules about drinking wine are not chichi, but sensible conclusions drawn from hundreds of years of experience of intelligent men. I learned also that these rules are not inflexible. It is standard practice, and good practice, to marry Chablis to shellfish, but the best Chablis I ever tasted was a superchilled bottle drunk in defiant gulps, unaccompanied by any food, on a very hot day when I was very thirsty. One morning at 3 A.M., tired and famished after eight hours at my writing desk, I ravished the kitchen and ate two cans of unheated Vienna sausages on Vermont crackers, together with a whole bottle of Chassagne-Montrachet '45. Barbarous? Not at all—merely an instance controverting Robert Browning, with

> *the time and the place*
> *And the loved one all together!*

One can learn, not only from such accidental successes (literally, *succès de fiasco*) but even from elaborate failures. I once attended a wine-tasting given by a gentleman whose reputation had been originally established on the football field, but who had graduated to higher things. With characteristic generosity he had assembled for us a dazzling collection of Rhines and Moselles, the finest labels and the most unbelievable years. The most recent of them belonged to the incomparable 1921 vintage;

but others dated from 1915, 1911, and I think even from 1900 and 1893. They had been bought, in a fit of enthusiasm, from a single cellar; and, with one or two exceptions, the entire potentially heavenly collection had faded. They had not turned or decayed; but their hearts had stopped. Yet not one of us said so. We muttered, every cowardly man jack of us, some polite vacuity—and went on drinking these noble ectoplasms, admiring the naked Emperor's new clothes. It may have been that we felt a flood of sympathy for our host in his misfortune, but I cannot help remembering that he stood six feet two in his socks and could have demolished any seven of us poor indoor creatures at a blow. Even at such polite functions as wine-tastings one learns a good deal about human nature.

I suppose no account of a happy marriage can be, except to the participants, notably interesting. I shall hurry over mine. Repeal came at the end of 1933; hence next year wine and I will celebrate the twenty-fifth anniversary of our legal union. (Don't send silver; glass will do, with the proper enclosures.) The changing embodiments of my spouse have on occasion disappointed me: some, the termagants, developed an acid temper; the reputed charms of others faded upon consummation. Many were not worth the bride-purchase price. With still others, though good of their kind, I found myself, after a decent interval of connubial experiment, temperamentally incompatible. I shall never learn to love the lady known as Vouvray, for example, and I gladly surrender all *rosé* wines to their admirers. Yes, we have had our ups and downs, wine and I, our misunderstandings and our reconciliations, our delights and our discords. On the whole however I think of ourselves as a model couple: faithful, mutually solicitous, still ardent, and, in the case of the lady, well-preserved.

The record of our union is contained in my Cellar Book, the earliest entry being that of October 17, 1935, at which time I seem to have laid down a dozen Morey, Clos des Lambrays '29 at a price ($28) that today induces wistful dreams. "Quite beautiful" is the notation under "Remarks": vague phrasing, but from the heart. The day before yesterday I binned three cases that for some years had been maturing their charms for my special benefit: Volnay, Clos des Ducs '43; Niersteiner Rehbach '43 (which may be *too* mature—it is such delicate uncertainties that give to wine drinking what hazards give to golf); and Piesporter Goldtröpfchen Schloss Marienlay '47. Between these two entries lies a third of a lifetime of adventures, each one drawn by the twist of a corkscrew from its horizontal torpor in the dim cellar to the vivid life awaiting it within the clear glass.

The drinking of wine seems to me to have a moral edge over many other pleasures and hobbies in that it promotes love of one's neighbor. As a general thing it is not a lone occupation. A bottle of wine begs to be shared; I have never met a miserly wine lover. The social emotions it generates are equidistant from the philatelist's solitary gloating and the football fan's gregarious hysteria. "Wine was not invented," says J. M. Scott. "It was born. Man has done no more than learn to educate it." In other words, wine is alive, and when you offer it to your fellowman you are offering him life. More than that, you are calling out more life in him, you are engaging in what might be called creative flattery, for you are asking him to summon up his powers of discrimination, to exercise his taste, or perhaps merely to evince curiosity or a desire to learn. I know no other liquid that, placed in the mouth, forces one to think.

That is why there are few better gifts to send a newly married couple than a case or two—or a bottle or two—of wine. It is not that, when drinking it, they will recall the donor—if you crave such vulgar satisfactions it is more efficient to send them a chair with a pair of spurs set in the upholstery. It is that, when drinking it, they will become more conscious of *themselves*, of their own capacity for joy. I doubt that you get the same result from a toaster.

It is for this reason that men of a wiser generation than ours left wine to their sons after their death. I cannot leave much, but I have carefully seen to it that I own more wine than I can possibly drink before I die. (This is not hard to do; forego a suit of clothes—no man needs to buy more than one every five years or so—and you have the wherewithal for three cases.) What good will three thousand dull dollars, which can at best yield five or six per cent, do my son as compared with a thousand inherited bottles of wine, guaranteed to generate cheer and laughter and good talk long after my last swallow?

But, if such considerations seem too rarefied, I retreat to my last line of defense, that of enlightened selfishness. I heard once, or perhaps read somewhere, that the palate is among the last of our organs to decay. I do not know whether this is so; I am not so great a fool as to hand over to the Inquisition of science a statement that has all the marks of a self-evident truth. Yes, our muscles give way at last to gravity's quiet, resistless pull; the best, the most joyful of our glands, in the end withers; the eye, the ear lose some of their fine quick power to seize upon the world; the limbs begin to ask What's the hurry? But I know men of eighty whose infirmities for the brief space of a bottle's emptying vanish as they sip their wine, their taste buds as lively as when they were one-and-twenty— nay, livelier. The pleasures of old age are few, but what one is more worthy of cultivation than a pleasure that the body, even in decay, can enjoy without enfeeblement, and judgment and memory still lift to the plane of the non-material?

I turn the pages of my Cellar Book. Two lines, appearing toward the end of *The Waste Land*, slip unbidden into my mind:

> *London Bridge is falling down falling down falling*
> *down. . . .*
> 　. . . .
> *These fragments I have shored against my ruins*

Mere Words

Babel and Babylon

At the pleasant-sounding address of Rockburne House, Alton, Hampshire, England, lives a youngish couple, Iona and Peter Opie. For some time the Opies have been dedicating their days ("all day every day") to a task at odds with much that our time deems really important. "We do not do anything else," Mr. Opie writes me, "except patch our clothes and hope one day some foundation will recognize our work." He goes on cheerily enough, "But that is the fate of most research workers, it seems. One does the work because one likes it."

The Opies—they have three children, James, Bobby, and Letitia—have spent much of their married life on a Mother Goose chase. Their shelves, for example, contain "two or three hundred" Mother Goose books. Authorities on eighteenth-century children's literature, they are the editors of *The Oxford Dictionary of Nursery Rhymes*, which is both lighthearted and learned. Assisted by five thousand erudite colleagues, all children, they are presently conducting a Britain-wide survey. This is expected to be published in a two-volume collection of the traditional lore, street games and rhymes that make up the autarchic literature of child-hood.

I doubt greatly that the Opies will get their foundation grant, but I wish them good fortune, for they have staked out for themselves a really civilized field of research. Per-haps as much can be learned from them as from all the child-development laboratories in the country.

Two years ago they published, after a decade of happy labor, *The Oxford Nursery Rhyme Book*. This is not to be confused with the earlier volume. It has no paraphernalia of scholarship. It is a collection of rhymes and riddles, baby games and ballads, tongue twisters and alphabet jingles, songs and lullabies, catches and prayers—all far more certain of immortality than the *Iliad*, unless the child mind of the future is deformed to the point where the imagination has been cut out of it by the surgeons of tele-vision and the comic strips.

This must be the largest collection of its sort in existence. Indeed, since J. O. Halliwell's *Nursery Rhymes of England* (1842) it is the only one that can claim to be both com-prehensive and freshly researched. Folklorists will recog-nize its value. A few thousand parents with taste and judgment will buy it for their lap listeners. And most of us will continue to be serenely ignorant of the fact that these eight hundred rhymes hold more humor, wisdom, fancy, and charm than a gross of young novelists, whether of the Bright, Dismal, or Shocking variety, could produce if rolled into one—an operation, come to think of it, that might be a pleasure to watch.

The Opies' book renders unnecessary all other editions

of nursery rhymes. It is a neat volume, about six by nine inches. This makes it a welcome relief from the Brobdingnagian monstrosities foisted upon us these days by certain juvenile publishers—or, as I do not wish by ambiguity to insult the children, let us call them publishers of juveniles. These consist largely of lots of bright-colored ink, white paper folded large, and a few carefully doled out words. There is a notion abroad that because children are small they therefore do not see very well. It is assumed that their attention must be caught by giant type and screaming full-page illustrations—the literary equivalent of the shrieking, bellowing, hollering, shouting, and roaring that make so many children's TV shows "lively."

The fact is that unless their visual taste has been coarsened by the comics, which are produced almost entirely by the antichild imagination, children prefer books suitable to their size. Particularly do they like small, numerous, nonflorid pictures. During the eighteenth and early nineteenth centuries hawkers cried from door to door their midget nursery-rhyme chapbooks. Some of these were no larger than 3 by 1⅛ inches. Embellished by tiny woodcuts, one to a page, they retain to this day a cottage charm no lurid four-color job can boast. We imagine that because grownups like Technicolor, children must. We forget that it takes time for taste to degenerate.

The Opies, who really know something about children in the natural rather than the exploited state, have illustrated their book by calling upon imagination, not the billboard paintbrush. For one thing almost every verse is illustrated. Thus the child is given an opportunity to enhance the pleasure of recognition by matching rhyme to picture. Also, because the world of the nursery rhyme is rich and crowded (it has added to our common stock more fictional characters than have Shakespeare and Dickens combined) many illustrations are needed to image it adequately.

But what makes the Opies' volume a special joy is the quality of the pictures. They have dared to throw overboard the whole post-Arthur Rackham tradition and to go back to "the precise miniature world of the Bewick-style engraving."

From dozens of forgotten peddler's chapbooks they have rescued the tiny fascinating woodcuts of masters such as Thomas Bewick (1753–1828) and his lesser brother John. Only to the sniffy adult are these "quaint." To the child they are just right. This is the way it should be: the little boys in top hats; the trundle bed, the windlass, the exact room interiors, as if seen through a peephole; the gentlemen in smallclothes and tailcoats; the animals drawn with modesty and love rather than hopped up in the Hollywood manner for the purpose of inspiring terror or convulsive laughter; the funny faces—but not *too* funny, no trace of the cartoon; the whole curious mixed atmosphere of literalness and magic, which is also the very heart and soul of the words themselves.

These old woodcuts are supplemented with one hundred and fifty loving designs by the contemporary wood engraver Joan Hassall. Her skew chisel works in the sly-grotesque Bewick tradition, tempered by the charming decorum of the early Victorian style. The result is a book whose illustrations bear the same absolute and classical relation to the text that Tenniel bears to *Alice in Wonderland*. There is no need (one man's opinion) ever to illustrate either book in any other manner

As for the text, the Opies, in contrast to many modern editions, give full versions. Jill's tumble ordinarily truncates the career of the notable pair; the fact is that there are three sequent episodes, with an unfamiliar but gratifying happy ending. Or, to take single lines: "All work and no play makes Jack a dull boy" is fair enough, but the less-known capping line, "All play and no work makes Jack a mere toy," is even more sagacious.

We think we know Mother Goose. What we really know are the tabloid versions of the last fifty years. I have nothing against Mother Hubbard and Tommy Tucker and Jack Horner, but they are overfamiliar members of a large family, rich in eccentric aunts and uncles and odd second cousins.

Before reading the Opie collection I had never met the three little ghostesses who ate buttered toastesses. Nor had I encountered the tale, terse and haunting, of Johnnie Norrie who

> *Gaed up three paper stairies*
> *And in at a paper doorie.*

I am not sure that I had even heard of the surrealist rat who

> *for want of stairs,*
> *Went down a rope to say his prayers.*

Listening to a pop song on the radio about Moses who supposes his toeses are roses I was shamefully ignorant of its being a nursery rhyme. I have also learned that the pig the piper's son stole was a pastry porker, not a real one; and that a puzzling episode in the life of the lipophobe Sprat concerns the time he sold his one-eared cat to buy—butter.

Little boys and little girls? Sure, but do you know what young men and young women are made of, made of? Ding, Dong, Bell? Of course, but how about this superior Scottish version with its wonderful, casually realistic final quatrain?

> *Ding dang, bell rang,*
> *Cattie's in the well, man.*
> *Fa' dang her in, man?*
> *Jean and Sandy Din, man.*
> *Fa' took her oot, man?*
> *Me and Willie Cout, man.*
> *A' them that kent her*
> 　*When she was alive,*
> *Come to the burialie*
> 　*Between four and five.*

In their researches the Opies also discovered that many old expressions had more point than their more familiar modern versions—one of the few possibly cogent arguments going to show that our ancestors had more sense than we have. For example, we appear to have forgotten the second balancing clause of "Charity begins at home but should not end there." "Seeing's believing" (a doubtful proposition upon which nevertheless the whole triumph of modern camera journalism is based) used to continue "but feeling's the truth."

The fascination of nursery rhymes lies partly in their simplicity. But it also lies partly in their complexity. This is felt by children as well as by grownups, though less consciously, and of course they do not spoil the whole affair by writing essays about it. Take this seven-second ring-dance jingle:

> *Sally go round the sun,*
> *Sally go round the moon,*
> *Sally go round the chimney-pots*
> *On a Saturday afternoon.*

In these four lines there is as much intimation of infinity as there is in Blake's

> *To see a world in a grain of sand,*
> *And a heaven in a wild flower*

and I consider the poetry superior. It is not only Shakespeare "who alone of us/Will put an ass's head in Fairyland." The children have been doing it for centuries. Categories are an adult invention, to which children, who feel that life is a flow, not a file, pay little attention.

Nursery verse is of course limited, like the ballads, but it is less limited than at first appears. What terror, for example, gasps out of these stanzas, with their dreadful iteration, sung to children when all England waited in fear of Boney:

> *Baby, baby, if he hears you,*
> *As he gallops past the house,*
> *Limb from limb at once he'll tear you,*
> *Just as pussy tears a mouse.*
>
> *And he'll beat you, beat you, beat you,*
> *And he'll beat you all to pap,*
> *And he'll eat you, eat you, eat you,*
> *Every morsel snap, snap, snap.*

(I understand, of course, that such vivid imagery is frowned on by progressive educationists, concerned that our children should grow up with a sense of security. It is interesting that so many well-intentioned people should be opposed to the realism of Mother Goose—people who are smartly contemporary with the same world-culture that has produced such energetically publicized phenomena as Communist-Fascist torture techniques, Communist Chinese brainwashing, the animal scream of the jet plane, the H-bomb, and rock and roll.)

In nursery rhymes one of the most interesting elements is the treatment of sex. There is a certain smarmy unreality in Mr. Disney's characteristically modern handling of the romance in *Snow White and the Seven Dwarfs*, just as there is a kind of leering Broadway knowingness in other contemporary juvenile treatments of the same theme. In the rhymes all is brisk, honest, aboveboard, almost adult:

> *Sing jigmijole, the pudding bowl,*
> *The table and the frame;*
> *My master he did cudgel me,*
> *For kissing of my dame.*

For the facts of life give me Mother Goose:

> *I peeped through the window,*
> *I peeped through the door,*
> *I saw pretty Katie*
> *A-dancing on the floor.*
> *I cuddled her and fondled her,*
> *I set her on my knee;*
> *I says, Pretty Katie,*
> *Won't you marry me?*

A new-swept parlour,
A new-made bed,
A new cup and saucer
Against we get wed.

I do not quite know what it is about most (though not all) of the TV shows and movies for children, as well as even the "good" comics, that gives an impression of spuriousness. I believe it has something to do with our advanced state of technical progress. The network factory, the Hollywood factory are waging war with the nursery at twilight and the neighborhood street filling with laughter as school lets out.

It is so tempting to substitute "effects" for charm, to utilize the gigantic techniques of all sorts of public-address systems instead of the simplicities of private communication. "A mother's own voice," say the Opies, "is worth more than four-and-twenty professional singers trilling on the radio"; and of course it is true. But its truth can only be recognized at the cost of the suicide of an industry; which is too much to expect. The producers of entertainment for children seem to *work* so hard. Battles, noise, orchestras, violence, a whole spectrum of repulsive color, Tin Pan Alley, choruses, pseudo-historical "authentic" costumes, live lions duller even than live actors, advertising, trailers, teasers, publicity premières, shanghaied child audiences, giveaways, prize contests, supertalented M.C. child-amusers who can sing, dance, shout, make faces, and get up every weekday at 5 A.M.—and it will all be forgotten while the cow continues to jump over the moon and children wonder how many miles to Babylon. Or is there a chance that Babylon will lose out and Babel win?

Small Excellencies:
A Dissertation on Puns

*A good pun may be admitted among the small excellencies
of lively conversation.*   JAMES BOSWELL

*The Seeds of Punning are in the Minds of all Men, and tho'
they may be subdued by Reason, Reflection, and good Sense,
they will be very apt to shoot up in the greatest Genius,
that is not broken and cultivated by the Rules of Art.*
                    ADDISON, *The Spectator*, MAY 10, 1711

*To trifle with the vocabulary which is the vehicle of social
intercourse, is to tamper with the currency of human intelligence. He who would violate the sanctities of his Mother
Tongue would invade the recesses of the national till without remorse.*   SAMUEL JOHNSON

*Debauched from sense, let double meanings run,
The vague conundrum and the prurient pun.*
                    TOBIAS SMOLLETT

*Of puns it has been said that those most dislike who are
least able to utter them.*　　　　　Edgar Allan Poe

*Where the common people like puns, and make them, the
nation is on a high level of culture.*　　　G. C. Lichtenberg

There is something to be said against puns. The man
who pounces with his pun upon something you have just
said reveals his attendance upon your words rather than
upon your thoughts. He derails your train of reflection.
Puns upset the dignity of speech, flout the etiquette of
serious communication, cut the ground of logic from under
us. We groan not only to convey disapproval but to cover
discomfiture.

To a great practitioner like late, blessed Christopher
Morley, a pun is language on vacation. But to the non-
practitioner it may seem more like language in agony, its
appeal more akin to the esthetic charms of the contor-
tionist's art.

The candid lover of puns will admit this charge. He will
cheerfully confess to a perversion, to a *preference* for language under stress, as Dali prefers a melted watch to the
correct time.

Surrealist punning, as we may call it, has a certain feverish, almost delirious quality. Thus there are wordplays
that *almost* make sense, teasing the mind as afterimages
tease the optic nerve. Often these hazy japes are the very
ones that stick fast in the memory, as the jingle *Punch,
Brothers, Punch* pursued the man in Mark Twain's story.

Marianne Moore has a famous definition of poetry: "Imaginary gardens with real toads in them." The phrase makes your head spin. You can almost grasp the meaning—but not quite. There are nightmare puns lacking all the poetical suggestiveness of Miss Moore's phrase yet with some of its odd, tantalizing effect on the mind. I remember one night during which I vainly tried to fool my insomnia by conjuring up dozens of these little lunacies. Some of them still return to haunt me. I find myself, glazed of eye, muttering, "Better osculate than never" or "Marionettes, repent at leisure." If they're rhythmic, it's even worse: "I could not love thee, dear, so much Loved I not Ostermoor" or "Anabolic, metabolic Comin' through the Rye."

Such puns are pointless and bare of amusement. But they are interesting to the lover of puns, as I have said, precisely because they expose the vulnerability of language to the attack of the irrational.

Let us take a few test cases of a more standard kind. In *Animal Crackers*, Groucho Marx recalled that when shooting elephants in Africa he found the tusks very difficult to remove—adding, however, that in Alabama the Tuscaloosa. To the contrapuntalist such a statement is quite irrelephant; to the propunent it is pleasing because it shows what language can produce under pressure, in this case language showing both the marks of strain and the strain of Marx.

I will give you another. Once on a television show called *This is Show Business* George S. Kaufman got himself mired in the word *euphemism*. After playing with it for a few seconds he turned to his fellow panelist Sam Levenson, declared, "Euphemism and I'm for youse'm," and closed

the discussion. Now this, like Tuscaloosa, was pure purposeless play, art for art's sake, like doodling, whittling,
singing in the bathroom, and chewing bubble gum. It
pleases the pun-lover precisely *because* of its denial of
meaning. Mr. Kaufman of course is no less a master of the
meaningful pun. One remembers his anguished cry at the
poker table: "I am being trey-deuced!" Among the greatest
wordplays of all time is his unsettling remark that what is
one man's Mede is another man's Persian.

Puns also please because in their commonest form they
seem to challenge the law of nature which tells us that two
things cannot occupy the same place at the same time.
They are condensations, like Lewis Carroll's portmanteau
coinages (chuckle + snort = chortle). Robert Benchley's
"Louisa M. Woollcott" is an example that comes to mind,
and later on, when we discuss the Meld Pun, we shall refer
to several such slight cases of merger.

Impromptu Puns, though not generally the finest, often
supply the purest pleasure. They are the May flies of language, living for a split second, dying to afford a moment's
small delight. Unrepeatable, they are less akin to literature
than to the more ephemeral arts—pantomime, conversation, making love. They are the work, or rather the play, of
a unique instant, and their whole effect flowers from the
miracle of unconsciously perfect timing. "A pun," says
Lamb, "and its recognitory laugh, must be co-instanta-
neous. The one is the brisk lightning, and the other the
fierce thunder. A moment's interval, and the link is
snapped."

I recall an impromptu pun of my own which, delivered
at precisely the proper moment, gave general gratification

at the time. Set down in print thirty-odd years later it seems to me almost devoid of wit. When I was a Columbia undergraduate the most brilliant student in the class was "Mike" Schapiro, now one of the country's great art authorities. I am putting it mildly when I say that Mr. Schapiro knew more than his professors and could outtalk them with ease. Somehow they did not always accept their defeats with complacence, a fact that now and then seemed to reflect itself in Mike's grades. Once, after he had won a particularly vigorous argument with the instructor, I muttered, "Another Schapyrrhic victory."

Such impromptus are successful for the unrecapturable moment only. You cannot judge them in cold blood any more than you can grade fragrances by memory. But, as we shall see, other puns, products of calculation, *may* be graded, just like eggs; and, as Fowler in his *Modern English Usage* reminds us, "only those who lack the wit to make them are unaware of the fact."

Bad puns are coined by those who are more ear-minded than meaning-minded; or who are professional gagmen, undermining the language systematically for profit. Bob Hope uses thousands like *Waves: Sailors who go down to the sea in slips.* This is passable but, like virtually all the puns that ride the air, it has a file odor. *In the Rainbow Room they dance the rumba to a tune that would Rockefeller Center. What did Cleopatra say when Mark Antony asked if she was true to him? Omar Khayyam.* Such puns depress us as do waxworks, and for the same reason—they are artifice acting like art. They are the product of dogged determination, they shine with the sweat of effort. "A bad pun," says Dr. David S. Stern of Philadelphia, himself a notable punster, "is as idiotic as all getout, which is what the listeners would like to do."

Yet, dismal as much current punning may appear, the general level is vastly higher than it has ever been. Progress has been steady. Take the first European pun I know, to be found in the ninth book of Homer's *Odyssey*. To fool the giant Polyphemus, the wily Odysseus has given his name as *Outis* (Greek for *Nobody*). When Odysseus later attacks Polyphemus in the cave, the latter calls to his fellow Cyclopes for help, crying, "Nobody is killing me!" (As they were all classical scholars in those days, he cries this in Greek.) His friends take him literally of course and make no attempt to aid him. Odysseus, who is telling the story and can say anything he pleases, calls this "my clever stratagem." It seems pretty primitive to us—though less so perhaps when we remind ourselves that our own "Dey's nobody here but us chickens" is merely a switch on Homer's wheeze, and a poultry affair at best.

To estimate our advance over Homer study James Joyce's *Ulysses*, constructed on the story plan of the *Odyssey*. *Ulysses* is crammed with wordplays whose richness and allusiveness are possible only because three thousand years of language growth lie between Joyce and his model. When you come to his *Finnegans Wake* the pun has expanded to include the whole book. I calculate that *Finnegans Wake* contains at least 50,000 puns in perhaps ten languages. Here punning has become cancerous. Joyce does not master the pun, he is mastered by it. It is as though his ear were distorted so that it could never hear single sounds but only a multitude of echoes. This affliction made Joyce the greatest punster who ever lived. It also

made his book unreadable except to a syndicate of glossolo-
gists.

Puns improved during the Middle Ages (there's a little
of the Schoolman's mentality in every punster) and began
to flourish during the Renaissance, with the development
of vernacular tongues and the advent of Rabelais and
Shakespeare. But even these lords of language are only
moderately superior to old Homer and his clever strata-
gems. The Bard, for example, is a punning fool, bringing
to the job far more enthusiasm than judgment. His wordplays, like his clowns, seem to us, with some exceptions,
tiresome. Yet he stands out as the best of a bad bunch. The
general level was about that of Queen Elizabeth I's "Ye be
burly, my Lord of Burleigh, but ye shall make less stir in
our realm than my Lord of Leicester." This may be to the
Queen's taste but it is hardly to ours.

The eighteenth century in England made further ad-
vances—Swift was an inveterate if sloppy punster. A friend
of Boswell named Dempster one day asked his own sister,
who dwelt in Kensington, whether currants and raisins
could be bought there. "O yes," she replied, "as currently
and reasonably as in London." (The reader will bear in
mind that the eighteenth-century pronunciation of *reason*
would sound Irish to our ears.) This eighteenth-century
gem is hardly brilliant, but on the other hand compare the
Greek-English pun, later quoted, attributed to another
eighteenth-century figure, Charles James Fox.

With the nineteenth century and the appearance of
Lamb, Sydney Smith, and other connoisseurs, puns began
to go places. Lamb's outright praise of the practice is the
first I know of: "A pun is a noble thing *per se*. It fills the

mind; it is as perfect as a sonnet; better." It was Lamb who wished his last breath to be exhaled in a pun: an inspiring, or rather expiring, thought.

As the Victorian age deepens, however, a certain let-down is observable. A few early Victorian puns are neat enough, such as Praed's

> *His partners at the whist club said*
> *That he was faultless in his dealings.*

(A couplet that cheers but hardly inebriates.) In general, however, the Victorians were heavy punners, relentless, ingenious, a bit grim. The tone was set by the comic poet Thomas Hood, probably the first Englishman to make a living solely out of commercial humor. Year after year Hood turned out thousands of puns, a few technically remarkable, most of them dreary.

> *Ben Battle was a soldier bold,*
> *And used to war's alarms;*
> *But a cannon-ball took off his legs*
> *So he laid down his arms!*

That was the kind of thing, exclamation point and all, that poor Thomas could and did provide by the ream, con-vulsing his audience. The Hood tradition was carried on by *Punch*, which even nowadays will print puns worthy of Homer. It is not that the puns are bad but that they are ruined by an old-fashioned build-up. Examples:

"There were no psychiatrists in medieval England, re-marks a writer. But it must be remembered that in those days the country was sparsely inhibited."

"An American dietician is exciting comment by experi-menting with various types of music during meals as an aid to digestion. Jealous rivals accuse him of playing to the calory."

Today the poorer among our airwave comics use puns as bad as Hood's. But their programs are the bargain basement of American humor and not at all fairly representative. The influence of such ingenious word-coiners as Walter Winchell and such humorists as Ogden Nash, Ring Lardner, S. J. Perelman, George S. Kaufman, and Peter De Vries, indeed the whole experimental drive of our language, has worked to produce a body of puns that surpass anything history has to show.

Let's look at a few exhibits, drawing them from both the past and the present.

The simplest pun is based on the re-use of a word with a slight shift in meaning: S. J. Perelman's "Doctor, I've got Bright's disease and he's got mine." It may turn on an almost undetectable alteration of meaning in the simplest word: Saki's "The cook was a good cook as cooks go; and as cooks go, she went."

The well-known wisecrack, "The self-made man adores his maker," supplies another example of the minimal-shift pun. This same witticism is polished to burnished perfection in Fred Allen's summary of a vaudevillian he disliked: "I know what became of Fay. The last time I saw Fay he was walking down Lovers' Lane, holding his own hand."

A pun involving not the slightest verbal distortion may have great richness. Take Sydney Smith's famous remark. Observing two housewives screaming at each other across a courtyard, he remarked that they would never agree because they were arguing from different premises.

Slightly more complicated than the identical-word pun

is the Homonym. Here the words match in sound but not meaning. The homonym pun is the basic pun. Shakespeare used it almost exclusively; as children we cut our punning eyeteeth (known as *bon mot*-lars) on it. It may be quite plain, like Alexander Woollcott's title for a collection of his theater reviews: *Enchanted Aisles*—which might also have been called *Alec in Wonderland*. I submit a home-grown sample of the homonym, plain:

> *The prideful Tern, about to be a mother,*
> *Reflects that two good Terns deserve another.*

Or, though plain, it may boast a fancy frill: "Days of Damon and Knights of Pythias" (O. Henry). It may be as fantastic as this classic by Christopher Morley. He and the late William Rose Benét were looking into the window of a wig shop showing two small wigs on their stands. "They're alike as toupees," said Mr. Morley.

The homonymous pun may be either congruent or near-congruent. A gentleman, crossing the English River Mersey and noting its muddy condition, remarked, "Evidently the quality of Mersey is not strained." I had occasion to note the cloudiness in a bottle of white Burgundy I had opened, and made a similar observation: "The quality of Meursault is not strained." Mine is the poorer pun but it was worth making. Nor do I blush, for

> *Malt does more than Miltown can*
> *To justify God's ways to man.*

The homonym may be broken up too, like light passing through a spectrum. Groucho Marx, in the original stage version of *The Coconuts*, introduced the orchestra leader as follows: "This is Emanuel. I got him from Emanuel Training School. He's Emanuel like." It may be far-fetched and yet perfectly homonymous, as in Ogden Nash's story of the hater of spring who appreciated the fact that his wife shot him with an autumnatic.

When the homonym is imperfect a certain wild touch of imagination is often present. Such puns depend on distortion. The distortion may be of varying degrees of complication. Change a single sound and you get Oliver Herford's "The more waist, the less speed." Change two letters and you get a name for New York's doctor-crowded Park Avenue: Malady Lane. Change a syllable: "The audience strummed their catarrhs" (Woollcott). Introduce an additional syllable: "The things my wife buys at auction are keeping me baroque" (Peter De Vries in an amusing *New Yorker* story about a compulsive punner).

So far we have been considering only single puns, depending on one word. We begin to approach structural complication when we get to double puns, whether homonymous or near-homonymous. Here's a good double pun of the kind that was fashionable in nineteenth-century America. At a dinner party a young lady was energetically flirting with her partner, whose name was Nathaniel. Her hostess-mother was listening with equally evident pleasure to the compliments of a Mr. Campbell. Noticing her daughter's overapparent liveliness, the mother frowned in severe reproof, upon which the daughter sent up a folded note on which she had written:

Dear Ma, don't attempt my young feelings to trammel,
Nor strain at a Nat while you swallow a Campbell.

(Of course for full effect Campbell must be pronounced in the English manner. These are the rhymes that try men's souls.)

Here is a well-constructed contemporary homonymous double pun, the handiwork of Sterling North: "A bustle is like a historical romance: both are fictitious tales based on stern reality." Perhaps that is more witty than funny; I now offer one that is funnier than it is witty, from S. J. Perelman's *Horse Feathers.* The secretary, who has been holding a caller at bay in the anteroom for some time, warns Groucho, "Jennings is waxing wroth," to which Groucho replies, "Never mind. Tell Roth to wax Jennings for a while."

When the homonyms are off-beat and require a double-take from the listener, they acquire some of the uncanny charm of echoes. Here is a first-rate doublet of this sort by F.P.A.: "Take care of your peonies and the dahlias will take care of themselves."

Even harder to forget is Mr. Adams' comment on an unhappy incident of the Spanish Civil War. It appears that some Basques, fleeing before the enemy, were penned into a narrow mountain pass and destroyed. Which, Mr. Adams brooded, is what comes of putting all your Basques into one exit. (Many-in-one charity drives now announce coyly that they are putting all their begs in one ask-it.)

You might imagine that one such Spanish pun would have exhausted Mr. Adams. By no means. Where there's Seville there's a way, as is demonstrated by his other Iberian jewel: "Those Spanish señoritas are a snare Andalusian."

Speaking of Mr. Adams, I recall that once when I was

M.C.'ing a quiz show called *Information Please* I warned the experts not to listen to whispered hints from the audience. "No eavesdropping," I said sternly. Mr. Adams raised his hand. "Adams-dropping O.K.?" he inquired. And now that someone's mentioned *Information Please* I will contend that many of the most diverting puns ever ad-libbed were shot into the air week after week by the four experts, to fall to earth I know not where. Once they were required to identify a certain Middle Eastern potentate. John Gunther confidently supplied the correct answer. "Are you Shah?" I ventured. "Sultanly," he replied.

We were speaking of double puns. Triple puns are as rare as tartar steak. Kipling somewhere refers to Persian as a language so constructed as to make triple-punmaking a common pastime. There is a suggestion of these Iranian possibilities in the verse of William Barnes, the Burns of Dorset, who was a close student of Eastern poetry. Barnes used the term "full-matching" to describe the decorative punmanship of the Persians in which all the sounds of a line are repeated, though with altered meaning. His refrain: *Ah! well-a-day! O wall adieu!* hints at the method. The Welsh repetition of consonantal sounds (*cynghanedd*), which Barnes also adapted to the uses of his beautiful dialect verse, is likewise a kind of punning, employed of course for effects of euphony, not humor.

There is a well-known example of French "full-matching." The story—doubtless invented—goes that a group of French poets were arguing one evening about feats of versification. The following problem was set: to compose an acceptable line of verse; to follow it with another line of verse which should repeat *exactly* every sound in the first line without repeating any of the words themselves; the two lines to form a comprehensible single statement. The poets were given thirty minutes to achieve this seemingly impossible feat. Only one succeeded. The winner—in one version it was Victor Hugo—came up with the following, in which line two is an absolute echo of line one:

> *Gal, amant de la Reine, alla—tour magnanime—*
> *Galamment de l'arène à la Tour Magne à Nîmes.*

Literally this tells us, as far as I can make out, that a chap named Gal, the Queen's lover, completed a high-minded tour or trip by gallantly going from the Arena to the Big Tower in the city of Nîmes. The statement will not be treasured by posterity but it is at least syntactically clear. It is also an incredible technical feat, possible only to a versifier with an ear furiously sensitive to the sounds of words and syllables. It bears the same relation to the ordinary complex pun that the geometries of Lobachevski or Gauss bear to that of Euclid.

As a further indication of the adaptability of French to punning here is a pleasant exercise in quadripolarity:

> *Paris est métropole.*
> *Le grand ours blanc est maître au pôle.*
> *L'Impératrice Cathérine aimait trop Paul.*
> *Amundsen aime être au pôle.*

Our own language, though flexible enough, is not quite so pliant as are the Romance tongues. For effects of comparable complexity one is compelled to the rather frigid artifices of the set-up pun, analyzed below. Yet, as I have remarked, deft triple plays, for example, do bob up once in a while, as flashy and memorable as comets. There is *Punch's* comment on the wit who complained that he was always hearing his own stories told back at him: "A plain case of the tale dogging the wag." This would seem to be a prose version of Keith Preston's neat "The Durable Bon Mot":

> *When Whistler's strongest colors fade,*
> *When inks and canvas rot,*
> *Those jokes on Oscar Wilde he made*
> *Will dog him unforgot.*
>
> *For gags still set the world agog,*
> *When fame begins to flag,*
> *And, like the tail that wagged the dog,*
> *The smart tale dogs the wag.*

A diabolical triplet I remember is the creation of the genial journalist Joe Bryan III. This goes back to the 1934 America's Cup races between Harold Vanderbilt's *Rainbow* and T. O. M. Sopwith's *Endeavour*. At that time *Rainbow* was experimenting with an unusually long boom. Mr. Bryan (having in mind that sound old proverb about supping with Old Nick) muttered, "He who would Sopwith *Endeavour* needs a long boom."

Such a triple can ennoble a whole life, but most are sad affairs. I cannot, for example, admire the chestnut about the mother who named her sons' cattle ranch "Focus" because it was "where the sons raise meat." The back of me hand to "Focus"—it's more triple than it's worth. Slightly less unacceptable is a triplet quoted by Punmaster Bennett Cerf: "Why was Pharaoh's daughter like a shrewd, cold blooded broker in a bear market? It's because she got a handsome prophet from the rushes on the banks." Triplets are ingenious but somehow not pleasurable. The contrivance behind them is too apparent, their wit efficient rather than meaningful.

Puns of the third order do not exhaust the field. There are complex puns whose structure almost defies analysis. Take Ogden Nash's sentence: "It reminds me of the visitor to the Chinese zoo who asked what language the aquatic carnivora talked, Pidgin English? and the keeper replied, No, Otter Confucian." This is as delightfully balled up as a piece of string the kitten has been playing with. The word *otter*, by the way, is a punster's favorite. Compare Mark Twain's "Information seems to stew out of me naturally like the precious otter of roses out of an otter."

Having noted examples of puns of the first, second, third, and other multiple degrees, we come to puns depending on the principle of combination. We may call these Meld Puns. A traditional example is Oliver Wendell Holmes' designation of Thomas Babington as the Macaulayflower of literature.

The Meld Pun is especially characteristic of our time. Its most noted practitioner is undoubtedly Walter Winchell (*Reno-vate*, etc.). Mr. Winchell's coinages are often pointed, economical, and witty. But his trick has been vulgarized by the kind of journalist who preens himself on such inventions as *cinemaddict* and *radiorator*. As Samuel Johnson remarked of Macpherson's poetry, any man can do this kind of thing who is willing to abandon himself to it. Such melds are as cheap as they are easy.

Nevertheless melds can be quite ingenious, as *alcoholiday* was in its time. Louis Untermeyer's term for composers who criticize and yet imitate Debussy—he calls them Debussybodies—is pretty. So is Christopher Fry's characterizing of a brilliant talker as "coruscating on thin ice."

A modest offering of my own in the field of the meld:

> *The Penguin is the fond mama,*
> *The Secretary-bird's the pa,*
> *And of this oddly mated pair*
> *The Fountain-penguin is the heir.*

The greatest meld of all time (also a compound or double pun) is by many connoisseurs considered the everlasting Everest of classic wordplays. It is credited to the famous trial lawyer of a bygone day, Joseph Choate. According to one version he was defending a case in Westchester County, a commuters' paradise lying just north of New York. The plaintiff's lawyer, driven to despair by Choate's silken imperturbability, finally addressed the jury: "Gentlemen! I sincerely hope that your decision will not be influenced by my opponent's Chesterfieldian urbanity." Mr. Choate rose and replied, "Gentlemen, I am sure that you will not be influenced either by my opponent's Westchesterfieldian suburbanity."

While we are considering puns in terms of their structure we might mention a rarely encountered variety, a kind of hypertrophied Spoonerism that depends on a syllabic reversal. Example: the Skid Row Saloon whose patrons entered optimistically and left mistyoptically.

We opened our discussion by considering the Impromptu Pun. This can at its best be the product of happy genius, but it can never be a work of art. That is, it is not pre-

determined; it is created out of nothing and dies almost
at once.

Polar to the Impromptu Pun is the Set-up or Circumstan-
tial Pun. This, to judge from my extensive correspondence,
is the favorite form of our time. It does not happen to be
mine, for in the excess of its calculation, it seems to me cold
and lifeless. But it is at the moment greatly admired and
therefore merits careful examination.

The Set-up Pun is to the standard pun as the subjunctive
mood is to the indicative. It is a citizen of the Land of
Make-Believe, whose national motto is "Just suppose." It
is akin to puzzles, riddles, and such contrivances on the
one hand, and to the art of fiction on the other. It offers
about as much valid commentary on human life as does a
well-played chess game. It is also related to Staircase Wit,
or what you would have said if you had happened to think
of it at the time.

In positive terms the Set-up Pun is a blend of narrative
and wordplay based on an imaginary contrived situation.
It is manufactured by working backward, just as Poe says
he wrote *The Raven.*

A small boy was accustomed to meet Patrolman O'Reilly
on the same corner each morning. He would buy a doughnut and feed it regularly to O'Reilly's grateful horse. One
morning the horse refused the doughnut indignantly.
"What's wrong with Brownie?" asked our urchin. To which
O'Reilly replied, "Oh, this is a horse of another cruller."
(The fertile mind of Roger Angell, one of *Holiday's* editors,
is responsible for this vivid slice of life. He also suggests
that an impoverished Monte Carlo gambler one day remarked to a friend, "Wagering against red in roulette is

my *bête noire*.") Mr. Angell is of course a brilliant per-
former. But that need not discourage us rank-and-filers, for
almost anyone can play this game. Let's see how it's done.
We begin by choosing some familiar phrase. Let's try
Am I my brother's keeper? Now the trick is to fiddle
around with the phrase, delivering yourself up to a kind
of freewheeling sound association. Obviously the most
fiddlable words here are *brother's* and *keeper*. Mumble a
few changes on *brother's*. Sooner or later you emerge with
blubber's. *Keeper* is even easier. Try shortening the long
vowel (standard procedure) and you come up with *kipper*.
Clearly we are involved somehow with the destinies of
a whale and a herring. A born Scheherazade like Mr.
Angell would now spin you a complete short story, with
subplot, minor characters, and love interest. We will content ourselves with a mere sketch. Thus: a whale and a
herring were regular visitors to a bar. One evening the
herring came in alone. "Where's the whale?" asked the
bartender. The herring drew himself up to his full height
and said pettishly, "Am I my blubber's kipper?"

And there you are—and, besides the Set-up Pun, you
have created a Shaggy Dog Story at the same time.

The central charm of the Set-up Pun (for its maker) is
that it is a work of art. It is not dependent on the accident
of casual conversation. It is pure contrivance and may be
polished till it gleams. You work with circumstances entirely under your control.

Nunnally Johnson, the pride of Twentieth Century-Fox
Films, writes me that one of their geniuses, identified only
as Mr. Kaufman, has for some years been brooding over a
Set-up Pun which requires little more than another war

with Japan. The season should be late fall and on a particular morning our forces would have hanged a small Japanese spy. In which case Mr. Kaufman would be on hand to remark, not implausibly, "There's a little Nip in the air this morning."

The attraction of the Set-up Pun, as we have noted, does not lie in its wit, of which it has little or none, but in its invention, which may be dazzling. Therefore the adept at these setting-up exercises is essentially a storyteller. The first-rate Set-up Pun is generated when an ingenious story combines with supercomplexity of language distortion. The two elements condition each other—the more complicated the pun, the more varied and colorful the elements of the narrative will be. I offer a classic by Bennett Cerf.

It seems that a relative and namesake of Syngman Rhee, visiting our country to learn the magazine business, got a job on Mr. Luce's most popular periodical. On his first assignment, however, he lost himself in the mazes of New York City. It took several days to track him down. At last the Missing Persons Bureau investigator found him in a Third Avenue bar and cried in relief, "Ah, sweet Mr. Rhee, of *Life*, at last I've found you!"

If you think this funny it is not so much because the climax is ingenious as because that climax is entirely out of proportion to the involved preceding narrative. In other words we have here the traditional humor of anticlimax, the foundation of the wonderful contraptions with which Rube Goldberg and Joe Cook used to make us laugh. The Set-up is really Build-up plus Let-down. The Set-up artist will devote his energies to the business of complicating his build-up without introducing any unnecessary factor. The elements at first blush appear inharmonious. But they are carefully brought into a single frame, the final effect of composition being secured by the last brush-shake, the pun itself.

Nunnally Johnson again supplies me with a striking example. (This is the work of the late Herman Mankiewicz, who once described himself as the only three-thousand-dollar-a-week film writer west of the Mississippi who did not own a painting by Utrillo.) In a world of infinite time, space, and possibility, the only world the Set-up punster cares to live in, the following situation, Mr. Mankiewicz predicted, would occur. Aboard a New York-to-Chicago train would be that excellent public servant, Congressman Emanuel Celler, together with some of his constituents. Aboard the same train (this is some time ago) are the members of the New York Giants and the Chicago National League team. Representative Celler strays off and his friends go in search of him. They find him in the club car dozing between Phil Cavarretta and Leo Durocher. It so happens that one of Mr. Celler's friends has a slight and rather charming accent, and it is this very one who exclaims, "There's Manny asleep between the Cub and the Lip!"

Back of such creations lies the ambition to play God, to rearrange the pieces on the board, to mold fate. Those touched with this passion will often go beyond mere fancy. They will force life itself to collaborate with them.

Hearken to this real-life story, sent me by Howard Cushman, himself no mean master of the Set-up Pun. A friend of Mr. Cushman's is Mr. Vilas Boyle, formerly a reporter on the New York *Post*. Once, during those old *Post* days, a group of determined journalistic colleagues succeeded, after a split second of effort, in dragging Mr. Boyle into a near-by saloon for refreshment. They took turns picking up the check for Mr. Boyle, having self-sacrificingly and in advance made up a fund for this noble purpose. As his admiring and attentive friends applauded his efforts, the co-operative Mr. Boyle steadily reduced, glass after glass, the liquid content of the saloon. After some time he explained that he had to leave. He did so, cheerfully but steadily. The remaining group of scientists had one final drink to toast the successful outcome of their careful experiment. They had wished to prove that a watched Boyle never gets potted.

Now no one will deny that it was worth going to a little trouble to arrange this *mise en scène* against which to project the unique dramatic talents of Mr. Boyle. Occasionally, however, life itself will act as stage manager, dramatist, director, even prompter. William Cole, who sways the publicity destinies of the publishing house of Alfred A. Knopf, writes me of a story he heard from George Jean Nathan. Once Mr. Nathan found himself in Dublin dining with some literary notables. Among them was the Irish poet George William Russell, who wrote under the pseudonym "A. E." Some dispute having arisen, Mr. Russell, flushed with wrath, stood up and pounded the table. Mr. Nathan remarked to the guest on his right, "A. E.'s Irish rose."

(Mr. Cole himself informs me that he waits in calm and certain expectation of the day when he will be taken to Police Headquarters, shown two sets of fingerprints, and be moved to comment, "Why, they're whorls apart!")

One of my valued correspondents, Cyril Sanders of San Francisco, writes me that his brother Murray once created a pun which, if I did not have entire faith in Mr. Sanders' veracity, would seem to have all the marks of an outstanding Set-up. The Sanders brothers were mining in New Mexico. Sitting in front of the Assay Office, they watched coming up the path some sort of insect with long waving feelers. By its side crawled a beetle which had somehow got tangled up, conceivably amorously, with its fellow insect. "Ah!" said Murray, "Antennae and Coleoptera!"

Akin to the Set-up Pun is the Literary Conundrum Pun, popular some years ago among the New York wits. The humorist and detective-story luminary, Alan Green, is something of a maestro in this dubious field. He will ask: The headline "Friars Kidnap Playwright Hart" suggests what famous novel by Dostoyevsky? Answer: *The Brothers Karamazov* (The Brothers Carry Moss Off). Or: Once in Russia a boss farmer came upon an idle peasant. He noticed that the hard earth needed loosening, picked up an implement, handed it to the peasant, and, calling him by name, gave him a curt order. What he said was the title of a Sir Walter Scott novel you read in high school. . . . Sure, that's it.

My own small efforts in the field of the Set-up Pun lack entirely the finish and ingenuity of such masters as Mr. Green, Mr. Mankiewicz, and Mr. Cerf. Yet they please me. As someone once said, I find it easy to curry favor with myself. For many years now I have been anticipating a tiny triumph which requires only two simple and easily-come-by ingredients. The first is a small elevator. The second is the presence in it of myself and the distinguished publicist and historian Herbert Agar who would at the moment be suffering from a fear of enclosed spaces. As Mr. Agar steps into the lift he remarks, "This elevator gives me claustrophobia." Secure in the knowledge that the reverse of claustrophobia is agoraphobia, or fear of open spaces, I will murmur, "Ah, perhaps you give the elevator Agaraphobia." (I may remark in passing that old Scrooge in *A Christmas Carol* suffered from Santa Claustrophobia.)

I have still another little private dream. I dream of the time when I shall be on my way to a restaurant in New York's Italian quarter, rummage in my vest pocket, and inform my companion blankly that I have mislaid the Spaghettisburg address.

I shall, of course, say it *risotto voce*.

Set-up Puns, even my own, please me less than puns that depend for their effect not on mere ingenious carpentry, but on the minor delight one gets from recognizing an allusion. The best of these involve a certain amount of learning, and it is probably the scantiness of my scholarship that explains my weakness for the Academic Pun, the pun that shows, in Christopher Morley's phrase, "the true bluestocking slope and curve." Mr. Morley himself was a past master at this sort of thing. I could offer a hundred specimens of these tiny morleycules of wit but will content myself with two. The English humorist Saki has a character, a brash young man named Clovis whom Mr. Morley has always supposed to be so called because he was so appallingly frank. Also Mr. Morley once described Walt Whitman as an ipsomaniac.

My learned friend, Professor Mortimer J. Adler, writes

me in one of his lighter moments that he and several dozen other heavy thinkers are now at work on a many-volumed study of the basic philosophical issues of our time. The treatise is known as a *Summa Dialectica* and can be achieved only by collective effort because, as Doctor Adler informs me, one scholar doesn't make a *Summa*.

A mere half-century ago the ability thus to pun via Latin was common, if not compulsory, among the well-educated. (Even today my friend the scholar-critic Basil Davenport, the Samuel Johnson of our era, can pun in Greek and, I make no doubt, in Sanskrit too.) There is the reputed—and threadbare—instance of Sir Charles James Napier's message to the British War Office after his capture of Scinde (or Sind) in India. He is supposed to have telegraphed one word—*peccavi*—which, as the class knows, is Latin for "I have sinned." Unfortunately this very beautiful pun belongs not to Napier, but to *Punch*, which printed it in 1844.

Equally apocryphal probably is the story of the gentleman, steeped in the *Odes* of Horace, who gave his opinion of movies and movie audiences by quoting the classical tag: *"Odi profanum vulgus et RKO."*

The time is long past when a tobacco broker (Jacob Brandon) could be generally admired for the wit shown in the motto emblazoned on his carriage: *Quid Rides*. It is doubtful if any humorous columnist today would venture to print the line that appeared in F.P.A.'s column after he had received more than a sufficiency of Christmas socks: *"Sox, et praeterea nihil."*

Still, if we are to believe Joe Bryan, reporting on our naval action in the Pacific, the ability to pun on classical

tags is still alive among some of us. A Ciceronian dive-
bomber pilot, anxiously awaiting one of the Navy's Cata-
lina planes long overdue with supplies, asked: "*Quousque
tandem abutere, Catilina, patientiâ nostrâ?*"

Basil Davenport sends me an English-Greek pun attributed to Charles James Fox. It is almost unbelievably
good, even judged as the result of calculation; and as an
impromptu utterance beyond praise. Mr. Davenport writes:
"Unfortunately it takes a little explaining, even to an American Hellenist, because of a slight difference in pronunciation, almost of accent; we Americans give Greek vowels
a sort of open, Continental value, while the English deal
firmly with them as an extension of their own language.
Anyway, Charles James Fox was presiding over a convivial
evening, when some drunk lurched into the table and both
spilled the punch and upset the candelabra, leaving the
guests both thirsty and darkling. Fox calmly said:

$$\text{Οὐδὲ τόδε οὐδὲ τἄλλο}$$

which means, of course, "Neither the one thing nor the
other," and which the English pronounce *Oudy toddy
oudy tallow.*

Let us return to our Latins.

The Hungarian Nobel Prize-winning biochemist Szent-
Györgyi once isolated a new sugar. The technical names
of sugars all end in -*ose*, as in glucose. His sugar being of
unknown structure, Szent-Györgyi suggested *ignose*. The
editors of the scientific journal *Nature* refusing to put up
with such trifling, he resubmitted *God-knows*. For a biochemist this is not bad.

The learned pun of course need not turn on a foreign

language. However it usually involves some special knowledge and assumes in the audience a well-developed bump of reference. Louis Kronenberger's remark about the interior decorator whose work was so easy to tell from Adam is a fair example. Another is S. J. Perelman's comment, in a parody-portrait of Arthur Kober: "I love the Mendelian characteristics he has inherited from his father Mendel." A little knowledge of English history supplies the key to Philip Guedalla's oft-quoted and sharply critical statement about the literary periods of Henry James: "The work of Henry James has always seemed divisible by a simple dynastic arrangement into three reigns: James I, James II, and the Old Pretender."

Such puns are "inside" humor, making a strong appeal to specialists only. Another beautiful example is Charles Poore's "More in Seurat than in Ingres."

At the opposite pole from these learned japeries stands the Unconscious Pun. Here the humor arises from misunderstanding or ignorance. The Ladies' Club chairman who introduced the speaker as an authority on Keats, adding that she had always been curious to find out what they were, was a first-rate unconscious punner. A subdivision of the Unconscious Pun comprises those misunderstandings that depend on dialect or language difficulties. In Frank Craven's *The First Year* (a comedy that merits revival) the anxious young wife, preparing for her first dinner party, questions her Negro maid: "Leota, did you seed the grapefruit?" To which Leota replies, "Yes, ma'am, Ah seed it."

As with the limerick, treated elsewhere in this book, the best puns are as unprintable as they are repeatable. All wit is an evasion of constraint; the pun doubly so; the Blue Pun triply so. It represents one of our ways of parading past Mrs. Grundy without being arrested for indecent exposure. As long as the pressure of censorship is maintained men, women, and children will continue to devote a surprising amount of mental energy to unseemly humor. Furthermore they are stimulated by an assured audience. The *double entendre* may shock but it rarely bores.

This dissertation would lose whatever slight value it has were it to neglect Blue Puns. Yet it would lose its distributability—precious to the author—were it to catalogue the finest of them. Under the circumstances I can hardly be more than suggestive.

We might begin our superficial researches with an anecdotal pun whose opening belongs in the raised-eyebrows department, but which closes in the purest odor of morality. The brash young man suggests to the blonde young lady that after the party she come over to his apartment for a whisky and sofa. To which she replies, "Don't care for a whisky and sofa—but I don't mind coming for a gin and platonic." That is very smart and modern and I must say I prefer it to the kind of bawdy pun our Elizabethan ancestors haw-hawed at. For an example of their elementary *double entendre* look up the last word of the last line of *The Merchant of Venice.*

In connection with Shakespeare, I recall that at the end of the great Shakespearian discussion in Joyce's *Ulysses,* Buck Mulligan invents a string of characters for a proposed Elizabethan play, each of whose names is a funny but not respectable pun.

In the *cabinet d'aisance* of that distinguished institution, the Players Club, gentlemen are often in an excellent position to observe a wall placard reading *More Haste, Less Speed.* In recalling this classic admonition (attributed, doubtless overgenerously, to the late Bishop Potter) I plead orthography as my defense and Frank Sullivan as my informant. Mr. Sullivan also reminds me that Mrs. Parker once summed up the sexual orientation of a celebrated French poet: "Yes, that was the trouble with Verlaine—he was always chasing Rimbauds."

Of such puns we may say that their special virtue is to be tried and found wanton. How pleasant, for example, is this minor effort by one Jack Thomas, apparently a very great man of whom Alistair Cooke writes me that his thought sequences are tied to the pun as a trolley to its electric wire. Mr. Thomas suggests as a subtitle for a guidebook: *Paris by Night and Bidet.* Which somehow reminds me of a story of Marc Connelly about Neysa McMein, whose memory for names was a bit shaky. One day she was rattling off to some guests in her studio a list of stage stars who were to be in a benefit she was helping to organize: "We've got Bea Lillie, Ethel Barrymore, Helen Hayes, Bobby Clark, N. B. Fields, the Lunts—" "Wait a minute," interrupted a listener. "Did you say *N. B.* Fields?" Mr. Connelly interposed suavely, "Certainly—would you expect a lady like Neysa to say 'W.C.'?"

I am depending on the obscurity of learned lingo when I pass on to you one of the most dazzling sexual puns I have ever encountered. This one comes to me from a Florida newspaperman, Walter Wadsley Anderson. He reports that around 1927 he and some friends were sitting around swapping puns, when the talk happened to turn to matters

involving procreation. A genius named Jim Hawkins settled the question by remarking quietly, "There's a *vas
deferens* between children and no children."

This, I must assume, is quotable, but the sad fact remains that the greatest loose puns are still compelled to
exist only in the world of the oral. Of such unquotabilia
one of the finest is to be found on pages 286–287 of *Ushant*,
the autobiography of the distinguished poet Conrad Aiken.
Aiken is without doubt one of the greatest punners alive.
His books, as well as his talk, glitter with gems. Some are
complicated, others simple enough to have been widely
stolen, such as the wire sent home by a lady who suffered
severely during an Atlantic crossing: *Sic transit.*

Mr. Aiken sends me an anecdote peculiarly suitable to
our age of Group Living. It is fairly well-known, at least
in academic circles.

Four dons were walking down an Oxford street one
evening. They were discussing group nouns: a covey of
quail, an exaltation of larks.

As they talked, they passed four ladies of the evening.
One of the dons asked: "How would you describe a group
like that?"

Suggested the first: "A jam of tarts?"

The second: "A flourish of strumpets?"

The third: "An essay of Trollope's?"

Then the dean of the dons, the eldest and most scholarly
of them all, closed the discussion: "I wish that you gentlemen would consider 'An anthology of pros.'"

Not closed—no. For a voice was heard behind them,
saying:

"But gentlemen, surely in thus beating about the bush
you have overlooked the obvious—a pride of loins?"

(The last voice you heard was that of the master himself, Mr. Aiken.)

I feel sure that my purer-minded readers, if any are still with me, are anxious to move on to a higher sphere. Let me respect their wish.

All puns are playful but some may put frivolity to serious uses. They may italicize the sobriety of a statement in a way barred to the more formal phrase. Shakespeare's

> *Golden lads and girls all must,*
> *As chimney-sweepers, come to dust*

draws its poignancy entirely from the pathetic little joke. The pun makes the poetry. Similarly the gravity of Franklin's "We must all hang together, or assuredly we shall all hang separately" is enhanced by its levity. The most far-reaching pun ever made we find in the sixteenth chapter of St. Matthew, verses 18 and 19, where Jesus calls His disciple Peter (petros)and says of him that upon this rock (petra) He will build His Church. Thus may a small ambiguity of language play its part in the founding of a great spiritual institution.

The serious pun can often do work with an ease impossible to more formal exposition. Bishop Warburton's "Orthodoxy is my doxy; heterodoxy is another man's doxy" supplies a well-known example. A nineteenth-century journalist, George D. Prentice, writing in the *Louisville Journal,* made a technical point unforgettably when he said: "A dishonest critic, by severing passages from their context, may make the best book appear to condemn itself. A book, thus unfairly treated, may be compared to the laurel—there is honor in the leaves but poison in the extract." This is truly elegant in its Victorian phrasing. Compare it with a modern critic's terser use of the pun—for example, the New York play reviewer who summarized *I Am a Camera* with: "No Leica!"

A pun may carry an entire story on its fragile shoulders. I am thinking of an ingenious crime yarn by Ellery Queen called *Diamonds in Paradise*, where the entire plot turns on the pronunciation of the title's last word; and also of *The Gold Bug*, where the crucial question of the language of the cipher is decided by a pun. Or it may be used effectively for the soberest of purposes, as in the highway admonition: Children should be seen and not hurt.

Increasingly puns are used to sell goods. The copywriter, fresh out of other arguments, will sell you a play on words, urging you to buy eyeglasses because of their specs appeal, or describing heat-resistant potholders as panhandlers. There is something a bit dubious about the enlistment of puns in commerce. The reason, I think, is partly that a pun is for play, not for persuasion. Also it may be that a punning slogan becomes less effective by repetition. The pun is of too fragile, too butterfly a nature to resist such continuous handling. However, my mild biliousness in this matter may spring from the fact that I once tried unsuccessfully to sell a slogan to a chromium company. I still think "There's No Plate Like Chrome" is fairly neat, in a small way.

Children's puns have a peculiar charm. It stems from the child's delight at discovering that language too is a toy. The child who puns is engaging in pure play, uncalculated, unstained by the exhibitionism of his seniors.

Christopher Morley once wrote me that his son, now a

learned divine, at the age of eight settled a problem raised
by a younger sister. She asked how wagon was spelled,
with one or two g's. He replied, "With two, of course;
every wagon has to have a gee-gee." This is fairly grown-up
stuff, but it is extraordinary at what an early age punning
will start. Mary Fairfax Gouverneur of Baltimore writes
that, someone having remarked, "Fall's coming," her three-
year-old granddaughter commented smartly, "Then you'll
have to get me a false face." That child will go far.

My own son, at the time not quite two and a half, treasured a friendship with the distinguished co-author of *Life
With Father* and other plays. Asked once what he was
having for lunch, he replied, "I am eating Russel Crouse."
The imp knew darn well it was Brussels sprouts.

I propose to end our discussion, first by considering the
levels of achievement possible within a given subject matter, and second by considering the levels of achievement
possible within the narrower confines of a single word.

First, subject matter. Let us select a small area—say the
pun based on geography.

When I was a child we chanted

> *Chicken-in-the-car*
> *The-car-can't-go*
> *That's-the-way-to-spell-Chicago!*

As punning nothing could be cruder or more pointless. The
chant merely represents the child's first attempts to put
into memorable form his pleasure in discovering that the
same sound represents two different things. Now let us
consider a slightly more advanced geographical jocularity:
"So long—Abyssinia!" It is, of course, an atrocity, yet let

us give credit to the man who first thought it up—at least he had detected a surprising near-homonym. Nevertheless only the simplest mind can extract pleasure from such a pun. It is meaningless, unwitty and stales on the first repetition.

Now—still confining ourselves to geographical puns—let us examine an Ogden Nash quatrain:

> *Our country, south and west of Hatteras,*
> *Abounds in charming female flatteras.*
> *Sweet talk is scant by Lake Cayuga,*
> *But in Tennessee, they chatta nougat.*

Here the same drive that produced the inane Chicago chant and the vapid Abyssinia drivel is at work on a higher mental plane. Mr. Nash began with his discovery of a grotesque but delightful homonym, hidden in the word Chattanooga. The problem was to clothe his discovery with wit and meaning, which are lacking in our two other examples. Rhythm, rhyme, perfect phrasing, and the sly appeal to a traditional American belief about Southern girls—all unite to solve the problem. We are a long way from chicken-in-the-car; but the child and the genius obey the same linguistic impulse and handle the same kind of material.

And now we go to work on a single word.

To enjoy any art properly we learn to discriminate, inclining neither to wholesale rejection nor to uncritical acceptance. To drive the point home and demonstrate the delicate differences between a satisfactory pun and a brilliant one, I shall ask you to consider four bits of wordplay. Each of the four is based on the same word. The word is *dogma.* Even the nonexpert will see at once that the pun must turn on the simpler word *dog.* Give me a familiar phrase about a dog. Correct. Our pun (Carolyn Wells') is at hand: *Every dogma must have its day.* Mildly witty but pretty simple. Let's see whether we can improve on it. We can do so easily with the help of Douglas Jerrold, who defined dogmatism as "puppyism come to its full growth." This is miles above Carolyn Wells. It makes a neater, more particularized statement about dogmas. In other words it has more meaning. Its construction, too, is far more interesting, involving a double pun, the second one turning on the literal and derived meanings of *puppyism.* The pun is first-rate. Can it be improved? I am not sure but I think I have one that's a shade finer. It's by Keith Preston:

> *A modernist married a fundamentalist wife,*
> *But she led him a catechism and dogma life.*

This also involves a double pun but a more unexpected one. Its statement is as meaningful as Jerrold's, both being pointed, sane comments on human life. It has the slight advantage over Jerrold's pun of being cast in rhyme. The form is a little tighter for that reason.

Have we exhausted the possibilities of *dogma?* Are you dogmatired? Only one more to go, but this one is the real thing. Its author is Philip Guedalla, the English wit and historian. My recollection is that he was defending the Catholic Church (or perhaps some other religious institution) from unfair and slanderous attack. He put it this way: "Any stigma will do to beat a dogma." I consider this double pun, by reason of the perfection of its form and the witty truth of its content, one of the greatest ever made.

How To Speak Videomatic
Televenglish

ONE OF THE PURPOSES of the French Academy is to confer immortality on distinguished old gentlemen at a time
when they would cheerfully trade the gift for an extra
decade of mere crude life. Another of its purposes is to
define and redefine the French vocabulary, to admit trembling new words only after the most severe examination,
and in general to fix the language.

We Americans are not only anti-academic but anti-Academic. Our interest in making immortals out of our great
men is tepid. When Stanton announced that Lincoln belonged to the ages, he was, though telling the truth, talking European, not American. The national imagination
trades in short-term futures. It was an American, Frank
Moore Colby, who remarked of H. G. Wells: "He is an-
noyed by the senseless refusal of almost everybody to
shape his life in such a manner as will redound to the advantage of the beings who will people the earth a hundred
thousand years hence."

Just as we reject the Academy as an immortality-factory, we reject it as a language-fixer. Our very professors of speech and linguistics, instead of being traditionalists, as one might suppose, are, many of them, free enterprisers who want our speech to develop unfettered and unhobbled. Should this development lead somehow to our all talking gibberish a thousand years hence, they would remain unperturbed—provided we *all* talk it. Usage makes right. Count noses in politics. Count larynxes in language, and let the slips fall where they may.

At this moment I am not controverting the policy of a verbal free market. I am concerned only to suggest that, while we have no formal Academy, we do have and indeed always have had one or more informal academies. In the nineteenth century and the first part of the twentieth our speech was largely influenced by the syntax and vocabulary of the orator, who was in turn influenced by the formal English of certain powerful British writers and statesmen. Even a popular orator like Bryan, whose strength sprang from his identification with plain people, used the best, that is the most academically approved, diction of which he was capable. The prose of Woodrow Wilson and Herbert Hoover, whether written or spoken, was similarly "correct." Such public men, from Daniel Webster to Hoover, did somehow furnish rough models of spoken English. They comprised a casual, an unsystematized Academy.

I would suggest that they have in our time been replaced by television-talkers. It is the aim of what follows to point out a few of the ways in which television (and of course its less picturesque elder brother radio) is influencing our tongue, setting certain standards of pronunciation and vocabulary, and generally acting as a national teacher of language.

Just as public address once harked back to the book, the schoolroom, and the legislative forum, so TV public address is based on the usages of *entertainment*. It is no accident that the first citizen of the land should be tutored by a movie and TV actor. The relationship is not only politically useful but deeply symbolic. In saying this, I intend no criticism of either Mr. Eisenhower or Mr. Montgomery. The public prose and public stance of our President seem to me far more honest and palatable than the public prose and public stance of a Webster or an Edward Everett. All I wish to emphasize is that television has inevitably mated public business and show business. Whether this union seems sterile or fruitful is for the individual taste to decide.

By Televenglish I mean the whole body of expression continually being created by thousands of highly audible authorities, including commentators, comedians, M.C.'s, singers, interviewers, newscasters, children's hosts, commercial announcers, staff announcers, and cartoon characters. This group, with us almost every hour of the day, unconsciously imposes upon the receptive viewer its own standards of speech. Its influence is far more powerful than that of our kith and kin, or of newspaper editorials, or of the movies which in their nature lack the repetitive impact of TV.

Let me give three minor examples of television's power to change and perhaps even fix the language.

The first has been widely noticed: the quiet assassination of the conjunction *as*. Winston cigarettes, which of course taste good like a cigarette should, have in the course of a year of successful advertising set the final seal of approval on the use of *like* as a conjunction. It *was* colloquial; it is now correct. Even academicians approve the usage, for the power of mass suggestion is too great for resistance. I am no Drew Pearson but I prophesy that within five years the man who boldly defends the heresy that *like* is not a conjunction will become the proper object of scrutiny by the Federal Bureau of Investigation.

My second example is drawn from the bards of television. I am fond of advertising jingles, largely because they are sung by anonymous voices that appear to have received some musical training, a training my naive ears are unable to detect in the highly regarded efforts of Mr. Frank Sinatra, Mr. Vic Damone, Mr. Eddie Fisher, Mr. Elvis Presley, and similar microphone maestros. I like the jingles also because they are often so much wittier and funnier than the lines assigned to real comedians. However, I was brought up to believe that near-rhymes are admissible only when used by professional poets to secure certain subtle effects beyond the reach of exact rhymes. The jingaleers of television, though otherwise worthy of praise, probably do not fall into this category. When they rhyme *gleam* with *sheen, time* with *fine, bosun* with *ocean* (this is the deathless contribution of Old Spice), and *new gasoline* with *Sky-Chief supreme*, I am forced to one of two conclusions. Either they really believe that *time* and *fine* are good rhymes, or they do not care whether or not they are. In either case, I am not worried about the effect on the future of poetry. What does interest me is that the simple and not especially important capacity of ordinary folk to match the sound of one word with another—this is particularly marked in children—may in the course of time become blunted by the vast unconscious influence of the singing commercial. For I cannot lay too much stress on the plain fact that the defective rhymes we hear ten thousand times a year are bound to have more influence on us than the neat heroic couplets of Alexander Pope. Television begins by being entertaining and ends by becoming authoritative.

While on the subject of the singing commercial we might also note that it can also actually deflect the course of musicology. In his brilliant book *The Public Arts*, which should be read by anyone at all interested in these matters, Gilbert Seldes makes the point that "D'ye ken John Peel" and the singing commercial for Pepsi-Cola share the same tune and that the latter's "diffusion is now so great that the original song has wholly ceased to exist."

Example Three: The speakers of television are following the lead of Sir Winston Churchill who quite deliberately pronounces all foreign words as if they were a kind of inferior English. Thus the *u* of *buoni* is dropped as too difficult or unnecessary, and *L'Aimant* rhymes with *Claimant*, which is at least in a weird way correct. I do not object to this forcible Americanization; it would be mere pedantry to talk like a real Italian or Frenchman. I point out merely that it makes the lot of the high school teacher of French or Italian just a tiny bit harder than it need be. He now has against him the entire authority of the perfume and spaghetti businesses—and their classrooms are in session night and day.

But Televenglish wields its power less by innovating than by confirming.

Up to recently the general understanding was that "platform English," that is, any words spoken *to* an audience, should be more carefully chosen, arranged, pronounced, and enunciated than those same words would be were they spoken *by* the members of the audience informally to each other. In television this tradition obtains in certain areas and has been displaced in others.

In general news commentators and professional announcers are taught to speak well, and do speak well. The *tone* (as in the Movietone voice) may be unnatural, but the words themselves are usually clear and traditionally correct. A John Daly, an Ed Murrow, an Eric Sevareid—all speak with ease, dignity, and clarity. They are, in the nineteenth-century sense, good models of diction. Certain journalese tricks may be open to question, such as the Lowell Thomas Interrogative: "His purpose? To explain American policy"; but these are minor points. However, the formally well-educated news announcer is a less powerful linguistic influence than the showman; and with the showman we must range a certain type of commercial announcer.

May I state at once that it is not the showman's business to speak in a way to satisfy a college professor? It is his business directly to amuse the audience and indirectly to sell his product. If clear, traditional English defeats either of these ends, he is quite justified in using an English that is neither clear nor traditional. He does so.

Showman's Televenglish is hard to analyze. It consists of several strands. The three major strands are the folksy, the genteel, and the smart. Of these the most important is the folksy. The showman either by nature speaks the English of the man in the street, even the man in the alley; or he deliberately imitates it in order to insure his popularity with a mass audience. In either case he uses his vast authority to confirm popular usage. In other words he *at once* makes respectable what, if television did not exist, might take years or decades to establish itself.

I run a small, quiet business called the Missing Sounds Bureau. In my files are certain little traditional English noises that have almost entirely disappeared from Televenglish. Among these are *wh* (generally rendered as a simple *w*); *our*, displaced by *ahr*; the *a* in *valuable*; the vowel sound in *you*, now either *ye* or *y'*; the old-fashioned *au* in *authority*, which appears to be analyzed into the indefinite article plus an interesting new word, *thority*; the participial *g* (the announcer clothes his larynx in homespun and chuckles his spiel about *smokin Blank cigarettes*); the *ll* in *all right* which our more successful M.C.'s know perfectly well is merely a misspelling of *awright*; the entire middle syllable of the nation's capital and first President; and especially the consonant *t*, living a half life at the head of a word but otherwise on its way out: *gennelmen, twenny, akshally* are excellent Televenglish. Amy Vanderbilt, who knows what is correct and has a keen ear for this sort of thing, has a vivid memory of a prominent girl singer announcing firmly that something-or-other was as gennel as a winner's breeze. One of our most highly placed public servants is convinced the word is *innerference*. One of our best-liked giveaway M.C.'s has popularized *congradulate* (he also feels *badly* when a contestant loses). I have become so used to having certain sounds omitted that the other night when Steve Allen (who speaks extremely well, somehow combining an air of good breeding with the necessary casual informality) correctly pronounced *vacuum* as if it akshally had three syllables, the word grated on my Televenglish-conditioned ear.

Televenglish develops by addition as well as by subtraction. *Idea* is enriched by a final *r; heart-rending* is more frequently *heart-rendering; by right* is given the dignity of the plural (*by rights*); *athletics* becomes *athaletics.*

The linguistic base of Televenglish consists of a rich compost of dialects as employed in the regions of Hollywood and Vine, Nedick's, the Stork Club, and Lindy's. Of late what is known as the Southland has been making its own special contribution. One begins to hear *i*-dea and *po*-lice more and more frequently. One correspondent writes me that during a broadcast of the Army-Navy classic the announcer gave *cadet* a really Deep South accent, making it *c*adet. *Ipse dixie.*

The pitchman implores you to "Have a Camel. They really got it." The charming young lady who tells us about the weather finds it necessary to preface her useful, neatly delivered information with "Hi there" (the influence of teen-age English is marked on television); we are told "how to use eyebrow pencil so it looks natural"; *parents* no longer exist, as against *folks;* the language of narrative develops in the key of "There's this ranch owner in this movie"; the evangelist, always on matey terms with his Saviour, tells us that "we're sinners but our Lord Jesus Christ paid the fine"; "the true facts" are always presented, presumably as opposed to the untrue facts. In all these cases the supposition is that the plain man will be pleased by having his vernacular given prestige by the highly paid, handsome announcer or entertainer. The supposition, I suppose, is correct; and the net effect of this confirmation by authority is the establishment of a grammar, syntax, and vocabulary diverging sharply from traditional or textbook models. We are privileged to be present at the birth of a new idiom.

The subjoined examples of show-business Televenglish are selected from the utterances of only our finest, highest-paid M.C.'s of the best quiz and interview shows. These gentlemen are the leaders, the Noah Websters and Fowlers of our time. What they say, goes.

They employ certain mandatory words and phrases, now becoming part of our general vocabulary: *but seriously* to indicate that what follows is to be duller than what has preceded; *definitely* for *yes; great* or *wunnerful* to express mild approval, or often merely to show that the M.C. has heard and noted a statement by the interviewee; *he's so* RIGHT; *I've got news for yuh; thing* as an all-purpose noun ("I wanna get back to that governor thing again, if yuh don' mind"); *that's for me; what's with——?*

Then there is the use of *very*, not as an intensifier but as part and parcel of the modified adjective. On *Person to Person* one night—when Mr. Murrow had relinquished his post to a hot entertainment "personality"—I noted within the space of three minutes *verydelightful . . . verylovely . . . verybeautiful . . . veryinteresting . . . veryveryfantastic memory . . . this is a verysatisfying and fun thing to do* (Televenglish for *I like to do this*) . . . *verywonder-*

ful. The guest on *Person to Person* delivered a *but seriously* message, counseling all aspiring actresses to "have a *wonderful, wonderful* education."

The magnificently elaborate quiz shows furnish interesting examples of vivid Televenglish. What is notable about these programs is that while the *content* is "cultural," the *tone*, set by the M.C., is in ingenious opposition to the content. Thus *money-winnings* becomes *a bundle*. An elderly lady-contestant to whom the M.C. has momentarily lost his heart is told, "You're a doll." (A movie star, currently undergoing a sincere attack of religion, refers to Jesus Christ as "a living doll.") Answers are given only to *queshuns*. The M.C. asks for a moment's grace so that he may "talk to the people"—an interesting usage, with its suggestion that somehow "the people" are a manipulable substance. Or he praises two earnest competing young scholars: "You guys really know your onions."

While Televenglish and English often seem to employ the same vocabulary, the *meanings* may have little kinship. Thus, Commercial Televenglish will speak of an *elegant fish-poacher*, a *terrific new Lanolin shampoo, amazing new Golden Mix, thrilling beef tenderloin, personalized service* (on air lines). To the linguistic traditionalist these phrases are puzzling or meaningless. But they are not addressed to him. They are addressed to the millions of good Americans who understand this new idiom; who would feel a real sense of loss if such adjectives as *terrific* and *amazing* were omitted; for whom there is something obscenely naked about an adjective not clothed with an adverb: a shampoo must leave your hair *radiantly alive*, a drink must be *deliciously different*.

I must again caution my audience (Televenglish: *the people*) against assuming that I am taking a superior attitude. Televenglish is a special language, now evolving as a medium of communication between a new kind of audience and a new kind of entertainment. Standard English would serve no purpose. It would confuse or even alienate large numbers of potential buyers of excellent products. One should not look down upon Televenglish any more than one should look down upon the spiel of the old-time sideshow barker or flea-circus impresario. The only difference is that the circus spiel, heard by few, developed into a minor special lingo suitable for detached study by the user of standard English. But with authoritative teachers by the thousands daily and nightly teaching Televenglish to 170,000,000 students, it is likely that in fifty years the Televenglish professor will be examining an obsolescent minority idiom known as English, just as today the academic linguist studies the argot of thieves or the slang of the hash-house counterman.

There Was an Old Man of Tobago

ONE HUNDRED and thirty-six years ago a certain J. Harris of London published *The History of Sixteen Wonderful Old Women*, a collection of succinct narratives of an elevating character. Here is one of them; it has been traced back to the mid-seventeenth-century nursery:

> *There was an old woman of Leeds*
> *Who spent all her life in good deeds;*
> *   She worked for the poor*
> *   Till her fingers were sore,*
> *This pious old woman of Leeds.*

Shortly after the literary debut of the lady of Leeds, John Marshall came out with *Anecdotes and Adventures of Fifteen Gentlemen*. It is here that you will find the happy-ending story of the noted valetudinarian:

> *There was an old man of Tobago,*
> *Who lived on rice-gruel and sago;*
> *   Till, much to his bliss,*
> *   His physician said this—*
> *To a leg, sir, of mutton you may go.*

The elderly Tobagoan, Edward Lear tells us, supplied the direct inspiration for his own first *Book of Nonsense*, and may therefore be considered the grandfather of the Limerick.

Since his day the Limerick has altered its tone, not always, one fears, in the direction of the higher morality. Its form, however, has remained basically the same, and perennially popular. Blank verse, the alexandrine, the heroic couplet—many classical meters ascended the heights on their iambic feet and are now outmoded. The Limerick stands firm.

Its origins are obscure. *Hickory, dickory, dock* is a kind of Limerick, its first and last lines suggesting ancient Westmorland shepherds' "counting-out numbers" that may go back to the Middle Ages. But it was not until Lear and his *Book of Nonsense* (1846) that the Limerick entered upon its triumph. Good poets—Tennyson, Swinburne, Rossetti —wrote Limericks, quite bad ones. In 1907–1908 the love of the Limerick had reached such a pitch of intensity that a true craze, as notable as tulipomania, swept England. In the fall of 1907 a Mr. Samuda, a tobacco king, ran a Limerick competition to advertise a cigarette. The first prize, for the best last line, was £3 per week *for life*. (Milton received £18 in total for *Paradise Lost*.)

Writers of the caliber of Robert Louis Stevenson, John Galsworthy, Arnold Bennett, Rudyard Kipling, Oliver Wendell Holmes; artists and scientists such as James Whistler and Julian Huxley; a most reverend collection of deans and bishops and vicars, including Monsignor Ronald Knox —all these have not disdained the lowly, sturdy Limerick.

Furthermore the reciting of Limericks has cheered the lighter hours of even such long-visaged and humorless greats as John Ruskin and Woodrow Wilson.

The origin of the term "Limerick" is as dark a mystery as the name Achilles assumed when he hid himself among women. There is a theory that the refrain "We'll all come up to Limerick" was once employed after certain extempore verses at convivial Irish gatherings, and that somehow "Limerick" became attached to the familiar five-line jingle; but 'twill not hold water. It would be much more reasonable, as has been proposed, to call the form "Learick," after its first great popularizer.

The power of the Limerick lies in the seduction of its form. As someone has put it:

> *Well, it's partly the shape of the thing*
> *That gives the old limerick wing.*

Let us examine what is probably the best-known (and also one of the best) in the language.

> *There was a young lady of Niger*
> *Who smiled as she rode on a tiger;*
> *They returned from the ride*
> *With the lady inside,*
> *And the smile on the face of the tiger.*

The first line introduces the main character, complete with setting. The second line, rhyme-linked to the first, expresses the major curve of action which is to precipitate the crisis. The third and fourth lines are shortened by a foot to suggest intensification and suspense, and a new rhyme is introduced to indicate a radical shift in the plot. The fifth line, offering climax and denouement in one, reverts to the original rhyme. Technically, its function is compound: to reflect in the suddenly lengthened meter the satisfaction of the reader who has been held in suspense by the staccato middle section; and, by its prosaic return to the pattern of the initial couplet, to give a sense of unity and completion. Or we may think of the initial couplet as the bow; the short couplet as the string; and the last line as the arrow.

There are few poetical forms that can boast the Limerick's perfection. It has progression, development, variety, speed, climax, and high mnemonic value.

The essence of the modern Limerick is contained in the climactic line. I say "modern" because Lear himself for the most part, when he reached his opportunity for climax, merely repeated his first line, rhyme word and all, with some slight, often pointless variation. To us this sounds tame to the point of anemia. To the Victorian Englishman it may have seemed understated humor.

At any rate, the bold exploitation of the last line represents the only crucial *formal* mutation of the Limerick since its Tobagoan beginnings. It is from our viewpoint a change for the better. Indeed, it may have saved the Limerick from death, for it opened new perspectives of surprise, oddity, and wit. It also supplied the needed technical base for the evolution of the most numerous of the Limerick's subspecies, to wit, the Indelicate or Unprintable Limerick. We shall say more about this anon. Anon. will have a lot to say about it himself, for, though towering minds have devoted themselves to the Indelicate Limerick, few have been willing to admit authorship.

We have stated that, except for the invention of the non-repetitive last line, the Limerick's form has remained traditional. With respect to tone and content, however, there has been a luxuriant evolution. The earliest Limericks, as we have seen, were homiletic. With Lear they become essentially picturesque and grotesque nonsense and more than half the effect is lost without the wonderful comic drawings. But the Limerick of the last half-century has gradually enlarged its domain. The evolution has followed several directions: toward pure wit; toward the macabre, the scabrous, the shocking; toward the play of ideas; toward the pun and other distortions and contortions of language; toward richness of rhyme; toward the merely unexpected. If a formula is desired we may say that, with certain qualifications, the trend, following that of light verse in general, has been from the polite to the sophisticated and from absurdity to wit.

There is a subtle difference between the pleasant but rather single-stringed oddity of Lear and his many followers and the sly modernity of Morris Bishop, unquestionably the master of contemporary Limerickists. Here is Bishop at his most episcopal:

> *Said a fervent young lady of Hammels,*
> *"I object to humanity's trammels!*
>   *I want to be free!*
>   *Like a bird! Like a bee!*
> *Oh, why am I classed with the mammals?"*

There is some willfully balled-up Freud (recall his theory

of projection) in this beautiful trifle by Ogden Nash:

> *A lady from near Rising Sun,*
> *She flattened her boy friend in fun,*
> *   Saying, Don't worry kid,*
> *   That's for nothing you did,*
> *It's for something I dreamt that you done.*

One of the marks of the post-Learical Limerick is a certain mock elegance of vocabulary which achives a tenuous but undebatable humorous effect. Here is a pleasing example, notable also for the neatness of the rhymes, from the first quarter of the century:

> *Certain pairs who had banns called respectively,*
> *Were married at Whitsun, collectively;*
> *   Said the parson in doubt,*
> *   "Let them sort themselves out."*
> *They are pondering now, retrospectively.*

The dandiacal phrasing of the last line of this one, again the work of Bishop, is similarly effective:

> *There's a vaporish maiden in Harrison*
> *Who longed for the love of a Saracen,*
> *   But she had to confine her*
> *   Intent to a Shriner*
> *Who suffers, I fear, by comparison.*

Mr. Bishop is a professor, and it is noteworthy that the Limerick, whether in its salubrious or ribald manifestations, makes a strong appeal to the donnish mind. In consequence the form has been impressed into the service of the intellect: Limericks have been used to comment on the Mendelian theory, on mathematics, on relativity, and on many aspects of metaphysics. Consider this well-known pair, the second member being by the learned and multi-talented Monsignor Ronald Knox:

IDEALISM

There once was a man who said, "God
Must think it exceedingly odd
 If he finds that this tree
 Continues to be
When there's no one about in the Quad."

A REPLY

Dear Sir,
   Your astonishment's odd:
I am always about in the Quad.
 And that's why the tree
 Will continue to be,
Since observed by
    Yours faithfully,
    God

After Lear the Limerick flourished so rankly that self-kidding became inevitable. Burlesque Limericks, devouring their own substance, are legion, but probably none is as calmly crushing as W. S. Gilbert's

There was an old man of St. Bees,
Who was stung in the arm by a wasp,
 When asked, "Does it hurt?"
 He replied, "No, it doesn't—
I'm so glad that it wasn't a hornet."

In Lear there is an element of the sadistic, or at any rate the punitive. It has remained for our own time to intensify this quality until it trespasses upon the macabre. Even Mr. Bishop, who harmlessly teaches Romance Languages and Literature at Cornell, has his Krafft-Ebing streak:

A ghoulish old fellow in Kent
Encrusted his wife in cement;
He said, with a sneer,
"I was careful my dear,
To follow your natural bent."

A book of Limericks called *The Listing Attic*, by Edward Gorey, appeared a few years ago. These are so appalling that I prefer not to quote them here. They are evidence of the bounds to which the Limerick may be pushed by an imagination at once febrile and cynical. Mr. Gorey thinks nothing of wrapping up such material as infanticide, simple murder, algolagnia, human vivisection, and the lynching of sexual deviants in a verse form traditionally consecrated to the innocent enjoyments of the nursery.

The enlargement of the Limerick's emotional and intellectual world has been paralleled by a multiplication of its linguistic resources. As examples of this development we may consider the Punning Limerick and the Limericks of Co-ordinated Orthography and Outré Rhyme.

We have traveled a long way from *The Old Man of Nantucket*, a simple-hearted Punning Limerick which appeared perhaps half a century ago in the Princeton *Tiger* and generated a series of increasingly doleful imitations. Even the confections of Carolyn Wells have a dated and mechanical air, though they are clever enough:

There was a young person named Tate
Who went out to dine at 8.8,
But I will not relate
What that person named Tate
And his tête-à-tête ate at 8.8.

The modern Punning Limerick is wilder, more surprising, and has a certain insouciance peculiar to our time. It explores a remoter area of linguistic territory. Its puns are untraditional and would have bewildered the earnest mechanics of the Theodore Hook-Thomas Hood school. A fair sample is this one by the ingenious David McCord, one of *Three Limericks for the Alumni*:

> *A native Executive Sec*
> *Of a Fund at Nahuatl Toltec*
> > *Has denied that his needs*
> > *Are for Mexican beads.*
> *Huatl please him? Nahuatl? A chec!*

The Limerick of Co-ordinated Orthography has a long lineage, has probably been overdone, and may have reached the end of its evolutionary course. I do not enjoy it, but I admire it. Here is a simple case:

> *A beautiful lady named Psyche*
> *Is loved by a fellow named Yche.*
> > *One thing about Ych*
> > *The lady can't lych*
> *Is his beard, which is dreadfully spyche.*

And here is a complex case, perhaps the most complex in the entire literature of the Limerick:

> *There was a young curate of Salisbury*
> *Whose manners were quite halisbury-scalisbury.*
> > *He would wander round Hampshire*
> > *Without any pampshire,*
> *Till the Vicar compelled him to Walisbury.*

As one or two of any readers may be somewhat bewildered by this, I hasten to explain that the English town of

Salisbury was of old called Sarum, and is frequently still so called by the more conservative natives. As for Hampshire it is generally spoken of as Hants.

Related to the Limerick of Co-ordinated Orthography is that of Outré Rhyme. A familiar example is the chestnut we used to chant as children, filled with a gleeful sense of sin:

> *A rare old bird is the pelican,*
> *His beak holds more than his belican.*
>> *He can take in his beak*
>> *Enough food for a week.*
> *I'm darned if I know how the helican!*

Though they rarely attain the pert good humor of this hoary classic by Dixon L. Merritt, modern Limericks solve far more advanced rhyming problems. As a Limerick traditionalist I cannot condone the metrical radicalism of the following example, but it has a certain charm as well as undoubted ingenuity:

> *A sleeper from the Amazon*
> *Put nighties of his gra'mazon—*
>> *The reason, that*
>> *He was too fat*
> *To get his own pajamazon.*

One of the most interesting problems in the construction of Limericks (for I need hardly state that Limericks are constructed, not written) is that of the impossible rhyme. The word "Limerick" itself I would have thought posed a perfect example. In my researches, however, I came across a solution (I doubt that more than one exists) that shows all the marks of clenched-teeth determination. It is a bad Limerick, but it is a miracle that it should exist at all.

> There was a young farmer of Limerick,
> Who started one day to trim a rick.
>   The Fates gave a frown,
>   The rick tumbled down
> And killed him—I don't know a grimmer rick.

And now for the Limerick's real *raison d'être.* "There are three kinds of limericks," says Don Marquis: "limericks to be told when ladies are present; limericks to be told when ladies are absent but clergymen are present—and limericks."

It is not easy to explain why the Limerick should have become what it has become: the perfect vehicle for the comedy of the indelicate, the obscene, and the scatological. The last line is of course inordinately useful. It is the mechanism of release, the lever of upset that sends Mrs. Grundy sprawling on her bottom, the surprise ending that suddenly divests humanity of its inhibitions. The end rhyme itself is at times the heart of the matter. When unprintable, it is all the more satisfying because it chimes so impudently with the decorous end words of the initial couplet.

The Limerick is well-suited to the small comedies of carnality, and most such comedies, despite the blown-up productions of Broadway and Hollywood, *are* small. It is especially fitted to express our rueful recognition of the fact that we are not only fearfully and wonderfully, but also absurdly, made; that the human body, though it may be the temple of the spirit, is also a kind of involuntary Fun House.

This recognition is tacit, rather than formally expressible. We seem at the moment to be willing to publish and read obscene novels, as long as the obscenity is ugly, serious, and dull. But obscenity that is merely frivolous and witty must be confined to oral literature, to the smoking-room story, and the recited Limerick. One remembers Macaulay's remark about the Puritan, that he hated bear-baiting, not because it gave pain to the bear, but because it gave pleasure to the spectators. It is not what shocks, but what shocks and diverts at the same time, that we censor.

The *locus classicus* of the Indelicate Limerick is Norman Douglas' collection. Its reputation seems to me undeserved. Its essence is not wit, but mere physiological candor, even mere scatological candor. While there are some ingenious rhymes to be found in it, the book on the whole is a bore that makes its strongest appeal to the phony Bohemian temperament and, quite properly and usefully, to the adolescent.

To theorize on this subject without quotation is to play *Hamlet* with the title role omitted. I have, after much dusty research, garnered a few Limericks of unimpeachable indelicacy, but which can, I think, be printed in these chaste pages. They will serve, in lieu of really forceful examples, to illustrate some of the foregoing remarks.

Here is Number One:

> *A striptease named Cubbard in Kansas*
> *Made a fortune by wiggling her Frances.*
> *When the censors got there,*
> *Miss Cubbard was bare.*
> *She explained, "I don't know where my fans is."*

Particularly to be noted here is the subtlety of the contrast between the elegant "Frances" and Miss Cubbard's endearingly folksy grammar. It is such touches that turn what might have been merely good jokes into small works of art.

Exhibit Number Two has a cold, legalistic charm:

> *There was a young lady of Wantage*
> *Of whom the Town Clerk took advantage.*
>> *Said the County Surveyor,*
>> *"Of course you must pay her;*
> *You've altered the line of her frontage."*

My third specimen, excellent in other respects, would appear to have a defective final rhyme:

> *The youths who frequent picture palaces*
> *Have no use for psychoanalysis;*
>> *And though Doctor Freud*
>> *Is distinctly annoyed,*
> *They cling to their long-standing fallacies.*

My final exhibit was composed by Heywood Broun, shortly after an operation. Its rhyming, unusual but correct, is particularly worthy of praise:

> *There was a young man with a hernia*
> *Who said to his surgeon "Gol-dernya,*
>> *When carving my middle*
>> *Be sure you don't fiddle*
> *With matters that do not concernya."*

Cleriheulogy

WHEN I WAS A BOY in high school we used to debate questions like: Which is mightier, the Pen or the Sword? Such arrogantly useless controversial calisthenics are, I understand, taboo under the new pedagogical dispensation which frowns on mental rivalry as nonconducive to Group Living. I cannot hope therefore to arouse much interest in the following small problem: Who in the long run benefits man more, the deviser of a new machine or the fashioner of a new form? Is there any way of comparing the achievements of those who thought of the motorcar with those who thought of the Gothic cathedral? How would you rate Kleenex, a machine for blowing the nose, against the sonata, a form for soothing the ear?

Aware that no answer exists in the back of any book, I do not pause for a reply. But I solicit a few moments of your attention while I extol the merits of a minor inventor whose main claim to the admiration of mankind is that he constructed a new verse form.

On March 30, 1956, there died in London at the age of eighty a literary and political journalist—a combination as common in England as it is rare with us—named E. C. Bentley. Bentley, from all I can learn of him, must have been a most remarkable man; perhaps most remarkable in that he preferred to make a casual, almost humorous use of his gifts, rather than an impressive one. His lifelong friend, G. K. Chesterton, has left us the best portrait of Bentley: "It was a poetic pleasure to see him walk, a little pompously, down the street and suddenly scale a lamp-post like a monkey, with the alleged intention of lighting a cigarette, and then drop down and resume his walk with an unchanged expression of earnestness and serenity." (Dickens had this same talent for fantastic clowning.) Chesterton also tells a delightful story of the days when he and Bentley were at St. Paul's School together. The High Master was perusing a Bentleyan version of the Dog in the Manger, which described the cattle as being prevented "from refreshing their own inner cows." It was this brilliant phrase that caused the High Master to exclaim, most perceptively, "That boy looks at the world standing on his head."

Bentley has been called "the father of the contemporary detective novel" by virtue of his *Trent's Last Case* (1913). This "acknowledged masterpiece" (Dorothy Sayers), called by Chesterton "the finest detective story of modern times," was described by its modest creator as "not so much a detective story as an exposure of detective stories." At this late date its merits need no recapitulation: it not only sounded the death knell of the Sherlock Holmes tradition, but it showed by quiet example that a presumably non-literary fictional form can combine harmoniously with a model prose style.

Though Bentley will be long honored for Inspector Trent, his name will not survive on that account. Had he *originated* the detective story, the case would have been quite different. However, Bentley did devise another literary form, far less consequential than Poe's invention, but one which may none the less endow him with a limited immortality. This is the Clerihew.

Elsewhere in this volume the attractions of the limerick are detailed. It is probable that, though the two are not otherwise comparable, as a permanently viable form the limerick will outlast the sonnet. The reasons are two: the limerick is peculiarly suited to the humor of bawdry, one of the enduring preoccupations of healthy men and women; and its composition is open to the limited poetical talent. The art of making stained glass is dead, that of whittling survives.

Bentley's clerihew is the only light verse form since the limerick that has "caught on," in the sense that it spontaneously attracts the efforts of nonprofessionals. This is truer in England than here, which I find a serious cause for regret. Perhaps these ephemeral words may induce some of my countrymen to try their hands at the clerihew. It is even easier to construct than the limerick and offers endless opportunities for mental amusement. During the time you normally spend reading the editorial page, you can create at least one passable clerihew that may be of real if microscopic benefit to the human race. For men become less human as they lose the talent for useless trifles.

When E. C. Bentley was a schoolboy of sixteen he was suddenly impelled, as by a daemon, to set down these remarkable words in remarkable order:

Sir Humphrey Davy
Detested gravy.
He lived in the odium
Of having discovered Sodium.

To invent and perfect an entirely new method of biography shortly after completing one's third lustrum is to enlarge the world's conception of precocity. Young Bentley's achievement may be estimated by recalling that it was not until Pascal was seventeen—a whole year older than Bentley—that he published his *Treatise on Conic Sections.*

In the course of his well-spent life, Bentley wrote many more of these captious capsule biographies—indeed three small volumes of them: *Biography for Beginners* (1905), *More Biography* (1929), and *Baseless Biography* (1939). In the fourth edition of the first of these collections, the author was listed as "E. Clerihew," a name, as he explained, "Those who happened to be listening heard bestowed upon me at my christening." His admirers, who had unconsciously been awaiting precisely this daring innovation in narrative verse, fixed upon it the term Clerihew, by which it has since been known and has, as its creator with pardonable pride stated, "seemed to find its way into the hands of connoisseurs of idiocy everywhere."

As I have said, Bentley wrote many more clerihews, but so consummate was his early talent one may doubt that he ever excelled, though he occasionally equaled, his summary sketch of the life and work of Sir Humphrey Davy. He lives in part by his own clerihumor, but even more splendidly in the inspiration he afforded thousands of happy followers. When he died, one of them, "Otto Watteau," spoke for us all:

Edmund Clerihew Bentley
Enthroned himself gently
Setting the whole country to work
On a quirk.

The range of Bentley's biographical research is as notable as the originality of his findings. The omnibus volume *Clerihews Complete* lists in its table of contents 107 separate and distinct historical personages. The tone of this vast vade mecum is set by the author's "Introductory Remarks" which must be quoted in full:

> *The Art of Biography*
> *Is different from Geography.*
> *Geography is about Maps,*
> *But Biography is about Chaps.*

Its range is indicated by the "Index of Psychology," affording a bird's-eye view of Bentley's all-inclusive intellectual curiosity. To suggest this to the reader, I transcribe that part of the index dealing with matters beginning with "D":

Delicacy (*Brigham Young*)
Diet, indiscretion in (*Milton, Henry I*)
Dilettantism (*Zinghis Khan*)
Dogs, dangerous (*Aeschylus, Laud, Maria Teresa*)
Domesticity (*Henry VIII, Ibsen*)
Done, not (*Stubbs*)
Dud (*George III*)
Dudgeon (*Herrick*)

Bentley has thrown new light on so many famous people that one is at a loss to select from amid so much wealth. Perhaps three examples will give the reader an idea of the Bentleyan method and his elegant art, so much less self-conscious than Lytton Strachey's and of course so much less diffuse than Maurois'. The best-known clerihew is perhaps his treatment of Sir Christopher Wren:

> *Sir Christopher Wren*
> *Said, "I am going to dine with some men.*
> *If anybody calls*
> *Say I am designing St. Paul's."*

Here is one of the few clerihews into which the personal note is permitted to creep:

> *I am not Mahomet.*
> *—Far from it.*
> *That is the mistake*
> *All of you seem to make.*

A hitherto undiscovered chapter in the life of Columbus:

> *"I quite realized," said Columbus,*
> *"That the Earth was not a rhombus,*
> *But I am a little annoyed*
> *To find it an oblate spheroid."*

Our final exhibit discloses Bentley as classical scholar:

> *"Dear me!" exclaimed Homer,*
> *"What a delicious aroma!*
> *It smells as if a town*
> *Was being burnt down."*

I do not wish to suggest that Bentley's genius should discourage us. On the contrary, once you have sat at his knee, you are ready to write your own clerihews. Such is the happy and accommodating nature of the form, it is highly probable that you will come up with something quite worthy of the master himself. His own son, N. C.

Bentley, no whit deterred by the eminence of his sire, once deservedly won a prize for this contribution to the history of the motion picture:

> *Mr. Cecil B. de Mille,*
> *Sorely against his will,*
> *Was persuaded to leave Moses*
> *Out of the Wars of the Roses.*

Ordinary mortals like you and me have written memorable clerihews. Here is a bit of musicology by M. Cassel:

> *Rachmaninoff*
> *Exclaimed to a fan—"Enough!*
> *What affliction that I*
> *Wrote the damned C sharp mi."*

An acute summary, by "Clarendon," of a great painter's career:

> *Paolo Uccello*
> *Was an unsatisfactory fellow.*
> *When his wife went to bed,*
> *He studied perspective instead.*

Ellen Evans contributes this psychiatric insight:

> *The idea of Europa's Bull*
> *Was a little fanciful.*
> *But Jove*
> *Was a queer cove.*

It is even possible to meddle successfully with Mr. Bentley's original rhyme scheme. Here is a variation by Diana Menuhin, wife of the great violinist:

Nietzsche
Was a cruel
Tietzsche
But Goethe
Wouldn't
Hoethe
Fly.

As a final demonstration that clerihews can be created by any conscientious person who can rhyme and who is willing to look at history without conventional prejudice, I subjoin a number of clerihews of my own, all composed under the influence of insomnia.

ABORIGINAL

Tecumseh
Lies under no odium, sir,
Even in comparison
With William Henry Harrison.

PRESIDENTIAL

A White House resident
Was Millard Fillmore, thirteenth President.
It's a mystery
How few were his contacts with history.

FASHIONABLE

The Brothers Ringling
Were quite used to mingling.
At tea in a zoo
They knew just what to do.

FISCAL

Madison Square Garden and Madison Avenue
Differ in their philosophy of revenue:
The first features punching,
The second expense-account lunching.

OF HUMAN BLONDAGE

Tommy Manville's complex
Researches in the field of sex
Are subsidized by a commercial operation
Involving materials for roofing and insulation.

POLAR

Admiral Byrd
Was never once deterred
(Any more than was the ice-crossing Eliza)
By an unfortunate tendency to coryza.

RETROSPECTIVE

Sweet Cohn and Schine!
For you I pine!
I miss you fellows.
Your act was better than Abbott and Costello's.

MAGICAL

Harry Houdini
Sawed a woman in two, the meanie,
Leaving neither fraction
Feeling any great satisfaction.

MARITIME

Stephen Decatur
Was no propitiator.
He would hurl his sextant
At anyone extant.

STENOGRAPHIC

Walt Whitman
Would hardly have cared for Pitman,
Sensing
No pressing need for condensing.

JACOBEAN

Henry James
(Whatever his other claims)
Is not always too deuced
Lucid.

SARTORIAL

Samuel Gompers
Found the labor movement in rompers.
After many changes and chances,
He left it in long pantses.

THEOLOGICAL

Said Descartes: "I extoll
Myself because I have a soul,
And beasts do not." (Of course
He had to put Descartes before the horse.)

HISTORICAL

Of Gibbon (the old prude
Who left footnotes in Latin because they were lewd)
It may be said:
His anecdotes remain lively though his language
   remains dead.

TERMINOLOGICAL

Andrew Jackson
Was given to Anglo-Saxon.
He addressed words unmailable
To any person available.

QUESTIONABLE

Harriet Beecher Stowe
Is said to have caused four years of woe.
Think it's plausible
She was that causable?

ALIMENTARY

The herbivorous Thoreau
Would emerge from his pondside burrow
Whenever he grew thinner,
And walk over to the Emersons' for a chicken dinner.

SARTORIAL

I am a votary
Of Dr. Johnson's coterie,
But waste no flattery
On Hedda Hopper's hattery.

CLERIHEWSFUL

Rhyme-linked,
Otherwise quite distinct:
Catullus,
John Foster Dulles.

POE-TATORY

Poe's curse
Was mixing stimulants and verse.
No sooner was Poe
Done with his old raven than he started
  on his Old Crow.

METAPHYSICAL

Hegel
Never ate a bagel.
Conversely, few Hegelians
Are to be found among Lindy's bagelians.

SPECTACULAR

Woodrow Wilson, addressing the masses,
Had a nervous habit of polishing his glasses.
Be under no misapprehension—
I am aware that this detail is barely worthy of mention.

LINEAL

Oliver Wendell Holmes
Would have helped writers of historical tomes
If Oliver Wendell
Had named his son, say, Oliver Mendel.

LITERARY

William Faulkner of Mississippi
(Known to more people than is Fra Lippo Lippi),
When Englished
Will doubtless be even more distinguished.

BIOGRAPHICAL

Harry Truman
Vexes some by being overhuman.
His life, it seems,
Would not have appealed to Parson Weems.

On the Utility of U-Talk

LAST YEAR there appeared an American edition of a book called *Noblesse Oblige,* edited by Nancy Mitford. Our reviewers greeted it with a certain amount of gentle kidding. Having abolished class distinctions by law and retained them in unadmitted actuality, we are naturally forced into a defensive position vis-à-vis the British, who have until recently been franker on the subject. And so, as part of our defense, we laugh at a people who actually dare to be as absorbed in matters of class as we are in something truly important, let us say, the World Series.

The subject of *Noblesse Oblige* is the language, more particularly the vocabulary, used by the English aristocracy. When first published, the little volume kicked up a cloud of dust, some of it not yet laid. The fuss started in Finland. Professor Alan Ross of Birmingham University published in Helsinki for Finnish philologists (I am not making this up) a paper called *U and Non-U: An Essay in Sociological Linguistics.* It was an attempt to define the language used by upper-class (U) Englishmen, language that sets them apart from non-U speakers. Miss Mitford, herself rather aggressively upper class and therefore just a shade non-U, commented wittily in an essay called *The English Aristocracy*. The two essays, with some other related pieces, made up *Noblesse Oblige*.

Why did uproar follow upon its English publication? Because (a) Miss Mitford and Professor Ross let the cat of U-vocabulary out of the closed bag of U-society; (b) according to her peers, Miss Mitford shouldn't have done it, because it is a private cat; (c) England is trying hard to convince itself and the rest of the world that its class system is on the way out; (d) anybody who thinks one way of speaking is better than another is a snob, isn't he, and snobs are bad people, aren't they?

The British tempest in a teapot was not repeated here, when an American edition of *Noblesse Oblige* was published. We should not have expected it to be. For one thing, we are ostensibly less interested in class distinctions —that is, few of us dare to say we are interested. For another, we are less interested in language. For the minority, however, who *may* be interested in language, I should like to set down a few comments on American U-sage and non-U-sage; and I hope that they will be challenged and corrected by better observers and scholars.

But before so doing I had better come clean and state that I believe there *is* an American U.

The American upper class is the lunatic aunt in the national attic. Both the family and the neighbors know she's there, but neither will own up to it. Superior manners are somehow supposed to betray our political democracy. This is a tenable notion only if we assume that political democracy and bad manners are linked. Governors who campaign with hillbilly bands and presidential aspirants who wear coonskin caps (surmounting tortoise-shell glasses) lend some color to this theory, but not enough for universal persuasion.

Yet a little quiet thought should convince us that ballot-box democracy and an upper class can jog along quite comfortably together. Indeed they have done so ever since the founding of the Republic, an achievement made possible in large part by aristocrats. We would all be a little less touchy on the subject if this simple fact could be taught to children in their first history class. Then, when they grow up to be voters, they may be able to exempt an admittedly U Adlai Stevenson from the admittedly non-U duty of kissing babies that do not belong to him—an example of barbarous manners apparently limited to twenty-five regular appearances per American century.

The present writer is by birth and training drastically non-upper class. That is what permits him to write, in non-U prose, about U's. Upper-class self-contemplation is a bit *infra dig.*, not quite cricket.

Our upper class is not to be confused with our most publicized, our richest, or our most powerful citizens, though it may be sparsely represented in all three groups. In his book *The Power Elite* Professor C. Wright Mills tries to equate this trio with what he thinks of as an emergent upper class. He sees this class—and his argument is often brilliant—as a cohesive, self-perpetuating group largely consisting of our ablest big-corporation executives, certain intelligent (and not necessarily well-publicized) politicians, and the intellectual cream of the admirals and generals. To these he adds a new crowd—the "celebrities" who, he believes, function as a kind of lightning rod to which the attention of the ordinary citizen is harmlessly diverted.

This Power Elite may exist. But even if it does, I do not agree that it runs the country, except intermittently, during the administrations of weak Chief Executives. Furthermore, I do not think it is identical, except to a minor degree, with a *genuine* upper class. To believe it is identical is to confuse ability with character and power with superiority.

Our upper class is less stable than that of England or France. It admits new members more frequently. On the other hand, it tends to lose members more frequently also. The weaker sisters are often seduced by the middle-class Circes of conformity and adjustment. Each such successful seduction decreases the U-will to persistence, for independence, sometimes to the point of arrogance or eccentricity, is a traditional *sine qua non* of a healthy aristocracy.

Is it possible to draw a profile of this upper class? Only roughly, and with many qualifications which the reader is begged to consider I am making in advance. Here perhaps are a few identifiable characteristics:

1. The unit of the uppers is not the individual but the family.

2. By our American standards this family is "old"; perhaps it has been here at least four generations.

3. It is generally of English or Scotch-English stock, or basically so.

4. It has won a certain respect in the community, a respect extended even to its less worthy members.

5. Its male members are usually Ivy League, West Point, or Annapolis.

6. They have not merely attended these schools; they have been educated there. A genuine U may not be mentally brilliant, but he believes, if quite unaggressively, in the value of an intellectual tradition. It is this characteristic alone which makes it impossible for most members of Professor Mills' Power Elite to be uppers.

7. Our *very* richest men are rarely uppers. But in the true U family there is generally *some* money, often inherited. A poverty-stricken upper sooner or later loses his stigmata.

8. Uppers often do nothing and (a faculty the rest of us have lost) do it very well. When they do something it is more apt to be professional than commercial. A few go into politics. Our first six presidents were uppers; the only others, I should think, have been Taft, Wilson, and the two Roosevelts. My own notion of a superb upper is John Quincy Adams, one of the most magnificent and least appreciated human beings ever born on this continent.

9. They are small in number, not generally prominent (in the newspaper sense), and reside in a few large eastern cities and their suburbs—mainly Boston (pre-eminently), New York, Philadelphia, Charleston, Richmond, perhaps San Francisco and New Orleans. Certain cities are by nature non-upper: Los Angeles is the key name here, Detroit is another. Chicago has a few survivals.

10. U's are not effusive and adjustment-mad on the one hand, or competitive on the other. Often highly emotional in their private lives, they do not appear so on the surface. The rest of us call them cold. They do not mind.

11. The final characteristic is the most difficult to phrase. It is even rather difficult to notice, because American uppers are developing a certain anxiety to seem no better (that is, no more distinguishable) than the next fellow. The weaker members of the tribe will often go to great lengths to camouflage those qualities in which they are superior. These qualities spring from a conscious or unconscious attachment to a dying code of behavior, ultimately derived from eighteenth- or even seventeenth-century England. This behavior is marked by: dislike of publicity; social ease, with "inferiors" as well as equals—uppers are not uppish; avoidance of display and of talk about money; a constant sense, occasionally absurd and boring, of family tradition; gentle manners, but when necessary, arrogant manners, which are not identical with bad manners; the ability, particularly of the women, to converse; the inability to argue, debate, or quote others' views as their own; a marked tendency to say what one thinks, rather than what is fashionable or pleasing; a great interest in physical well-being and strength and grace of body; relatively notable attachment to the past, sometimes exaggerated into a tedious antiquarianism; an almost instinctive capacity to recognize their peers wherever and whenever encountered; and, finally, certain linguistic habits and traditions.

It is these last I should like to discuss briefly.

Let me state at once my awareness of the fact that sufficient usage can eventually make the ugly, the repulsive, the unclear, the evasive, the discordant perfectly correct; and I am not in the least impressed by this circumstance, which seems so greatly to please our professors of linguistics. I am not urging anyone to imitate, let us say, the speech of Adlai Stevenson. It would be foolish and vain to try. I merely say that it is more admirable than certain other kinds of speech, because more efficient, cleanly, and memorable; and for these reasons it is worthy of detached study, study quite unrelated to "snobbery."

I have not known many U-speakers. In one of my trades —entertainment—they are virtually nonexistent, though there are a few English actors resident among us who are genuinely U and several more who are excellent U-mimics, which they should be, as that is part of their business. Writers are usually non-U in their speech and many of the most popular and successful ones are non-U in their writing. (An exception is Mr. John Marquand.) My observations are drawn therefore from limited experience. But this experience is more fruitful than would have been the case had I been U myself, with wider access to U-families. Such families generally are not self-perceptive. The fish does not notice the water. (Miss Mitford is an odd fish indeed.)

Roughly speaking, I would say that American U-sage is marked by:

1. Avoidance (unconscious if upper U, conscious if garden-variety U) of the smart or topical phrase, and of trade jargon and slang. Qualify this last: there is a special U-slang, derived largely from certain U-sports, particularly the hunt. There is also a special U-slang learned in certain Ivy League colleges or gentlemen's preparatory schools.

2. Avoidance of language fidgets. A U does not fiddle with his face. (Observe how many TV speaker are victims of such small tics.) Similarly he does not fiddle with the language. He economizes, often to the point of sparse-

ness. He does not preface his sentences with "Well . . . ." To say anything a U-speaker will as a general rule use about 20 per cent fewer words than will a non-U.

3. Preference for the direct and simple, even the common or what the non-U speaker would call the vulgar.

4. Often an inability to use *rich* or *striking* language; the wonderful inventiveness of our vernacular (when it *is* wonderful) is entirely non-U. The English of Ring Lardner is, in its coinages, its humor, and it vividness, non-U. However, in its economy and directness it is U. Lardner himself came of a near-U family though most of his later interests and associations were non-U.

5. Certain peculiarities of pronunciation, though not many, as most of our pronunciation differences are matters of region, not of class.

6. Certain minor peculiarities of syllabic accent.

7. Freedom of vocabulary. Longshoremen and U-speakers use Anglo-Saxon monosyllables casually. (So do young American novelists, but for different reasons.) My own class, the middle, is relatively circumspect in its speech.

8. Neatness of enunciation, not to the point of the Oxford or Noel Coward "clipped" accent, but in general an avoidance of drawling and slurring. Except of course in the South—Southern U-families seem to me to speak badly, but that may be because my ears are Northern.

9. A special pitch and tonality, varying with the region, but essentially distinct from that region's non-U. This is a point rather difficult to illustrate without the use of linguistic technicalities. I shall not illustrate it.

Suppose we begin with a few examples as to which

there can be little debate. *Black tie* (or often *dress*) is, generally, U, which does not mean it is not also the preferred form of many non-U speakers; whereas *tux* is not only non-U, but perhaps even sub-non-U. *Long dress*, I am told, is more or less U; *formal* is non-U, or perhaps non-U undergraduate jargon, a special non-U subdivision; our great Midwestern and Western colleges are mints of non-U-sage. The simple *how do you do?* is proper and has descended to the rest of us (probably) from U-speakers; *pleased to meet you* and similar unhappy phrases are non-U. U introductions are usually terse and consist of the names of the two principals; *meet the missus, the wife* we need hardly discuss. Jocular introductions (*meet the ball-and-chain*) are sub-non-U. In England, Miss Mitford tells us, *mirror* is non-U as opposed to U *looking glass*; but this usage applies here only among certain conservative New England families. *Curtains* is U, *drapes* non-U, *draperies* is a limbo word. *Pardon me* is vaguely non-U, as is *I beg your pardon*; but I am not sure that *excuse me* or *sorry* are at all decisively U.

Non-U speakers are given to various euphemisms (or perhaps we should say non-U-phemisms) for *bathroom* or *toilet* (this latter word, itself a euphemism, seems hardly to be used at all). *Toilet paper* is in general usage (I do not know quite how to recast that statement), but *toilet tissue* or *bathroom paper* would suggest non-U. In this connection we might note that most advertising copy is non-U, particularly when it is supposed to be exceedingly U. *Rumpus room* and *den* are non-U. *Children* is U as opposed to non-U *kids*. In Hollywood, where only the purest, undefiled non-U is current, a *cook* is generally a *house-*

keeper. There is something non-U about *passed away* for *died*.

The most ordinary phrases are often the most crucial. U will often use *woman* where non-U will use *lady*; U *parents*, non-U *folks*. *Have you got?* and *have you?* are both correct, but the first is a mite non-U. The word *weekend* is interesting: U-speakers often prefer *Friday to Monday* and many who do use *weekend* will accent the second syllable as against non-U *week'end* (either stress is correct). The tendency to accent the first syllable of certain words, by the way, is often a non-U identifier: *cig'arette, mag'azine*, are non-U. So are *ice' cream* for *ice cream'* and *Moth'er Goose* for *Mother Goose'*. But *ar'istocrat* seems U as against *arist'ocrat*: either is acceptable.

The scholar-critic Basil Davenport tells me that he feels *commence* is generally non-U as opposed to *begin*; but I think this a bit subtle. I am not sure of the U for *to date* (a girl), but there is no doubt the phrase itself is decisively non-U. *To keep company* used to be non-U, but today one rarely hears the phrase except among elderly non-U's. *To go steady* is perhaps sub-non-U.

The U-speaker avoids like the plague (a phrase he is apt to avoid like the plague) all modish phrases, such as *I couldn't care less, I couldn't agree more, educated guess, calculated risk, I needed that one* (after a drink), *to know the score, 'n stuff, no percentage in it, the psychological moment, I've got news for you, that's for sure, it doesn't add up, you can say that again, out of this world, —— or else!, a fun scarf*; also vogue words: *psychosomatic* and other cheap Freudianisms, *upgrade*, a *character, tycoon, reaction*.

The world of advertising and popular journalism is rife with such phrases, even though many men in these trades are U by birth and education. (It is interesting that the Luce periodicals are managed in large part by U-men, who do their successful utmost to employ and develop a writing style that will conceal their impeccable origins.) Please do not accuse me of political bias when I say that the leaders of our present Administration are prolific users of non-U English. Probably it is part of the homey, cozy, honest-American middle-of-the-roadness which is the presumed hallmark of the Republican Party as at present constituted. The late Senator Taft, on the other hand, spoke (for a politician, I mean) relatively U-English.

Vase is interesting. The nearer you are to the correct French pronunciation the more likely you are to be non-U; most U-speakers rhyme the word with *face*. On the other hand, the U-pronunciation of *lingerie* is apt to stick fairly close to the French; non-U is something like *lonjeray*.

I am on debatable ground here but I think U will say *May I have coffee?* whereas non-U will often preface the last word with *my*. A man who orders *a coffee* in a restaurant has probably spent some years in France; but the usage is gaining generally.

To *name* one's country house, particularly jocularly, is a trifle non-U, unless, like Alexander Woollcott's *Wit's End,* the joke is really witty. But a traditional and unexpressive name for a large estate (Mr. Baruch's *Hobcaw*) is England-county-family U.

To call the *maître d'hotel* the *maître D* is blatantly non-U. It is, once again, pure Madison Avenue in origin; all such knowing phrases have a non-U coloration.

To refer to *my wife* is more or less U; *Mrs. Smith* is non-U; *Mrs. S.* sub-non-U.

Professor Ross has an interesting footnote on the phrases used in casual toasting. English U-speakers used to say nothing, which does seem the best form. (In general, when there is no need to say anything, U-speakers say nothing.) *Cheers, down the hatch, bottoms up*, and similar locutions are all perfectly pleasant, perfectly acceptable, and perfectly non-U.

The use of first names among people who have just met each other is increasing among us: it is non-U and probably derived from the entertainment industry.

A U-man will say *view* rather than *viewpoint, good-bye* rather than *'bye now*. Jocularities such as *see you in church* or *don't do anything I wouldn't do* are pathetically non-U and would be repulsive if they were U.

Conference (in business) used to be elegant; then it became non-U and gave way to *meeting*. Unless a businessman is really attending a meeting, *he's busy* would appear the honest U-phrase to be used by the receptionist.

U-talk is often brutal as compared with non-U talk: *poor* is U-sage, *underprivileged* non-U-sage. The jargon of sociology and editorial journalism is responsible for a good deal of this kind of circumlocution.

Non-U's, particularly the ladies, often love the exaggerated phrase: I cannot conceive of a U saying, "I *despise* garlic!" *Tasty*, as applied to food, I find non-U; also the phrase *to go to theater*, perhaps a Yiddishism, as are *this I've got to hear, I told him off, but good*, and similar fashionable locutions.

Our professional students of language have quite properly called upon us to admire the venison richness of our vernacular, the coinages of a Winchell, the inventions of the hard-working journalists of *Time*, the close-to-the-people vocabulary of Ring Lardner. Well and good. But in the excitement of this linguistic Popular Frontism, the quiet, steadying, braking influence of U-speech tends to attract small notice. Concision, understatement, exactness, even conventionality of expression (if the convention is a noble one) are not to be sniffed at. Why not give the underprivileged gentleman a fair shake?

I recollect the exact moment when this became clear to me—the moment that I decided that, despite the New Grammarians, correct usage had its value. As a young man —I was nineteen—I got my first teaching job in a private school. The principal—Herbert W. Smith is now seventy-one, and I should like to record his name here—was interviewing me in his office. He asked my permission to make a necessary telephone call to one of the teachers. To the switchboard operator he said, "May I speak with Miss Jones?" Something about the question struck me as odd. I realized what it was: I would have said "May I speak *to* Miss Jones?" The difference is not unimportant. It is not only a matter of exact meaning, though it is that also. It is a matter of courtesy, even morality. The clearest English is often *good* English, in both senses of the term. It respects the communicatee just as it shows that the communicator respects himself.

My view may seem stiff-necked but here it is: no matter how many people say *to, with* is better. And it will remain better even though every English speaker on the face of the earth should reject *with* and embrace *to*.

A Letter to the Editor of

Holiday

Dear Ted:

On several occasions you have asked me to set down some notions on the art—if it is an art—of letter writing, together with some counsel to our readers against those moments in which pen, ink, paper, and the Postmaster General are enlisted to repair or confirm friendships.

In this matter I claim small authority. As a letter writer I am not even middling good. On the other hand I am a model correspondent. I answer all letters on the day of receipt, usually (in this respect only resembling Shaw) on postcards, for I cannot help feeling that, considering their contents, most sealing of envelopes is a waste of time, as is so much frantic packaging in general. I answer mail promptly not because I am either efficient or markedly courteous, but because the sight of a clean desk pleases me; and it pleases me because it gives me the illusion of accomplishment; and that particular illusion is necessary to many a professional writer who is never quite sure that he has done what more respectable citizens call work. A clean desk seems for a few precious instants to make me part of the business community.

Yes, I am a good correspondent. But I am a poor letter writer because, making my living by my pen and on occasion by agitating my vocal cords and lower jaw, I find it necessary to husband my thoughts. A good letter is a proof of surplus in the writer's temperament. All I can do is admire the prodigality of such letter writers as Dickens, Keats, Byron, Santayana, Thomas Wolfe—those Niagaras of excess energy who never needed to budget their mental expenditures.

No, I must be content just to answer the mail. But this is not letter writing. It is a mere series of transactions. Such transactions, increasing in number with each passing year, perhaps make smoother the world's work. But surely they do not bear witness to the mind's play. They lack at least two marks of the first-rate letter: personality and uselessness.

A good letter is an exercise of the ego, a modest letter writer a contradiction in terms. That is why one should be wary of letters that hew too closely to the characters of their recipients. I want to hear from *you*, not you relative to me. Do not exercise upon me the talents of the salesman, nor inquire oversolicitously about my well-being or that of my family. If you are too tactful you will not touch me; if too persuasive you will not persuade me. (The obvious exception here is the love letter, in which sender and sendee merge into one.)

Many men, handicapped by the nervous habit of public

statement, lose the capacity for private expression. Their audience-sense is overdeveloped at the expense of self-awareness and even—I use the word literally—self-interest. The letters of Gladstone, like his remarks to Queen Victoria, are all addressed to a public meeting. A good letter writer has nothing to offer but himself. It is his own personality, with all its quirks and quiddities, that he drops into the mailbox. Such a letter is one of the many ingenious inventions man has devised so that he may talk about himself, the analytic couch being the most up-to-date. By and large more memorable letter writers seem to crop up in Protestant than in Catholic communities, perhaps because Protestantism lacks the office of the confessor.

There is a letter I recently came across written by George Santayana* to the Marchesa Iris Origo on the death of her son. It is not a "letter of condolence." Indeed it hardly seems to take into account the Marchesa herself, or the state of her feelings. Instead it is an honest expression of the writer's own thoughts on death. These thoughts Santayana, as a philosopher, felt to be the best gift he could send his friend. The letter contains himself; and because this self was an interesting one the letter is a good one. But it would never receive a passing grade in a manual of correspondence.

(I must break off, Ted, to walk down for the mail and answer it.)

To resume: I think the kind of letters I have in mind, which are essentially self-revelation, should not be written in expectation of an answer. They may *inspire* one; they

---

* *The Letters of George Santayana*, edited, with an introduction and commentary, by Daniel Cory (Charles Scribner's Sons, N.Y., 1955).

must not exact it. They are not like dinner parties, to be exchanged and returned on what a friend of mine calls a retaliatory basis. "The letter which merely answers another letter," says Mark Van Doren, "is no letter at all." *
Many of the best I can recollect receiving I would not think of answering, any more than I would think of replying to something overheard. Indeed the pleasure of reading a good letter is akin to that of eavesdropping, as its writing is a kind of licit indiscretion. Lately, reading some letters exchanged by Lytton Strachey and Virginia Woolf ** I was gratified to note an occasional, if self-conscious, note of bawdiness. One would never from their immaculate works have suspected such an amiable weakness in either of these rarefied minds. (Although, come to think of it, Ted, I remember an anecdote about Strachey bearing on this point. Once, asked what he considered the greatest thing in life, he inclined his reedlike body, complete with owl eyes and spectral beard, and, in his elegant, high-pitched voice, languidly piped: "Why, passion, of course.")

Literary people, like Strachey and Virginia Woolf, no longer write letters for posterity, though they may keep them for publication. The full-dress letters of antiquity are not letters at all, but essays fitted with the accessories of dateline, salutation, and signature. They may be interesting but they lack the salt of indiscretion and the spring-water smack of spontaneity. Very few of the classic letter writers who wrote with one eye on posterity contrived

---

* *The Selected Letters of William Cowper,* edited with an introduction by Mark Van Doren (Farrar, Straus and Young, Inc., N.Y., 1951).
** *Virginia Woolf and Lytton Strachey Letters,* edited by Leonard Woolf and James Strachey (Harcourt, Brace & Co., N.Y., 1956).

also to retain the note of the personal and the purposeless. Of those who did, Horace Walpole seems to me supreme. We do not know how many letters this shrewd eighteenth-century elegant wrote. About four thousand have survived. Even a skeleton selection * bears witness to a curious ability to put his entire self into his correspondence and yet to take due account of the need to conserve and enhance his reputation for generations to come.

Walpole's letters were eagerly read in his own day for a reason that would not obtain so strongly were he our contemporary. You recall that he was the youngest son of Sir Robert Walpole, First Minister for twenty-one years. He was rich, knowledgeable, close to power. Consequently, knowing everyone and being, though a spectator, in the dead center of large events, he always had news to impart. Today's news is the cheapest of commodities. It is in such long supply that it is thrust upon one. Immediate obsolescence is built into it as more carefully calculated obsolescence is built in to one's motorcar. Thus nothing happens that is not at once everyone's property—the sheerest, the blackest communism. Few any longer own, like Walpole or Byron,** a little corner in events from which they may dole out novelties to friends. The newspaper and the broadcaster have made harder the path of the born letter writer.

All rapid communication has, of course. Letters are bridges, and the art of bridgebuilding is bound to decay when there are no more rivers to cross. The art of letter

---

* *Letters of Horace Walpole,* selected by W. S. Lewis with an introduction by R. W. Ketton-Cremer (The Folio Society, London, 1951).
** *The Selected Letters of Lord Byron,* edited with an introduction by Jacques Barzun (Farrar, Straus and Young, Inc., N.Y., 1953).

writing flourishes when literacy, highly charged personalities, and primitive communications all happen to occur simultaneously. Such a period was the eighteenth century in our country and Western Europe. Today we have wholesale literacy and personalities are not lacking. What is lacking is isolation, geographical or mental or both. Perhaps a certain kind of unhappiness, not too overwhelming, provides a fertile seedbed for letter writing. As Nietzsche says, "Any man who does not write books, has plenty of time to think, and lives in unsatisfying society is likely to be a good letter writer." These three conditions are hard to come by today: our neighbors are incessantly eager to adjust to us, as we to them; the communications people have benevolently relieved us of those tedious bare hours in which reflection might occur; and everybody writes books.

The greatest letter writers, among plain people as well as the highly educated, seem to have thrived on impediments. Carbon paper, the typewriter, the duplicator, automatic filing systems—all seem to make letter writing so easy that some of the delight fades out of it. Perhaps the splutter of the quill pen and the dim light of the smoky oil lamp were helps to composition. At any rate, while labor-saving devices have enlarged the body of epistolary communication they have not greatly nourished its soul. The mere act of letter writing could not have been easy for Jefferson, Franklin, or Abigail Adams; but they seem to have produced letters difficult to match today. Not impossible, however. Try the Holmes-Pollock correspondence—though that of course goes back fifty years; or Proust's letters—though they also are of near-historical vintage.

On the other hand, Ted, wouldn't you agree that in the matter of *preserving* letters we show more wisdom than our ancestors? They seem to have saved everything. As Frank Moore Colby says, "Never burn an uninteresting letter is the first rule of British aristocracy." One good consequence of the omnipresence of cheap and easy communication is that our attics (which we don't have anyway) are no longer cluttered with boxes and trunks containing old letters that no one will ever want to read. We do not hold them in superstitious reverence; and the man who retains carbon copies of his personal correspondence appears a little odd or at any rate old-fashioned.

Without a doubt the best letter writers today are children—before they have been taught the proprieties of correspondence. They have all the virtues—spontaneity, honesty, directness. I don't know, Ted, whether you have looked into the latest *divertissement* * of our good friend H. Allen Smith. In this astonishing collection of literary productions by moppets there are at least a dozen letters that posterity will not willingly let die.

The loser in a class election, bidden to send a message of congratulation to the winner, inscribed this on the blackboard:

Dear Class:

I congratulate Mildred Stokes on her election as the class leader. She is a much better one for leader than I am. Fooey.

Priscilla Caulkins

Or perhaps you care to make a note of this correspondence between two third graders:

---

* *Write Me a Poem, Baby*, by H. Allen Smith (Little Brown and Co., Boston, 1956).

Dear Judee: I luv you. Do you luv
me? Jimmy.

The answer:

Dear Jimmy: I do NOT love you.
Love, Judy.

The best letters I have ever received from grownups
did not come from professional writers or people in any
way distinguished. They came from people who were
naturally intelligent; who found themselves mildly, not
tragically, at odds with their environment; and who had
not read enough literature to distort the slant of the style
of their own minds. Because they had no public character
to sustain, they wrote with utter frankness; and because
they were a little lonely and a little unhappy—but not to
the point of self-pity, which would have spoiled everything—they made me a free gift of themselves. All of us
have had this experience of receiving remarkable letters
from people whose conversation may be far from brilliant
and whose achievements in life are not notable. "Joe writes
a good letter," we say, noting the fact as a special talent
unconnected with high performance in any other field.

Other than these "natural" letter writers, my best correspondents have been the comedian Fred Allen and the
poet-novelist Vincent McHugh. You knew Fred and you
know Vincent. Perhaps you'll tell me some time just what
it was in Fred that emerged only in his letters—all, you
recollect, typed without benefit of capitals, most of them
wittier than anything he ever said on the air, all obviously
tossed off without much premeditation. I wish I had a little

magpie blood in me—I never thought of saving them. My impression is that a really fat collection of Fred Allen's correspondence would place him among the classic epistolary masters of the last hundred years.

Vincent McHugh's letters have the tone of the finest talk and at the same time—because he is incapable of using a worn phrase or remodeling another man's notion—they come pretty close to being informal literature. I thought I'd end this missive—practically an object lesson in how not to write a letter—by quoting a few lines from the last note I got from him. Anybody would be happy to receive a letter beginning thus:

> I am glad you and I are alive in a new year. I'm getting a little indignant about these people who up and die without an aye or no; without even having the decency to ask my consent; with the most indelicate disregard for my feelings. Just die. And there they are looking at the ceiling, usually in some place I can't get to, looking deaf as a dog to all the questions I'd meant to ask them, the news I had for them alone, the word of this or that I'd intended to write. *Non compos* and no soap. I hope I'll never live to see the day I'd do a thing like that.

There's always the problem, isn't there, of how to work in your own daily experiences without sounding either egotistic or diary-ish. It's hard to do, and yet such material is the very stuff of a good letter. Vincent's final paragraph, short, unstudied, brings him vividly to my mind—and that's what I want a faraway friend (he lives in San Francisco) to do when he takes pen in hand. Here it is:

> Enough. I must get out and return a pair of Japanese binoculars I rented to pick up the *Monterey's* white flank as

she came out of the fog the other morning. Helmsman borrowed them at the last minute; I had to pick her up with my still bleary morning eye, hideously unused to daylight. I was wedged against the tugboat's pilothouse, shooting the ship with a Filmo against waving gulls and the sun's red eye. Hands completely numb with cold. But I guess I got her. Felt good to climb aboard through the No. 10 port into that warm ship.

The sentences are charming. The important thing however is that they suddenly materialize the writer. I was about to add, "as if on a television screen." But the comparison is inexact. A good letter transmits a private image; electrical impulses, almost as if the laws of physics had built this into their nature, a public one.

Best to you, Ted.

Kip

P.S. All well here.

Under the Reading Lamp

The Bubble Reputation

LITERARY reputations ebb and flow, answering to hardly discoverable tides and moons, or rise like Lazarus to a second life. What makes an author's name live, waver or die, or sometimes persist in a cocoon of suspended animation? Why are some writers revived, others exhumed? Who are the resurrection men? What part does accident play in the establishment of an author's fame?

A reputation may stand high with literary men. It may stand high with the general public. Or it may (Shakespeare) stand high with both. The English poet John Skelton (c. 1460–1529), prized by the first group, draws a blank with the second. A complication arises when a reputation must be assessed on the wing—that is, during its passage from the first group to the second. For example, for some years after his death in 1924 Franz Kafka enjoyed increasing popularity, but largely with other writers. A few years ago however his short stories were added to the Modern Library series, a sign that Kafka had broken through to the general public.

Many reputations cannot be said to be either alive or dead with either group. They exist in limbo. Thus Longfellow's *Evangeline* is not highly regarded by the knowledgeable. Nor is it read by the public. The schoolroom however continues to pay it a kind of wax-flower tribute.

Then there is the confusion caused by mere geography. Just the other day I learned with amazement that Ethel Voynich's *The Gadfly*, a best-seller of two generations ago that one would have thought as dead as Sallust, has for years enjoyed sensational popularity in the Soviet Union. In 1952 UNESCO reported that throughout Russia and the Iron Curtain countries the most widely translated American writer was—Jack London. With us *The Call of the Wild* is still read, but it requires little more than a sad leafing-through of a recent Jack London selection (*Tales of Adventure*, edited by Irving Shepard, 1956) to make one feel the remoteness of this romantic forerunner of Ernest Hemingway.

One country's classic is another country's bore. Many authorities regard the fourteenth-century Persian Hafiz as one of the world's greatest poets. In English he is next to unreadable. Another familiar example is our own Shakespeare. In the seventeenth and eighteenth centuries the French thought him barbarous. They are still a bit reluctant to place him on a level with Racine. But to us Racine in translation, despite the apologetics of Lytton Strachey, does not read like a classic. The tariff of misunderstanding is so high that many reputations never get beyond the home grounds. On the other hand, some gain by emigration: the French in Baudelaire's day thought better of Poe than we did; and today think even better of Faulkner than we do, exalted as his reputation is.

It works the other way also: the Atlantic is a two-way ocean. The German poet Rainer Maria Rilke died in 1926. His reputation has steadily grown, but far more spectacularly among a fairly numerous American coterie than in his own country. In the year of his death only one of his books was in print among us; since then perhaps fifteen titles have appeared. Translation is not always a barrier.

The case of Sören Kierkegaard (1813–1855) is even more spectacular. The posthumous enlargement of Kierkegaard's reputation is a phenomenon not confined to the United States, but we might say that it is here being given its most systematic development.

Sören Kierkegaard was not a clergyman. Indeed he hated "official Christianity" and, rather than take it from priestly hands, died without receiving the sacrament. But he did have a degree in theology and has probably influenced certain branches of modern Protestant theology more than any other figure since the days of Knox and Calvin. The modern German philosopher-theologians Heidegger, Jaspers, and Barth owe much of their inspiration to him. Franz Kafka (himself, as we have noted, recently rediscovered) was among those who rediscovered Kierkegaard. The French existentialist school acknowledges him as one of its basic sources. His influence in our own day is probably similar in scope to that of Nietzsche during the nineteenth century. Yet, as far as England, France, and the United States are concerned, he was for generations after his death known only to specialists. The

American *Cumulative Book Index* lists eight works by and about Kierkegaard from 1912 to 1938. Since then there have been over sixty. The Princeton University Press is gradually Englishing the complete works of this melancholy Dane who, one hundred years after his death, has suddenly become a major god of advanced modern thought. Something dark and bleak in the contemporary mind turns, as iron filings to a magnet, to the Kierkegaardian view that to be a Christian is to be "alone in a small boat in 70,000 fathoms of water."

Who or what is responsible for these booms and booms-lets? Are they part of the changing current of the time? Are they fortuitous? Are they set in motion by an identifiable person or group of persons?

Let us try to answer the last question first, confining ourselves to major and generally familiar resurrections of reputations.

Probably the most striking example is Herman Melville. In a sense *Moby-Dick*—and thus Melville himself—was *given* to us by the judgment and devotion of a few unregarded literary men, notably Raymond Weaver and Carl Van Doren. Today *Moby-Dick* is included, as one of only seven novels, in the classic set of *Great Books of the Western World.* This would have been inconceivable forty years ago—and remember, Melville died in 1891. How did this come about?

When *Typee* was published in 1846 Melville awoke to find himself famous. *Omoo* (1847) and *Mardi* (1849) were also fairly well received. But *Moby-Dick* (1851) and *Pierre* (1852) were both stillborn. Melville's reputation declined. By the seventies he was already in obscurity, and by the time he died he was so little known that *Billy Budd* (now generally ranked after *Moby-Dick* and assuredly a masterpiece) was not even published until 1924. In its obituary, *The New York Times* called him Henry Melville.

One should not make too much of this obscurity, for during his lifetime his books continued to sell steadily—up to his death about fifty-six new editions and reissues of his work had appeared. He was not "appreciated" but he *was* read, and does not at all present the classical picture of the poverty-stricken author—he was no Poe. In fact, when his widow died she left $170,000, though very little of this flowed from royalties.

The year after his death Arthur Stedman with some difficulty managed to get *Typee, Omoo, Moby-Dick,* and *White-Jacket* published in a group; and these books did continue to reappear here and in England up to 1919. It is this date, however, the centenary of his birth, that really marks the re-emergence of Melville, not as a minor writer of exotic adventure novels, but as a major writer of classic dimensions.

The clan Van Doren, which was distinguished long before it became famous, is mixed up in this re-emergence. Carl Van Doren, at that time a Professor of English Literature at Columbia, had heard of *Moby-Dick* but had never read it. To his younger colleague, Professor Raymond Weaver, Carl suggested that a book on this nineteenth-century author might be feasible. Weaver poked about in dusty bookstalls for Melville first editions. He found several of *Moby-Dick* (or so at least the story goes) for from 25 cents to $5. One of these, which Weaver claimed to have bought for 50 cents, he gave to Carl's brother Mark. In

1928 Mark was in sore need of cash to pay for an operation on one of his sons. He got $500 for the *Moby-Dick* and paid for the operation. It is possible therefore that 50 cents' worth of *Moby-Dick* was indirectly responsible for the winning, twenty-nine years later, of an eighth of a million dollars by the young Charles Van Doren. (In 1947, by the way, Mr. Dauber, a rare-book dealer, sold a mint copy of a first edition of *Moby-Dick* for $1,200.)

In 1921 Raymond Weaver's *Herman Melville: Mariner and Mystic* appeared and created a sensation. From that moment on Melville's reputation leaped skyward. Critics both English and American—Frank Jewett Mather, Jr., Van Wyck Brooks, Lewis Mumford, Percy Boynton, Viola Meynell, J. W. N. Sullivan, John Freeman, Grant Watson are just a few—contributed to its rise. These have been followed by dozens of closer though perhaps dryer commentators. The drama of this resurrection is best felt by reflecting on the fact that from 1912 to 1921 there were two books published by or about Melville; that from 1922 to 1927 there were 27; from 1928 to 1940, 90; and since then possibly a hundred.

It is easy enough to say that Melville would have been rediscovered anyway, just as it is easy to say that some one, had Einstein not existed, would have worked out the theory of relativity. The fact remains however that Einstein *did* work it out; and that Carl Van Doren and Raymond Weaver *did* do the spadework that endowed the American people with a new classic.

The Henry James boom, which shows no sign of abating, is not quite as clear a case. During his lifetime (1843–1916) James was famous, influential, and even, with cer-

tain titles, fairly successful. But no one will contend that
at any time during his career a critic could be found who
would say, as the contemporary scholar Leon Edel says,
"With Henry James the novel in English achieved its
greatest perfection." The great James revival is the work
of the last twenty-five years and must be laid largely to
the account of a dozen or so brilliant American and English critics, among them Leon Edel, Lionel Trilling, F. W.
Dupee, Philip Rahv, Edmund Wilson, Stephen Spender,
Newton Arvin, Edna Kenton, T. S. Eliot, R. P. Blackmur.
The excitement stirred up by these dedicated men was so
great that the commotion even reached the ears of Hollywood and Broadway. *The Heiress* actually made money as
a play and a movie, and other dramatizations (particularly
a brilliant one of *The Turn of the Screw*) have also done
moderately well. Perhaps some idea of the extent to which
James has now penetrated the consciousness of the average intelligent (not "high-brow") American reader may
be gained from a statistic I can myself vouch for. My own
edition of the selected *Short Stories of Henry James* appeared during wartime, in 1945, when the boom had
attained considerable but perhaps not major proportions.
From that time to the present this edition has sold a total
of slightly under 60,000 copies. This excellent sale is not
due to the editor, or even to the publisher. It is the work
of Henry James himself, more powerful dead than alive,
and to the devoted labors of a small group of men and
women who know great literature when they meet it and
who have succeeded in transmitting their love and enthusiasm to a fairly extensive public.

The sources of the Melville and James booms are trace-

able; in other cases this is not so. The English novelist
Anthony Trollope died in 1882. A few of his novels, particularly *The Warden* and *Barchester Towers*, have never
failed to attract readers. But his general reputation suffered
a severe setback when his posthumous *Autobiography*
(1883) revealed that he had written his many books in
the spirit of an efficient businessman and had received
such and such a sum of money for each one. The late-
Victorian public could not stand this affront to its tender
sensibilities. Trollope's stock went down. But about fifteen
years ago a Trollope boomlet got under way, more marked
in England than here. Previously out-of-print novels re-
appeared; some of his lesser-known works (*Orley Farm,
Rachel Ray, The Way We Live Now*) came out in attractive new editions; the critics and biographers went to work
on him. Thirty-five Trollopes are now available in the
handy *World's Classics* series, more than at any time since
1940. Today I would guess that Trollope is about as well
regarded as any Victorian novelist except Thackeray,
Dickens, and perhaps, strangely enough, George Eliot,
though the latter still remains less a popular favorite than
the special darling of a few influential critics such as F. R.
Leavis. I would guess further that Trollope's reputation is
still on the upgrade.

What caused the rise in the Trollope market? Hard to
say. Certainly no one man, not even a coterie. Many
critics would ascribe it to the circumstance that Trollope,
better than any of his contemporaries, supplies us with a
well-ordered, comfortable, prosperous, unworried, unhur-
ried, unharried world—a perfect escape-hole for many
tense twentieth-century readers. But that is only part of

the story. If a man is big enough, and Trollope is big, it may often take several generations before all of him can be seen. Our own time has discovered that only a part of Trollope is cozy, that indeed the finer part of him is most uncozy indeed, that such hitherto neglected novels as *The Way We Live Now* cut to the very heart of what was unhappy and even morbid in the presumably nicely padded Victorian Era.

In other words Trollope is now undergoing the same fruitful re-evaluation that Dickens underwent, beginning many years ago with Shaw and continuing with Edmund Wilson's decisive *The Two Scrooges* (1941).

Dickens of course is a fixed star; from *Pickwick* on he has never stopped selling. During his lifetime he was the most popular novelist the English-speaking world had ever seen. But, and here is the point, there was less unanimity as to his purely literary pre-eminence. Trollope, for example, had many misgivings about Dickens and pointed to Thackeray's *Henry Esmond* as the best novel in English. But, though it is hard to pin such things down, I should judge that today his literary standing, apart from whatever may be the actual number of his readers, is higher than it has ever been. Again this is due to the work of many contemporary critics and scholars, climaxed by the last-word two-volume life by Edgar Johnson (1952). It is, more profoundly, due to the fact that we of our century are able to see in Dickens, as we see in Trollope, more things, or at least different things, than were visible to his contemporaries.

It is possible that these revivals or enhancements of fame are connected with a general reawakening of interest

in the great Victorians, a reawakening that we may date
as far back as Lytton Strachey's *Eminent Victorians* (1918)
and *Queen Victoria* (1921). It is quite true that during the
last decade or two a large number of excellent Victorian
studies have appeared, beginning with Lionel Trilling's
Matthew Arnold (1939) and continuing with a spate of
books on the Brownings, Stevenson, Wilkie Collins, Carlyle, Ruskin, Mill, Newman, Gissing, Meredith, George
Eliot, and others. But somehow these figures have not
stirred from their dignified immobility. There is—at least
to the present body of general readers—some spark lacking
in them. They do not speak to us; or perhaps what they
have to say is something that only a later generation will
want to listen to.

Sometimes, as we have seen, one or two men (if the time
is waiting for them) can revive an author. Sometimes a
group can do it. Sometimes, though rarely, even a publisher can do it. But in the domain of revival there are
many more failures than there are successes. In the last
few years, for example, there have been laudable attempts
to bring back to popular notice such imposing names as
Kipling and Conrad and such undeservedly neglected ones
as Ford Madox Ford. But so far there has been no great
stir. It will be interesting, for example, to see whether
anything happens as a consequence of the recent reissue,
in Mr. Knopf's splendid Vintage Books, of Ford Madox
Ford's *The Good Soldier*. Fifteen sensitive and well-read
critics have subscribed to a single statement about it:
"Ford's *The Good Soldier* is one of the fifteen or twenty
greatest novels produced in English in our century." This
is a fairly defendable thesis; but I should be surprised, as

well as pleased, if *The Good Soldier* were suddenly to become widely read.

These are relatively recent names. Perhaps it is difficult to revive a writer unless he has been in his grave a fairly long time. The not-too-long dead seem to lack appeal. When John Galsworthy was in his prime a new novel would sell its hundred thousand copies without difficulty. Today the total annual sales of all the books of this Nobel prizewinner probably approximate only a modest fraction of this figure. *The Forsyte Saga* is firmly established; the balance of his work we seem willing to forget. Yet it is a possibility that when another twenty-five years have passed—Galsworthy died in 1933—we may return to him because he will then have the added attraction of being a historical figure. He will have the freshness that comes of being sufficiently remote, as is the case with Trollope.

Galsworthy's reputation is additionally handicapped, for his name is linked with a whole generation that is momentarily in the doghouse of fame. People tend to forget groups as well as individuals. The Georgian School of English novelists (Barrie, Wells, George Moore, Arnold Bennett, Galsworthy, Conrad, Hugh Walpole), once so popular and powerful, is today rather out of fashion, its solid qualities awaiting rediscovery. To this make one exception: one great Georgian (after all, he was born way back in 1874) survives not only in the flesh but with a constantly growing reputation—Somerset Maugham.

Yet even this reputation owes something (but let us not exaggerate the something) to the efforts of a few men and to the vagaries of chance. Like Ford's *The Good Soldier*, Maugham's masterpiece *Of Human Bondage* suffered from being published during wartime, in 1915. It may seem incredible today that such a book should receive little attention; but a World War is tough competition. Theodore Dreiser praised it (I believe shortly after its publication, but it may not have been until 1919) but nothing could save it from what seemed like oblivion. Then in 1923 a young journalist, Marcus Goodrich, on the play-reviewing staff of the New York *Tribune,* interviewed Maugham, one of whose plays was currently enjoying a Broadway run. In answer to some queries as to his personal life, Maugham replied, "You'll find it all in *Of Human Bondage.*" Goodrich went home, read the book, and began talking about it to his friends. Probably he was the first to point out that *Of Human Bondage* is autobiographical, a circumstance which, though quite unimportant, was in part responsible for the interest later taken in the book. Goodrich in 1925 wrote a full-page rave (I can still remember it) in the *Times,* entitled *After Ten Years: Of Human Bondage.* Other critics rediscovered the novel at about the same time, but I think it is probably fair to give Mr. Goodrich the greater part of the credit. From 1925 on *Of Human Bondage* sold by the thousands and has never stopped selling.

(I might add as a footnote that Marcus Goodrich's own novel *Delilah,* which has enjoyed a kind of subterranean high repute since its appearance in 1941, is itself worthy of the most valiant efforts of the resurrection men—a remarkable book.)

But I digress. We were talking about the resistance to revival exhibited by any generation of writers who are caught in the middle: they are neither long enough dead,

like the Victorians, to offer the attractions of relative unfamiliarity; or so recently dead (Dylan Thomas, George
Orwell) as to arouse the championing instincts of the up-
to-date critics.

For example, the whole group of American writers who
were in the ascendant during the twenties and thirties—
Dreiser, Anderson, Lewis, Hergesheimer, Tarkington, Cab-
ell—seem for the moment in a kind of eclipse. Perhaps
they suffer from the handicap of having made almost *too*
great an appeal to the readers of their period. They date
because they were so successfully contemporary. Of them
all, I would select two names as most likely to resist the
tooth of time during the next fifty years: Sinclair Lewis,
who will be saved by one man, George F. Babbitt; and
Willa Cather, who will be preserved by the grace of her
style and the exactness of her sensibility.

Note that these are all novelists. Novelists, even first-
class ones, have a harder time of it than do poets. They
date more evidently because of the partly journalistic
nature of their materials. But Robert Frost, who is of the
Dreiser generation (he was born in 1875, Dreiser in 1871)
has never enjoyed higher esteem than he does now. (It is
true that he also enjoys the advantage over Dreiser of
being alive.) E. A. Robinson, on the other hand, who during the latter part of his life stood on a level with Frost,
today appears to be undeservedly neglected.

Part of Frost's fame (the unimportant part of it) is due
to his personal qualities; he is a legend in his own time.
(He is also a great poet.)

But there *are* writers who preserve their reputations less
through the absolute excellence of their books than

through the persistent force of their personalities. Nobody reads *Rasselas* or *Lives of the English Poets* (excellent works, both of them), but everybody has heard of Samuel Johnson. It is easy to say—and true—that he was lucky in his biographer; but only a personality of the most crushing force could have attracted such a biographer. In somewhat the same way Bernard Shaw has imposed himself on the Western world. I suppose he is, taking everything into consideration, the twentieth-century writer with the largest general reputation. Shaw was a brilliant writer, an even greater master of English prose than he was of the drama; but today the image most of us have of him is that of a dominating, delightful personality rather than of the magnificent artist he undoubtedly was. To some extent I think this is true of the dazzling reputation enjoyed by Ernest Hemingway, traceable as much to the colorfulness of his personality as to the qualities of his prose.

So far we have talked mainly about those revivals that are more or less the product of the determined and conscious efforts of definite individuals. But the seesaws of literary reputation are often a matter, at least in part, of sheer accident. Fortuity joined hands with Rossetti to make Fitzgerald's previously unregarded *Rubáiyát* as mandatory as antimacassars in every Victorian drawing room. The works of Aristotle were saved from a dark cellar. No less providentially Montaigne's *Journal* of his Italian travels was found generations after his death in a worm-eaten coffer in his château. Tacitus we owe to a single copy discovered in a Westphalian monastery; otherwise, true to his name, his voice would have been forever silent.

Of Livy's great Roman history we possess only thirty-five books of the original 142. A dozen wild tales tell us how the lost books were found and then lost again. Stumble across them, and you are lodged immortally in the memory of scholars.

A prime example of laggard rediscovery is provided by Robert Herrick, the English clergyman-poet who suggested gathering rosebuds while we may. His *Hesperides* (including *Noble Numbers*) was published in 1648. That was in the very middle of the Civil War, and England had little time for Herrick's lovely trifling. The result was that he was forgotten for 175 years. In 1823, after a sleep that makes Rip Van Winkle's seem like insomnia, Herrick awoke in a second edition, looked about him, and became a classic.

If you seek posthumous literary fame, there appears to be an added advantage—a kind of surplice value—in being a clergyman. Let me submit three more examples.

John Donne (1572–1631), Dean of St. Paul's, was the greatest of the Metaphysical poets. His poems were published in 1633, shortly after his death, and became widely known and liked. During the next century however his reputation suffered, his strange sensibility according ill with the skeptical common sense of the eighteenth century. Samuel Johnson's disapproval set the tone, which continued for almost 150 years, even though during the nineteenth century Donne enjoyed the favor of some of the Romantic poets. Grierson's great edition of the *Collected Poems* (1913) began to lay the groundwork of reassessment. But it was not until almost another decade had passed that this reassessment assumed measurable proportions. We may consider T. S. Eliot's essay *The Metaphysical Poets* (1921), setting them firmly in the direct current of English poetry, as a more or less decisive date. Ezra Pound and the Chicago magazine *Poetry* re-enforced the growing interest in Donne. Before 1923 the number of items by or about Donne rarely exceeded one or two a year, but since then there has been an annual average of thirty published items. In 1931, the tercentenary of his death, at least ten books and fifty-one articles about him saw the light; and he had become a hero to a whole school of American poets, including the Southern Agrarians and Hart Crane.

So far however Donne's stock had risen only among the highly literate. Its rise had been traceable to the purposive efforts of individuals. Then came the stroke of pure chance. In 1940 Ernest Hemingway's best-selling novel *For Whom the Bell Tolls* appeared. Its title and magnificent epigraph were taken from Donne's *Devotions XVII*. Hemingway had no special interest in the revival of Donne; but he had quoted better than he knew. I echo *Time* for January 13, 1941: "After some 300 years, Ernest Hemingway's best-selling novel, *For Whom the Bell Tolls* (whose title and magnificent motto are by John Donne), had made Preacher-Poet Donne a best seller. U. S. customers could not buy a volume of Donne's works for love or money. The bookstores had sold out completely. Consternated publishers . . . confessed that Best-Seller Donne was O. P." Since then he has continued to be popular; a goodly number of new editions is issued yearly.

Or consider the case of the Reverend Edward Taylor (c. 1644–1729). Taylor served as pastor in the little hamlet of Westfield, Massachusetts, wrote remarkable religious verse in the Donne manner, and died without anyone's being aware that with him had passed, as one critic has said, our finest poet before Bryant. Almost three centuries after Taylor's birth, the scholar Thomas H. Johnson unearthed more than three hundred of his poems that had been lying doggo in the Yale library. They were published for the first time in 1937—a bit like a bequest from an uncle whose existence one had not even suspected.

Or take a more modern instance, that of the English poet Gerard Manley Hopkins (1844–1889). His life was brief and quiet; his posthumous life bids fair to be long and rumorous with fame. In 1866 he became a convert to Roman Catholicism and two years later was inducted into the Jesuit order. It was then that he burned all the verse he had hitherto written. But he began to write again for a public of three: his friends Robert Bridges, Coventry Patmore, and Canon Dixon. It was not until 1918, twenty-nine years after Hopkins' death, that Bridges, his literary executor, published the *Poems.* A second edition appeared in 1930 and from that point on Hopkins has been continuously reprinted, his correspondence, notebooks, and other papers have been edited, and many books have appeared about him. He stands today, in the opinion of many, as one of the most original metrists who ever lived, and possibly one of the greatest of all nineteenth-century English poets. An extraordinary career.

I have, come to think of it, one more clergyman on my list of resuscitations. This one is a theologian, Jonathan Edwards (1703–1758). He has of course always figured in any history of our colonial beginnings. But in 1930 Carl

Van Doren edited *Benjamin Franklin and Jonathan Edwards: Selections From Their Writings.* From that time on Edwards has come to be more and more seriously considered, though mainly within the quiet walls of the academy, as one of our greatest philosophers. It is doubtful, however, that a man whose most famous sermon is called *Sinners in the Hands of an Angry God* will ever be precisely popular.

Incidentally Carl Van Doren's unpretentious book of selections may have been in part responsible for the upgrading of Benjamin Franklin, an upgrading that received its great impetus in 1938 when Van Doren's classic biography was published. Franklin's complete works are now in preparation by the Princeton University Press. I do not suggest that Franklin has not been continuously read, merely that during the last thirty or forty years his literary and historical stature has increased enormously.

The post-mortem literary careers of these clergymen and theologians are lively enough. But they seem tame compared to that of a man of thoroughly nonecclesiastical spirit, to wit James Boswell. Boswell used to be known as the biographer of Samuel Johnson. Today he dwarfs his giant hero. To understand how this has come about we raise the curtain on a three-act comedy-drama, written by Messrs. Fate, Chance, and Providence, entitled

THE BOSWELL PAPERS

ACT ONE

SCENE I: Auchinleck, Scotland

James Boswell died in 1795, strongly disapproved of by his family. His three executors did not receive permission to publish any of the papers entrusted to them. Time passed. In 1822, Boswell's two sons died. The family mansion at Auchinleck was left to two great-granddaughters. They too were leery of anything connected with their black-sheep ancestor. They even turned to the attic wall a picture of Samuel Johnson. (*Slow music.*)

SCENE II: Boulogne, France

About 1842, an English traveler, Major Stone, was making a purchase in Boulogne. He found that his packages were wrapped in parchment on which was written the name James Boswell. He bought the shop's entire supply of parchment and found that he possessed over one hundred letters from Boswell to Sir William Temple, one of his three executors. They were published in 1857 and again in a complete edition, edited by Professor Chauncey B. Tinker, in 1924.

ACT TWO

SCENE I: Malahide Castle, near Dublin, Ireland

In 1873 great-granddaughter Emily Boswell married Lord Talbot of Malahide Castle. Emily's sister and coheir, Mrs. Mounsey, died in 1905 and her Auchinleck property, including a number of old manuscripts, passed to the heir of Malahide, the Honorable James Boswell Talbot. So much for background.

In 1920, four years previous to his edition of Boswell's Temple correspondence, Professor Tinker had sent a letter to the London *Times*, requesting information about his subject. He received an anonymous communication saying, "Try Malahide Castle." He assaulted the castle and was shown three large boxes of Boswell papers, two of which had never been opened. But Tinker was a mere American, not rich— in short, he got nowhere with the blue-blooded Talbots.

Heavy-hearted, he published his own incomplete edition and told others of his find. A New York collector who sent a cable offering $250,000 for the manuscripts did not even receive a reply. It is vulgar to do business by wire. Besides, if that much was offered sight unseen, more might be got by waiting.

Enter the hero of this story, Lt. Col. Ralph Heyward Isham, wealthy, handsome, beautifully mannered, unimpeachably backgrounded—and a shrewd, resourceful manipulator. Slowly, carefully, Isham made friends with the Talbots. Finally, as the American editor F. A. Pottle puts it, "Lady Talbot persuaded him that they ought to sell the papers." In 1927 Isham surrendered with good grace and took title for a large sum. The collection was published as *The Private Papers of J. B. from Malahide Castle.*

SCENE II: The Same.

In 1930 an old box in a carriage house, supposedly full of croquet equipment, was discovered to be full of manuscripts. Isham, a magnificent sportsman, bought these too. In 1937 another box was found in an attic. In 1940 two more chests turned up in an old unused garret storeroom. "Having started on the trail," writes Pottle, "[Isham] had no choice but to follow the spoor to the very bottom of his bank account."

SCENE I: Fettercairn House, near Aberdeen, Scotland

Meanwhile Professor C. Colleer Abbott, doing literary research in Scotland, found occasion to examine some papers in Fettercairn House, an estate belonging to Lord Clinton, a direct descendant of Sir William Forbes, another of the three original executors of James Boswell's will. In an attic (where else?), tied up helter-skelter in bags, bundles, bean sacks were more than 1,600 items pertaining to Johnson, Boswell, and other eighteenth-century worthies. Abbott announced his find in 1936. Question: who owned the papers? After much wrangling, the courts ruled that half belonged to the gallant Isham, who had thoughtfully provided himself with an assignment from the Talbots, in case any more croquet boxes should turn up at a time when his pockets were empty. The other half belonged to a hospital which was the now-bewildered heir of Mrs. Mounsey (remember her?). Isham, by this time automatically conditioned to the act of purchase, bought this half too.

SCENE II: New Haven, Connecticut

The Old Dominion Foundation (a Mellon institution—who would ever have thought that Boswell and aluminum would ever have anything to do with each other?) supplied Yale with the money to buy the Fettercairn collection from Isham. The work of publication of *The Private Papers of James Boswell* in the trade edition is proceeding merrily, six volumes have so far been issued, and James Boswell, over one hundred and fifty years after his death, makes the best-seller list as

THE CURTAIN FALLS

Boswell of course could never have predicted his post-humous reputation and he was probably fairly pleased with his contemporary one. But the annals of literary history are full of writers who flatly and in print assured their readers that only posterity would judge their work properly. Some of these (Horace and Shakespeare, to select only from among the greatest) scored a bull's-eye in prediction. The great majority possessed less clairvoyance.

The clearest-sighted of all is perhaps Henri Beyle, who used 171 pseudonyms and who is known to us today as Stendhal. The history of the growth of Stendhal's reputation (he died in 1842) is so complicated that volumes have been written on it. Indeed in France the interest in Stendhal is so great that his present bibliography, in its vastness, its variety, and its attention to detail, almost rivals that of Napoleon. Yet during his lifetime his books had little success; even Balzac's warm praise (1840) of *The Charterhouse of Parma* was insufficient to establish Stendhal firmly in the French pantheon. But something in this man refused to die. A long succession of critics, scholars,

bibliographical researchers, fellow-novelists, even statesmen, kept hammering away at Stendhal's rehabilitation
until today there are many who would agree with the
English critic Martin Turnell that he is the greatest of
French novelists. What is most interesting about this long
upward climb is that Stendhal predicted it with brilliant
accuracy. He wrote during his lifetime, he said, for "the
happy few," and he was correct. But he also wrote, "I hold
a ticket in a lottery whose grand prize is this: to be read
in 1935"; and he was no less correct.

So far we have been in the main recalling those reputations which owe their revival to the stimulus of professional literary men, or to the workings of chance, or to a
combination of these two factors. There are at least two
other ways in which such revivals may come about.

Let us consider first the influence that may be exerted
by the nonliterary.

For example, Garrick, an actor—though a literate one—
may have done as much as any single person in the latter
half of the eighteenth century to revive Shakespeare's
fame, which happened at the time to be in pretty dubious
shape.

Or consider the Case of Mary Webb and the Prime Minister. During her short career the now-almost-forgotten
Mary Webb published five novels of English rural life.
They had their admirers—*Precious Bane*, her best book,
won the 1924–1925 Femina-Vie Heureuse prize—but their
sales were what publishers term modest. On October 8,
1927, Mary Webb died, filling no great space on the obituary page. On April 25, 1928, Stanley Baldwin, then Prime

Minister, publicly eulogized her work. Next morning she was aureoled in posthumous glory. So great was the rush that within a few hours her books, once unsellable, were now unbuyable. Bigwigs such as Baldwin, Chesterton, and John Buchan wrote introductions to new editions. Then the flurry died down and Mary Webb's reputation slowly shrank to its proper dimensions. (She was an excellent minor local colorist.) A Prime Minister had started a boom. But even Prime Ministers are powerless to sustain one.

The Webb-Baldwin affair however does suggest that the general public will often place its innocent trust in the literary pronouncements of politicos, golf champions and Hollywood stars rather than in those of men who have given their lives to books. No one knows how much Shakespeare owes to the approval expressed some years ago by Gene Tunney. So dazzling are our toys of communication that we confuse our admiration of them with admiration of those able to exploit them. Yet a statement on life or literature is no sounder because its circulation is multiplied by bits of ingenious hardware—iconoscopes, electronic tubes, rotary presses, and the like. But it sounds sounder, if only because it is louder. Our ears are tuned to high-number decibels.

For example, if I were seized with a passion to revive, say, James Fenimore Cooper, I would not lobby among the critics. I would try to persuade Mr. Eisenhower to issue a public pro-Cooper statement. A few words from him and *The Last of the Mohicans* would vault onto the best-seller lists, briefly. In fact, the more nonliterary the authority (provided he is publicity-hot), the greater the instantaneous influence he is apt to exert. Even more magical than the nod from the President would be one from a money-winning race horse.

But pressures subtler than the say-sos of popular heroes may work to revive authors who appear to be beyond resuscitation. Take Henry Adams, grandson of John Quincy Adams, great-grandson of John Adams. Henry was born with a one-hundred-piece, sterling-silver service in his mouth. At once he set to work to make a career out of being dissatisfied. He became more and more positive that both his life and his era were failures. Had the world during his long lifetime (1838–1918) taken an unarguable turn for the better, he would have felt bitterly frustrated. But events played right into his hands. His great *History of the United States During the Administrations of Jefferson and Madison* (1885–1891) was neglected. His now-classic *Mont-Saint-Michel and Chartres* (1904) was hardly taken seriously. Flushed with failure he refused to allow the despised public to read his autobiographical masterpiece *The Education of Henry Adams*. In 1907 it was published privately for that hardy breed, his friends.

In one of his last letters, to Charles Milnes Gaskell, he says: "I once wrote some books myself, but no one has even mentioned the fact to me for a generation. I have a vague recollection that some young person *did* mention an anecdote to me that came from one of my books and that he attributed it to someone else."

In 1918, in a state of sardonic elation over what Jimmy Durante calls "de conditions dat prevail," Henry Adams, having carefully worked himself into relative obscurity, passed to his distinguished ancestors. At once fate started to double-cross him. The *Education* was published posthumously and in 1919 an unfeeling jury awarded it the Pulitzer Prize. His books began to be talked about by the intellectual vanguard. In the thirties they came into their own. Adams' gloom, his patrician disgust with what he considered American materialism, his conviction that the world was headed for the demnition bowwows, inevitable mechanization, and disintegration—all fitted in neatly with the mood of a decade sunk in the Depression and staggering toward Munich. What revived Adams was History itself, which seemed to be confirming the bleakest of his prophecies. He would have been delighted to know that his reputation had at last been established through the friendly offices of disaster, and that he is today the philosophical *Wall Street Journal* of those speculators for whom the future is merely one enormous bear market.

History spoke kindly to Stephen Crane too, but also only after his death. In 1900, when he was twenty-nine Crane's life ended. Two years later there was not a single edition in print of *The Red Badge of Courage*. In 1953 there were six, and the film version had at least made the title familiar to millions of us. Crane is a remarkable writer and there has been no lack of critics ready to say so during the last thirty years. But his present high standing is probably due to another factor. It is a war product. His fame rests largely on *The Red Badge of Courage*, one of the best novels ever written about battle. It was after World War I that his reputation began to rise. In the thirties it fell, only to rise again during and after World War II. It may have receded a bit at the moment; another war may well provide the setting for another comeback.

Such connections between history and literary fame are

not absolute. No matter how many future holocausts sweep the world most war novels will remain fixed in their graves. History lends its aid only to the first-rate. It helped Adams. It helped Crane. And in the same way, during the Nazi invasion of Russia it caused tens of thousands of Americans to turn again to Tolstoy's *War and Peace.*

Emily Dickinson was first-rate, but during and after her inaudible, almost invisible life (1830–1886) history did not even brush her with its wings. Only among the saintly contemplatives do we find lives of a privacy as pure as hers. She may have had a frustrated love affair; we are not sure. The rest of her life seems completely eventless—that is to say, it was filled with wild joys, terrors, disasters, ecstasies, disappointments, and surprises, all of them staged within her mind. At twenty-six, dressed in the symbolic white that she ever afterward wore, Emily retired to her Amherst house and garden, and stayed there. Year after year on odd slips of paper she wrote thousands of brief poems. Only five were published during her lifetime, and they anonymously. She must have been afraid of fame, even posthumous fame, for she left instructions for all her manuscripts to be destroyed.

These arrangements for obscurity would seem to have been perfect. Yet they failed. Today, sixty-eight years after her death, Emily Dickinson is ranked by many as the greatest woman poet who has ever lived; by many as one of the greatest of all nineteenth-century poets; by many as the best American poet; and by other good judges as one of the dozen poets of the last hundred years who have most influenced contemporary English and American verse.

The story of how this came about is too long and twisted

to tell in these pages. Her testamentary instructions were of course disobeyed. After her death three small volumes appeared in 1890, 1891, and 1896. They were simply too brilliant to be completely neglected and even sold pretty well. Critics as responsible as William Dean Howells praised them. Nevertheless no one at the turn of the century could have prophesied that by 1930, after the publication of several other volumes by and about her, she would be hailed as one of the finest poets who ever used the English tongue. It is true that her style is peculiarly "modern," that she controls an idiom that seems quite contemporary, that the ironical-mystical cast of her mind is currently modish—but, all that having been said, we must add that the main reason for Emily Dickinson's freakish post-mortem success story is simply that as the years go by all sorts and conditions of men find themselves responding to her strange and beautiful verse. In his *Emily Dickinson* Henry Wells says: "Such revivals as the recovery of Gerard Manley Hopkins or even the belated cult of John Donne appear almost ephemeral beside the steady pressure exercised by her sure skill upon the artistic ideals of the best of the younger writers."

She could bury her life. Bury her genius she could not.

Literary archaeology is apt to be brisk in a period and country such as our own. The search for a tradition is the finer face of the coin whose ugly one is chauvinism. We have now accumulated enough past to make ransacking it possible, and a public sufficiently numerous and sensitive to make the effort worthwhile. We have taken note, for example, of the recent unearthing of the Reverend Edward Taylor and the rediscovery of Jonathan Edwards. The new

evaluation of Emily Dickinson, Crane, and Adams is part
of the same urge to tap our past.

Sometimes the urge borders on the antiquarian. Hector
St. John de Crèvecoeur (1735–1813) was a French traveler who lived among us from 1754 to 1780. His *Letters
from an American Farmer*, published first in London in
1782, were popular enough in their faraway day. Then
virtual silence for over a century, a silence broken only by
the praise of Hazlitt, who missed nothing, and a mention
by Lamb. Not till 1904 did the first accessible reprint
appear. Several reprints have been published since then,
together with a number of biographical studies. Crèvecoeur is now firmly established as a sort of minor minor
classic; I mention him only to indicate the intensity of our
twentieth-century passion for exploring our beginnings.

To this same enthusiasm we may in part ascribe the
high esteem Count Alexis de Tocqueville currently enjoys.
This Frenchman is the author of the most searching book
ever written about our country. *Democracy in America*
appeared in two parts, in 1835 and 1840. Good judges recognized its quality at once and throughout the nineteenth
century, with some ups and downs, it held its place. Then
history again helped out. Our own time saw the fulfill-
ment one after another of Tocqueville's amazing forecasts
of our development. Consequently during the last twenty-
five years interest in *Democracy in America* has mounted
steadily, climaxed in 1945 by the appearance of Phillips
Bradley's truly magnificent edition, published by Alfred
A. Knopf.

It is the revivals like those of Emily Dickinson and
Stendhal that are most interesting. They are less the result

of accident than of natural need, the need of readers for a writer they unconsciously are unwilling to let die. Perhaps the purest example in our own literature is Thoreau.

Thoreau today is an international classic. There are many who feel, with E. B. White, that though their shelves contain many books, *Walden* is the only book they own. Thoreau's essay on civil disobedience was instrumental in determining the lives of both Tolstoy and Gandhi and so may be said to be one of the few American works that have actually changed the course of world history. I would dare say that *Walden* and *Huckleberry Finn* are the two books that reflect most deeply and most clearly the basic tensions involved in being an American.

Thoreau died in 1862. His *Week on the Concord and Merrimac Rivers* had been published in 1849 in an edition of 1,000 copies. Several years later less than 300 had been sold. Thoreau took back the remainder, and wrote in his *Journal:* "I now have a library of 900 volumes, over 700 of which I wrote myself". One would assume that *Walden,* a far more striking book whose qualities seem to cry out from the very first page, would have done better. It did— but just barely. Nevertheless after his death Thoreau began to make his way, slowly, unspectacularly, surely. Posthumous works appeared year by year. Americans found in him what they were looking for—"nature" in the sixties, seventies, and eighties; then the philosopher of simplicity; then, more recently, the political radical, or rather anarchist; and finally in our own time the author of a kind of antimaterialist bible, the truest spokesman of the powerful idealist strain in the American character. The centennial of *Walden* (1954) marked a high point in Thoreau's reputation. It had taken just a hundred years for its complete establishment.

When, reflecting on the durability of reputation, we raise our sights and, instead of generations or centuries, begin to think in terms of millenniums or even vaster cycles of time, we are driven to admit that even the greatest of literary names can never hope to enjoy security of tenure because of the very nature of language. Languages die; they are but temporary inventions, and translation, though a useful preservative, is in the very long run a transient one. The more one reflects on the comparative longevity of human achievement, the more one tends to agree with the great English mathematician, G. H. Hardy, who believes that Archimedes will be remembered when Aeschylus is forgotten. The last enduringness is reserved, not for Shakespeare, but for those odd chaps who discover things like the Pythagorean theorem or the innocent-faced equation $E = mc^2$.

Yet time may have its edacious way even with those who deal in what may seem to be absolute truths, as valid on Mars as on Earth, as true for our descendants a million years hence as for us today. In his minor classic, *A Mathematician's Apology*, G. H. Hardy tells a story about Bertrand Russell whose *Principia Mathematica*, written with Alfred North Whitehead, is undoubtedly his securest claim to immortality. It seems that Russell once had a horrible dream. He seemed to be in a room on the top floor of a great library, about 2100 A.D. "A library assistant was going round the shelves carrying an enormous bucket, taking down book after book, glancing at them, restoring them to the shelves or dumping them into the bucket. At last he came to three large volumes which Russell could recognize as the last surviving copy of *Principia Mathematica*. He took down one of the volumes, turned over a few pages, seemed puzzled for a moment by the curious symbolism, closed the volume, balanced it in his hands and hesitated. . . ."

Some Day

ONE OF MY manila folders is labeled Some Day. (Sounds like a bad popular song.) This folder, an example of wishful filing, holds notes on books I'd like to write, promissory notes all made out to Self, and all bearing the same due date: When I Get Around to It.

Most professional scribblers keep a Some Day file. Perhaps it gives them an illusory sense that thus they shake hands with their futures. They regard the file with sentimental affection, for in it is often placed, or buried, their better parts. What a writer writes measures his ability, or the compromise his ability must strike with that universal horse-trader, the world. But what he would write if only he could is the yardstick of his dreams.

I am not so fatuous as to conceive that my own Some Day file could interest today's, much less tomorrow's literary investigator. Yet my excuse for opening it in public is not quite free of immodesty. Unabashed, I aver that it contains a number of ideas for books that *ought* to be written, that, done by men better equipped than myself, would

353

prove interesting to the general reader. In any case, if you happen to know anyone who feels like writing a book, have him look over my free samples.

Someone ought to do a job on dead writers. I mean *really* dead writers, unresurrectible writers, writers who have nothing whatsoever to say to us, writers to whose minds we have probably forever lost the key. Most literary men who discourse on forgotten classics wish to show that *they* at least are capable of connoisseurship; or else they want to sell a corpse to a reluctant public. My notion is different. I believe that dead men tell tales about the living.

We differ from our forefathers not only in our responses but in our nonresponses. Our field of vision is in part defined by what we are blind to. What has died out in us, or is dying, sheds an eerie light on what is alive in us.

My book, then, would be a kind of negative anatomy of ourselves. I would select perhaps a dozen writers, good writers who are also dead writers or who at best are saved from dissolution by classroom embalming. I would not try to revive these writers, my thesis being that they are unrevivable. I would merely try to isolate those qualities in them that make them inaccessible to us.

Take Walter Savage Landor, for example, Carlyle's "unsubduable old Roman," leonine, irate, litigious Landor who to his ninetieth and dying year kept the bright impracticality of a froward child. The story goes that once, furious with his cook for supplying a bad dinner, Landor threw him out of the second-story window into the garden, only to lean out of it the next moment, exclaiming in horror: "Good God! I forgot the violets!"

Landor's human personality is still full of bounce; his literary personality has gone flat. At one time he was ranged with Shakespeare. Today, except for a handful of lyrics and a few set pieces from his *Imaginary Conversations*, he is by and large unreadable. Yet dozens of his contemporaries still charm. Why should this be so?

Landor is a perfect example of the faults and virtues of a rigidly classical education, as we are examples of the faults and virtues of a nonclassical or even an anticlassical education. It is not his references that alienate us. These may be looked up in a classical dictionary. It is his attitude to life, discoverable in no encyclopedia. Our ears are deaf to his Greek-and-Latin-founded "grand style" because the tone of antique grandeur itself is beyond our auditory range. Our ideas of the lofty, the noble, and the heroic differ radically from Landor's. His ceremonial sentences offend our politics; their very shape and texture are aristocratic. Landor wrote to please people like himself, classically educated gentlemen of leisure. But we have our own notions of leisure and of the gentleman; and they accord ill with Landor's.

To the question, Why does Landor seem to be writing in a dead language, even these obvious answers are suggestive. They tell us something about ourselves. So would studies of such presumably unresurrectible classroom greats as Spenser, Scott, Dryden, Addison and Steele, Smollett, Meredith, and Ruskin—to cite only English writers.

In the same way we might learn even more if we took less remote instances. Why, for instance, should such recently departed figures as Galsworthy or Knut Hamsun seem suddenly about as far from us as the Venerable Bede? A close look at a few fossil or now-fossilizing modern writers might be more revealing than most scrutinies of the contemporary literary scene.

The word "contemporary" suggests the title of the next item in my Some Day file. This is a novel to be called *The Contemporaries*. It would be a story about a passion, precisely as Balzac's novels are about passions. Passions have their lives and their deaths; the money obsession that dominates so many of Balzac's fictions seems merely quaint to a period like ours, irretrievably committed to the income tax. But the passion for *contemporariness* is a real passion of our time, startling in its range and intensity. I do not mean merely the desire to be up-to-date or "well-informed," which is a normal human attribute in any period. I mean that almost religious veneration of *today*, a profound sentiment that finds expression in our journalism, our advertising, our mass communication, our politics of improvisation, and particularly in certain remarkable personalities of the time, hero-men of the momentary.

These heroes had their immediate progenitors, great figures such as Edison, Rockefeller, and Ford, mental mutants, born without a sense of the past, a new type of human being, the ahistorical man. I know leaders in the field of mass communication today whose superlative brilliance flows from a powerful drive to deny the past; showmen whose decisions are intuitively right because they are not, any more than is their audience, confused by tradition; journalists whose mesmeric power stems from their ability to convince themselves and their public that what has just happened is, for that reason alone, overwhelmingly interesting.

It is these men who would crowd the pages of my novel, *The Contemporaries*, supermen of the short view, marvelously inventive, as vital as a Renaissance hero, fascinating just as Dreiser's now-dated business titans were fascinating in their era.

Most writers prefer to write books the public will buy, and it is sheer affectation to pretend the contrary. It is not, despite Dr. Johnson's shallow dictum, a matter of money, for there is no money in writing, in the sense that there was a short while ago money in making and selling Davy Crockett hats. It is a matter of self-assurance. A writer wants to be bought, and presumably read, that he may feel his life is worth living. The maker and seller of Davy Crockett hats knew that his life was worth living, for his activity at once received the stamp of social approval. But a writer is not so sure. He has to be convinced, and readership is the only really clinching argument.

Nevertheless many writers secretly cherish the idea of writing *one* book that they know cannot sell. (Frequently they do succeed in writing a book that cannot sell, but it is rarely the one they had in mind.) The unsalable book is their concession to that part of them, and it is only a part, that dares to do without social approval.

My book would be unsalable because it would take a position at the moment rather unpopular. It would defend the thesis that the secret of happiness, if any, lies in *un*-peace of mind—that is, in fairly continuous, productive, useful mental activity, though not necessarily of a highly intellectual order. Many best-sellers are currently purveying mental and emotional Novocain. My book, bucking this trend, would almost surely fall flat.

It would fail for another reason. It is to be a book about the English essayist, William Hazlitt. Now Hazlitt is not a genuinely dead writer. Any intelligent twentieth-century American can read him with pleasure. The fact is, however, that few do so.

Hazlitt's was a career of successful unpeace. His erotic and domestic life was tragic; he was unsparingly attacked in the public prints; from a worldly point of view he was a failure, not even a picturesque failure; he does not seem to have possessed any notable charm of personality; he had more than his share of neuroses; and he died at fifty-two saying, "Well! I've had a happy life!"

The purpose of the book would be to explain Hazlitt's dying utterance. The explanation is that Hazlitt's mind was so lively that all experience, even unhappy experience, gave him a kind of stimulus that at least bordered on happiness.

Then I want to do two books for children. Now, there's another oddity about professional writers—seventy-five per cent of them yearn to write a juvenile. Secretly each of us thinks he could turn out something a little better than *Alice in Wonderland.*

My better-than-Alice book is to be called *The Other Park.* It will be *very* long, perhaps 100,000 words, with a *great* deal happening, and *hundreds* of characters. We grownups, who have little time for such minor matters as the use of the mind, should quite properly read digests and similar material; whereas children, who have more time, should be given long, leisurely, old-fashioned books with real covers.

Anyway, *The Other Park* is to be a fantasy of big-city life. Its story concerns what goes on in Central Park in New York City after twilight, which is when its *real* life begins. That's when those cold-looking statues, including Balto the dog, come alive; when the old pretzel woman reveals her true identity—she's a good witch; when the tunnels that give out only dull echoes during the day answer all your questions correctly; when we meet the denizens of the zoo being informal—there's an untrained seal I'm fond of, for example; when the mischievous people who keep hidden during business hours—who do you suppose spatters the noses of boys and girls at the drinking fountain?—emerge; and Cleopatra tells the story of her Needle; and the carrousel ponies are free to gallop; and the wise old carp who lives in the reservoir recalls the old days when there were real sheep in the sheep meadow . . . had enough? O.K. But the children might like it.

The other book for children is more practical. It might be called *Liking Poetry.* I have found from experience that, while you can tell adults *about* poetry, you can't make them like it if their minds, as with most of us, are closed to verse. But you *can* make children like it, if you catch them at the right age—eight to fourteen is best. At that age they are still very close to the primitive bases of poetry, they respond to rhythm, image, rhyme, fancy. If you can hook them at this time, you may be able to restore to at least a few of their generation a pleasure which both children and adults of a hundred years ago quite naturally and simply enjoyed. A book such as the one I have in mind can do only a little toward this end, but I think it's worth doing. Not because poetry is "cultural," but for a deeper reason, connected with the fact that if we should ever lose completely our feeling for verse, we should at that moment have cut ourselves off from a part of our origins, for we sang and chanted long before we reasoned or persuaded. I wouldn't put it quite that way to the children, however.

War and Peace,
Fifteen Years After

ABOUT fifteen years ago I wrote an introduction to an edition of Tolstoy's *War and Peace.* I wrote it after six months of careful study of what is universally acknowledged, often by people who have actually read the whole book, as one of the greatest novels ever written. This introduction, now that I have reread it, gives the impression of being almost as long as the novel. I must have been infected by Tolstoy's own mania for inclusiveness, for in it I tried to say everything—and of course failed. No final statements about a first-rate work of art are possible. The work itself is the final statement. That is one reason for its first-rateness.

Now, after fifteen years during which the whole world has experienced its own very real wars and even a certain reasonable facsimile of peace, I have reread Tolstoy's masterpiece in about eight virtually uninterrupted hours. It is a good way to read it. Indeed it is the only proper way, for no novel was ever written to be studied. I do not say it *should* not be studied, merely that such was not the author's intention.

So, I plunged into these wide waters and then began to swim as rapidly as I could. By so doing I avoided the mental lockjaw that often afflicts the man who sits down deliberately to read a "classic." Often the poor fellow is so rigid with preconceived reverence, so stuffed with the unyielding upholstery of other men's opinions, that (a) he does not know whether or not he is enjoying the book and (b) he does not know what to think of it when he has finished it. It is like being introduced to a great man. You and he are not really shaking hands. You are shaking hands with History or some other paralyzing abstraction.

Rereading a classic entails other dangers and difficulties. You are afraid that you may not find there what once you found. Or, on the other hand, your enjoyment may be clouded by nostalgia, by the sense of familiarity, pleasant but sometimes mentally blurring, that overcomes you when you revisit the scenes of your childhood.

We would probably all enjoy classics a good deal more if the publishers could be induced to issue them casually, with a changed title and an unfamiliar author's name. But this is too much to ask: literature, like commerce, is subject to the Brand Name complex.

At any rate, I tried hard to reread *War and Peace* as though it were a new book sent me for review. This is impossible, of course, but even the attempt brought with it certain rewards that were not mine fifteen years ago.

Perhaps I can pass on to you a few of them. I am especially anxious to do this for it seems clear that this book, by virtue of the film version now available to tens of millions of people, is in for a re-revival. What all the world's finest literary critics find difficulty in doing, Anita Ekberg and Audrey Hepburn will accomplish with ease.

In a way writing about *War and Peace* is a self-defeating activity. Criticism in our day has become largely the making of finer and finer discriminations. But *War and Peace* does not lend itself to such an exercise. If you say the book is about the effect of the Napoleonic Wars on a certain group of Russians, most of them aristocrats, you are not telling an untruth. But you are not telling the truth either. Its subject has been variously described—even Tolstoy tried his hand at the job—but none of the descriptions leaves one satisfied.

You can't even call the book a historical novel. It describes events that are part of history, but to say that it is about the past is to utter a half-truth. *Ivanhoe, Gone With the Wind*—these are historical novels. Kipling (a part of him, I mean) has suddenly become for us a historical novelist: Gandhi made him one. But the only sections of *War and Peace* that seem historical are the battle pieces. War is now apocalyptic; it was not so in Tolstoy's time. Austerlitz and Cannae are equally historical, equally antique, equally part of the springtime of war. Now our weapons think for us; that is the revolutionary change that has outmoded all previous narratives of conflict.

But, except for these battle pieces, *War and Peace* is no more a historical novel than is the *Iliad*. Homer is not history, not Greek history, not Trojan history, he is—Homer. So with Tolstoy.

No, you say little when you say that *War and Peace* has to do with the Napoleonic Wars, Borodino, the burning of

Moscow, the retreat of 1812. As a matter of fact the vaguer
your critical vocabulary, the less precisely you describe
the subject of *War and Peace*, the nearer you get to the
truth. It is really—yes, let us use un-twentieth-century
words—about Life and People and Love: those abhorred
capital-letter abstractions that irritate our modern novelists
and against which they persistently warn us.

Another impression I got from my rereading was an odd
one indeed. That is to say, I did not seem to be reading a
"work of art." In a sense, Tolstoy is not an artist at all, as,
let us say, Virginia Woolf, Hemingway, Faulkner, Proust,
are artists. He does not appear, at least in translation, to
have any "style." There is no such thing as a Tolstoyan
sentence or a Tolstoyan vocabulary. The poor chap has no
technique. He knows nothing of flash-backs, streams of
consciousness, symbols, objective correlatives. He introduces his people flatly and blurts out at once their domi-
nant characteristics. He has unending insight but no subtlety. Compared to such a great master as Henry James,
or such a little master as Kafka, he seems deficient in sheer
brain power, the power to analyze, the power to discriminate.

He never surprises you. All his characters are recognizable, most of them are normal. Even his villain, Anatole
Kuragin, seems merely an impetuous fool compared to the
monsters of labyrinthine viciousness that our Southern
novelists can create with a touch of the pen.

He isn't even a good storyteller, if by a good storyteller
one means a master of suspense. You do not read *War and
Peace* in order to see "how it comes out," any more than
you live your life in order to see how it will end. His people

grow, love, suffer, die, commit wise or foolish actions, beget more people who are clearly going to pass through the same universal experiences; and that's about all there is to the "story." There are plenty of events, but they are not arranged or balanced or patterned. Tolstoy is not a neat writer, any more than your biography or mine is neat. He is as shapeless as the Russian land itself.

I found myself struck with the originality of *War and Peace*, but by a kind of reverse English. It is original because it is unoriginal. Kafka is original. Faulkner is original. Eudora Welty is original. In fact most of our most admired modern writing is original, full of strange people, strange feelings, strange ideas, strange confrontations. But Tolstoy portrays pleasant, lively, ordinary girls like Natasha. His book is crowded with people who are above the average in intelligence or wealth or insight—but not extraordinarily so. He balks at portraying genius: he makes of Napoleon a fatuity, and of the slow-thinking, almost vacant-minded Kutuzov the military hero of the war. And when he writes about war, he does not describe its horrors or its glories. He seizes upon the simplest of the truths about war and sticks to that truth: that war is *foolish*.

Tolstoy has a genius for the ordinary, which does not mean the commonplace. It is this ordinariness that to us moderns, living on a literary diet of paprika, truffles, and cantharides, makes him seem so unusual. When we read him we seem to be escaping into that almost forgotten country, the real world.

Another odd thing—Tolstoy does not seem to have any "personality." Many fine writers are full of personality, Hemingway for instance; but the *very* finest write books that seem to conceal themselves, books like the *Iliad* or *Don Quixote* or *War and Peace*. I do not mean that Tolstoy writes like an impersonal god, but that he seems to intrude into his book only in the sense that he and the book are one and the same. I believe this effect of desingularization springs from his instinctive refusal to load any scene or indeed any sentence with more meaning than it will bear. He has no "effects." He is unable to call attention to his own mastery. He knows what he is doing, but he does not know how to make *you* know what he is doing. The consequence is that, despite the enormous cast of characters, everything (once you have waded through the rather difficult opening chapters) is simple, understandable, recognizable, like someone you have known a long time. In our own day the good novelists tend to be not very clear, and the clear novelists tend to be not very good. Tolstoy is clear and he is good.

To the professional literary critic *War and Peace* is an irritating book. It is irritating because it forces him to say simple things, such as those I have already said. Any sympathetic critic of Faulkner will inevitably find himself saying quite profound things. Indeed that is one reason for his popularity among the technicians of criticism. But *War and Peace* forces you into nonsophistication.

For example: *War and Peace*, I need hardly say, is not a transcript of life. Nothing could be more alien to it than the photograph or the tape recording. But the one thing you find yourself saying as you read it is, "Yes, this is the way life is." Not "the way life was." Not "the way Russian life was." Not "the way these aristocrats, so different from plain, down-to-earth American me, must have been." But

—the way life is. And, as you say it, you feel rise up in you
a peculiar satisfaction, a pervasive, unanalyzable sense of
the richness, the palpability of human experience. This is
not the only thing a good novel can give you, but it is a
great thing none the less—and of how many novels of the
last twenty years that you have read can you say the same?
The Man in the Gray Flannel Suit is about life as it is—
that is to say, a narrow sector of life as it is—but once you
have recognized the simple identity, nothing else happens
to you, no welling up of emotion, no throat-catching sense
of richness. You *spot* the reality in such a book. But spot-
ting is not an emotion, it is a parlor game. That is what
most current best-sellers are: pleasant invitations to a parlor game.

On rereading *War and Peace* after fifteen years, I came
upon another equally obvious fact. Here it is: when you
reread a classic you do not see more in the book than you
did before; you see more in *you* than there was before. A
lesser book on rereading often reveals new subtleties. A
great one is more like an instrument of self-discovery. Thus,
fifteen years ago, I did not see at all plainly that *War and
Peace* is, among other things, about love—love between
men and women, love of country, but more especially
Christian apostolic love. Fifteen years ago Christian apostolic love did not, as it happens, occupy any great place in
my mental world. Today, as it happens, it occupies a
greater place. The Bomb is responsible for that, of course;
it is the severe teacher who is making clear to all of us, one
after another, that hatred is destroying our whole world,
that, as Auden says, we must love one another or die. A
platitude? Yes—but for many of us a relatively fresh and

new platitude. And, curiously enough, the addition of that platitude to our emotional stock enables us to see in *War and Peace* what was there all along, the fact that this is a preachment in story form of the original, not the contemporary, Christian doctrine.

And this doctrine is not mere moralizing. It is the foundation of Tolstoy's aesthetic theory, if we may use such un-Tolstoyan jargon. Somewhere in his notebooks Tolstoy writes: "The first condition of an author's popularity, the means of making himself beloved, is the love he bears to all his created characters."

In a letter to one of his friends Tolstoy sets down another deceptively simple statement: "I have read [Turgenev's] *On the Eve*. This is my opinion of it: writing novels is useless in general, and even more so if those writing them are dispirited or do not have a good idea of what they want to get out of life." If this last clause is admitted to be true, how much of the contemporary novel, in Tolstoy's view, at once becomes "useless"?

War and Peace is written by a man who knew what he wanted to get out of life, or at any rate spent his life in a relentless search for it; and his characters are all engaged in the same search, most of them, as with us, unsuccessfully. But it is precisely because Tolstoy will not settle for a subject matter any less serious than this that he continues to engage us, even to engage Hollywood, after so much time has elapsed.

It is an unusual thing to read a novel by a grownup who refuses the temptation to be merely interesting or entertaining; who does not use his novel to prove a private thesis; or to work off a resentment; or to recall his youthful sufferings; or to cure himself of his obsessions; or to educate

himself by the mere exercise of writing. *War and Peace* is
not Tolstoy's *mechanism* of self-comprehension; it is the
result of this comprehension. He dares to write a long
story—a story, not a philosophical essay—about the meaning and value of human life. This is the platitudinous subject that most modern novels are either afraid to touch,
or touch with bitterness or frenzy or incoherence. How
many of our best-selling novelists, many of whom are admirable in other respects, would be interested in setting
down such a dialogue as that in which André and Pierre
debate how men should live well?

It is because Tolstoy is *continually* reflecting on such
questions that he is able, it would seem without calculation, to break our hearts and suddenly enlarge our minds
with those moments of "crystallization" for which he is so
renowned. The face of the little Princess Lise, dead in
childbirth, says, "What have you done to me, and why?"
Prince André hears Natasha's happy voice at the window
at 1 A.M.—and his life turns on its base. At the Peronski ball
Natasha disregards the entrance of the Tsar—she thinks
only of whether she will be chosen as a dance partner. Old
Prince Bolkonski is dying; he does not speak of his beloved
Russia, or of his family, or of his approaching death. But
he says to his daughter Mary, to whom he has always been
a tyrannical task master: "Put on your white dress. I like
it."

A half dozen of such moments, such summatory sentences, would make the fortune of a dramatist. But Tolstoy
offers hundreds of them; he knows and *loves* his characters
so well that he cannot help seeing always, describing
always, the shattering moment of truth.

Crime and Punishment

UNLESS he has been thoroughly briefed the English-speaking reader who enters *Crime and Punishment* for the first time may well believe he has strayed into a lunatic asylum. It is not merely the *oddity* of the characters. English and American novels are crowded with odd characters who do not faze us at all. Dickens' people, for example, are sufficiently odd. But we accept them, and for two reasons. The first is that they are exaggerations of a recognizable reality. No one has ever met Uriah Heep, everyone has met a fawner. The second reason is that you are reassured by the author, who from time to time nudges you as if to make clear that he too realizes that the characters are queer fellows.

The people of *Crime and Punishment* however do not seem to be exaggerations of a familiar reality. They seem to be a *new* reality altogether. And Dostoevski, unlike Dickens, does not reassure the reader by agreeing with him that the characters are eccentrics. On the contrary, Dostoevski seems to be saying, "This is the real world as

I know it. If you think it freakish, that points to a mental limitation on your part."

In our Western world when two people meet for the first time they act a little like dogs, who cautiously smell and circle each other before establishing closer relations. In *Crime and Punishment* when two people meet for the first time they at once go into an emotional undressing act. Marmeladov accosts Raskolnikov in a bar and within two minutes is engaged in a full confession. "I am a beast by nature," he remarks to this perfect stranger, and goes on to explain, "I drink because I wish to multiply my sufferings." We think it proper to hide our weakness or our baseness from others, as well as from ourselves. But Dostoevski's idea of a life story is that it is something to be shared at once with someone else. Thus all the major characters in *Crime and Punishment* are in turn confessors and confessees, and analysts and analysands.

A man weeping into his beer and telling you his troubles is for us a stock cartoon character. But not for Dostoevski. For him *the confession is standard behavior.* It is in itself a mode of experience, perhaps more important than the action that precedes it and forms its content. Insofar as our modern literature is confessional in nature it has been deeply influenced by Dostoevski. Sherwood Anderson in the tale, Eugene O'Neill in the drama are examples that spring readily to mind.

To us especially, with our activist drives, the characters in *Crime and Punishment* may seem crazy, for the simple reason that they are always thinking. Most of them are poor, but they are rarely shown doing any work. They live in St. Petersburg, but they take little notice of their environment. They do not, like us, see life as progressive movement. No one is interested in what anyone else *does*, or wants to do, or in what his social or financial position may be. They have no *careers*. They do not ask each other any of the questions we are used to asking. One American, casually meeting another, may ask him what his business is. In *Crime and Punishment* the question is more likely to be something like: "Do you believe in God?" They meet. They unpack and compare their souls. Reflection is with them a normal activity; with us it is unusual if not vaguely suspect.

To a degree the explanation lies in Dostoevski's own partial vision: he sees people, not in the round, but as spirits, souls, sometimes devils. But it lies also in the history of prerevolutionary Russia. In this book one of the characters, Razumihin, speaking of his countrymen, remarks: "For almost two hundred years we've had practically nothing to do with practical affairs." Like virtually all generalizations in Dostoevski, this is an exaggeration. But not an absurd exaggeration. Pre-Communist Russia was essentially Byzantine, hierarchical, static. "Practical affairs" was the specialty of a small class. Peter the Great is properly so-named not only because he was a great ruler but because by virtue of his "sensible," Western viewpoint, he was a great *exception.*

Hence at first *Crime and Punishment* baffles us because all the characters seem to be philosophers or psychologists or prophets rather than "normal" people. But it baffles us also because these people appear to have no reticences. Not only do they say the first thing that comes into their heads but also the first thing that comes into their hearts; and, even beyond this, they are continually crossing the thin threshold that divides them from their unconscious selves and dredging up conversational material from the very subcellars of their souls. They do not obey any of the rules of ordinary social intercourse. If a man feels like talking for ten pages, he does so; and the other fellow listens with what to us seems impossible patience. There is no single *tone* to their talk. They will switch in a moment from civility to quarrelsomeness, from quarrelsomeness to repentance, from repentance to cruelty. In general they have passions, but no ruling passion. They are compendiums of emotion. Nothing is more difficult than the task of summarily characterizing any one of them. It is like trying to trap a whirlwind.

From this it follows that, from the Western viewpoint, there are no heroes or villains in Dostoevski. This makes us uneasy. As novel readers we are used to the convention by which we can identify ourselves with the good guy and hiss the bad guy. Raskolnikov commits a brutal crime, or rather two of them, but it does not proceed from this that he is evil. Even Svidrigaïlov, who at first seems the incorporation of unmitigated malice, finally kills himself *because* he has been unable to commit the crime of rape against Dounia, *because* he cannot succeed in being all devil. We might almost say that he commits suicide in a fit of bad temper at discovering that he is good. As for Sonia, she is undebatably good. But she is not a heroine. She is a saint, which is very different, something to which we are not accustomed in our novels.

If the characters at first encounter run against the grain of most of our accepted notions of the identifiable, what shall we say of the form and plot of *Crime and Punishment*? They appear to be no less remote from what we would normally expect.

In the first place, we are told that this is one of the supremely great novels of the world. But this supremely great novel is sheer melodrama, melodrama seemingly of the kind we have been taught to smile at. It is made up of elements which teeter on the edge of the absurd: the prostitute with the heart of gold, the woman who protects her honor with a pistol, the libertine who does everything but twirl his moustaches. Borrowings from the thriller, from the tale of terror, abound: there is blood in every other chapter, there are ghosts, nightmares, deathbed scenes, deliriums. We have been taught to think that material of this sort belongs to the imaginative childhood of the race, or that it is proper only to the literature of blood and thunder. Yet it is clear that Dostoevski is not a child and not a yellow journalist, but just about as clear a case of genius as has ever existed.

But if he is a novelist of genius, he is, we may say, a mighty queer one. What novelist of genius introduces one of the major characters (Svidrigaïlov) three-quarters of the way through the book? What novelist of genius would dare to write an immensely long novel in which there is virtually no relief from intensity, no humor, no balance of themes, no interludes of calm, a book all one huge exclamation point?

We are told that the form of *Crime and Punishment* is that of the detective story. Its admirers claim it to be the greatest detective story ever written. It probably is. But what are we to say of a detective story in which the criminal is known virtually from the first page? In which he commits so many blunders that there is no possible chance of his escaping detection? In which the "facts" of the case are of practically no importance as compared to what is going on in the mind of the criminal? In which the suspense turns not on the discovery of the *murderer* but on the discovery of the *motive*—the motive about which the murderer *himself* is not entirely clear? And finally one in which the murderer is his own detective?

This last point is the most astounding of all. Raskolnikov's urge to kill is overpowering; but so is his urge to confess, to punish himself. Indeed, one might almost say that he kills *in order to confess*. The crime and the punishment are contained in the same person. Raskolnikov is not, except in a formal sense, arrayed against the law. He is arrayed against himself. He is criminal, victim, detective, judge, executioner all in one, though he calls in supernumeraries—Porfiry Petrovich, Sonia, Svidrigaïlov—to assist him or stimulate him in one or the other of his functions.

So: *Crime and Punishment* is a detective story—unlike any ever written. It is a ten-twent'-thirt' melodrama—unlike any ever written. It is a tale of terror—unlike any ever written. It contains all the ingredients of the novel of sensation—and is obviously not a novel of sensation.

Now the question presents itself squarely: if the characters are crazy and the story itself a lurid melodrama, why does it grip us like a steel vise? Why, particularly on a second or third reading, does it impress many not merely as a masterly study of the criminal mind, which it unarguably is, but as a masterly study of the *human* mind? More than that: why is our initial sense that here is a world of freaks existing in an atmosphere of fantasy replaced gradually by a weird feeling that Dostoevski is describing a large part of *the real world of our own time?*

For the final paradox of *Crime and Punishment* (and this is even truer of *The Brothers Karamazov*) is that it is *convincing*—not only convincing in its own terms, as a poem like *Kubla Khan* might be convincing, but convincing as a picture of checkable reality.

Here we touch the inner core of Dostoevski's greatness. He was a visionary. By that I do not mean that he had ecstatic hallucinations, though he claimed, probably truly, that in his epileptic fits he did have them. I mean first that he saw into the human mind as only a few—Socrates, Jesus, Buddha, Blake—had done before him; and second, that he saw into the future, perhaps without knowing it. Entirely apart from the fact that he is a supreme master of a new kind of dramatic narrative, he is overpoweringly impressive in these two other ways: as a psychologist and as a prophet. As they say in the advertisements, no other novelist can make this claim.

It was Freud who first pointed out that Dostoevski was a Freudian. Ever since then the point has been belabored *ad nauseam.* But because the statement is familiar does not make it any the less true.

Freud is still a fighting word. Let's not use it. Let us say, more generally, that most of the major discoveries about the human mind made during the last sixty years (with the possible exception of Pavlov's conditioned reflex) are to be found in dramatic and unsystematized form in Dostoevski's major novels. Others anticipated some of them: the Oedipus complex is stated in a perfectly casual way by Diderot in his *Rameau's Nephew*. (Perhaps Sophocles might be given a little credit too.) The Marquis de Sade, though a bad writer, detected—and exaggerated into an absurd philosophical system—our universal masochist-sadist impulses. But in Dostoevski the whole armamentarium is discoverable: projection, identification, sublimation, the unconscious, the censor, ambivalence, the dream-work, the psychoses, the sense of guilt, suppression, paranoia, symbolization, substitution, the father-image . . . the jargon is dreadful, one hates to use such barbarous shorthand, but there is no help for it. It is all there, much of it in *Crime and Punishment*, and the only way to refute the contention that Dostoevski is a psychologist of genius is to deny *in toto* (which many of course do) the findings of modern psychological science. If you do deny them, however, you must find some tenable explanation of the fact that Dostoevski's novels have impressed so many millions of people as persuasive pictures of the human mind at work.

In a way *Crime and Punishment* is not a novel at all. It is one long psychoanalysis. It is, as an analysis, successful from one point of view and a failure in another. It is successful as insight, unsuccessful as therapy—for, in my opinion, Raskolnikov's religious conversion in the Epilogue, his return to mental health, is about as unconvincing as the happy ending in a Victorian novel. Dostoevski's various solutions to the tragic human predicament, whether Pan-Slavism or primitive Christianity or theocracy, seem to me confused and incoherent. He cannot minister to a mind diseased. But he knows how the disease works.

His kind of greatness in perception does not spring from research or even power of intellect. It comes, like certain kinds of greatness in the history of science, simply from noticing what has been there all along. Dostoevski did not "discover" how the human mind acts; he merely observed it, but observed it *really*, freshly, without any dependence on previous patterns of observation.

We often say something and then are astonished at what we have said. That is today a commonplace observation. But it was not so commonplace when *Crime and Punishment* appeared. The characters in this book are continually astonished at what comes out of their mouths. Name the novelist or dramatist who before Dostoevski had the sense to make this universal human habit a staple of his characterization. Again, Dostoevski makes one of his people (I think it is Raskolnikov) say "innocent" when he means to say "insolent." A Freudian slip, we comment wisely; but Dostoevski came long before Freud. Or take Raskolnikov's rationalization of his hatred of Svidrigaïlov: "I shall not let my sister make this sacrifice for me" when what he really means is "I shall not let my sister share another's bed."

I have given three minor examples of his psychological acumen. I could, any reader could, multiply them by a thousand. It would be tedious to point out how accurate is the symbolism of Raskolnikov's dreams, how unrelenting is Dostoevski's uncovering of our sadist-masochist drives, how penetrating is his exploration of the dualism in human nature.

But it is not tedious to read about. On the contrary, it is almost too exciting. As we make our way through this inferno of human motives, we suddenly feel a hand fastening itself upon our own hearts, and we know that we are there, we are in the picture, we are partially Raskolnikov and Svidrigaïlov and Marmeladov. We are all potential murderers, alcoholics, rapists, creatures of sin. Where else will you find these potentialities so pitilessly, so frighteningly actualized as in Dostoevski's novels?

Conrad objected to Dostoevski on the ground that he is morbid. He *is* morbid; but what he shows us is that morbidity is one of the unconfessed conditions of our fallible human nature. He forces us, as modern psychology does in its more systematic and logical way, to revise our whole conception of the abnormal.

It is usually with a kind of reluctant fascination that the attentive reader of Dostoevski at last admits that such a world as that of *Crime and Punishment* is no mere creation of an overheated brain. The admission is forced out of us, as we have seen, by our recognition of Dostoevski's intuitive knowledge of the night-side of human beings, of their unconscious drives, of those furious capacities for emotion which are ordinarily inhibited by the universal censor we call society.

But it is forced out of us also by another recognition—that of Dostoevski's alarming prescience. His world is not half as unfamiliar as we should like it to be. It bears a disquieting resemblance to precisely those elements in our own environment that most alarm us. It is because Dostoevski incorporates not only our permanent unconscious *individual* fears but also our current conscious *societal* fears that he exerts upon us a double grip.

Raskolnikov was a romantic totalitarian; Stalin and Hitler, to name merely two outstanding examples, were practical totalitarians. Raskolnikov's head, not a particularly strong one, was turned by Napoleon, the first great embodiment in our time of the amoral will to power. Twenty years later Nietzsche, acknowledging Dostoevski as his master, was to formulate his theory of the Superman and to point out the horizon that lay beyond good and evil. The whole bloody sweep of modern totalitarian history, with its apocalyptic tropism, its reliance on power, its denial of Christian ethics, its assumption that people are divided into masters and slaves, its redefinition of crime, its deification of the State: all this is shadowed forth in Dostoevski's four great novels, much of it in *Crime and Punishment*. The entire *philosophical* justification of a Hitler or a Stalin is to be found in Chapter 5 of Part III, in which Raskolnikov explains his ideas to Razumihin and Porfiry Petrovich.

Even the techniques of totalitarianism—brainwashing, mental inquisition, forced confession, denunciation—are foreshadowed by Dostoevski. It is as if he wrote with the future already cloudily alive in his imagination. Raskolnikov anticipates all the strange, tortured men of our time who have been victimized by the idea of social regeneration through cataclysm, and who have in many cases survived to repent publicly their fanaticism.

But Dostoevski's prophetic insight goes even deeper. He is the dramatist of the Displaced Man, Colin Wilson's Outsider. The breakup of Christendom has been attended by a vast deal of social and material progress. But it has also resulted in a curious and troubling phenomenon: the struggle for status. In the twelfth century you were born into your place in society. You may have been miserable, and probably were, but at least you knew where you stood; your obligations both to your fellow man and your God were plainly laid down. Today that is no longer universally true. The consequence is a gigantic but by no means clear-cut cleavage between the Insiders (those who have a stake in society, a place, a respected position, and a modicum of power) and the Outsiders, who are trying to achieve status, or have given up the struggle, or are in rebellion against the idea of status altogether.

Most of Dostoevski's characters—Raskolnikov is an excellent example—are statusless. One of his novels is called *The Humiliated and Insulted*; but all of them might be so called. Another of his titles is *Notes from the Underground*—and that too describes his whole work. His people are deprived of a sense of belonging—not only by poverty, for not all of them are poor. Society gives them no proper place; their particular kind of brain is ill-adjusted to the demands of the time. Yet it is often this very Displaced Person (Raskolnikov, Stalin, Hitler) who has great gifts of energy, mental concentration, will power, and even executive ability. Such a person, rejected by the society that surrounds him, will, as Raskolnikov tries to do, change it by force. The force may be merely a symbolic murder, as in *Crime and Punishment*, or it may be a wholesale bloody revolution.

Our world is full of Raskolnikovs, men and women who want to *be*, to feel their individuality, but who do not have the trick of it. Most of them succumb and live out their lives in a kind of twilight stupor. Others may turn to crime or revolution, unless society is wise enough to point out to them other and better ways in which they can achieve self-expression. Raskolnikov murders, he says at one point, "for myself, for myself alone." Society tells him he is nobody. He insists that he is somebody; and his poor half-crazed mind can conceive only of murder as a way of becoming somebody. If he can possess nothing else, at least he can be *the sole owner of a crime.*

All this is not as farfetched as it may seem. Perhaps we will some day realize that the almost universal current acceptance of war and violence *as a normal way of life* is rooted less in political maladjustments or ferocious evangelistic nationalisms, and more in a general frustration of personality. "Only to live, to live! No matter how—only to live!" cries Raskolnikov.

At any rate all our philosophies of bitterness, such as existentialism; all our outcries (D. H. Lawrence) in defense of the living organism as against the repressive forces of statism or conformity; all this is to be found in Dostoevski. That is why, though at first he seems strange, at last he seems familiar. He is describing a land in which, unhappily, we are at home.

Yet, so many-sided is the fascination of this book, it can make its appeal to readers who may be baffled by its psychology or who remain unconvinced of Dostoevski's power of prophecy. For it remains a great and terrifying story. It can be read as a vision, it can be read as a thriller, it can be read on several levels in between these two. On all planes you are gripped by the intensity of Dostoevski's powers of description, by his genius for describing suffering and pain, by his dramatic force. You may dislike much in Dostoevski's character (he seems to have been a thoroughly unpleasant person), but you cannot help being moved by the heartrending scene in which Katerina Ivanovna forces her children to sing and dance in the street. You cannot escape the mesmeric power of Raskolnikov's confession to Sonia. You cannot fail to follow with a beating heart the sinister chess game that Raskolnikov and Porfiry Petrovich play against each other.

The reader is, against his will, caught up in this hellish world. Once caught, he cannot escape. As you read on you lose awareness of the "real" world. It is with a gasp of bewilderment that you emerge from *Crime and Punishment's* murky pages and, looking back, realize that its entire action has taken only nine days. One seems to have lived and suffered a lifetime.

Seven Authors in Search of

a London

1386?

HE WAS SQUATTY, big-nosed, his eyes hooded with sharp watching of the humors of men; comfortably paunched; like his time, hardheaded; his demeanor easy, for he had been a page in the household of a countess, a courtier, a diplomat, a courier to the royalties of Europe; yet not servile—he had unpursed his fine of two shillings after beating that scurvy Franciscan friar in Fleet Street; and full of business, too, as was proper for a prosperous vintner's son who for twelve years had been Comptroller of the wool customs at Wool Wharf, had been a Justice of the Peace, had served his term at Westminster's Parliament, and, as Clerk of the King's Works, surveyed the drainage system of an ever-busier London.

A sound man of affairs he was; like all his fellows, a good and sometimes fearful son of the Church; a respected burgess to whom the King himself was civil and whose son would climb to even higher estate. A poet too. Not as good, perhaps, as his friend Gower, whose verse, being more moral, would surely lodge longer in men's minds.

Above all, a Londoner. For all his visits to the stately courts of the continent, this was the city, the flower of all cities. He had been born in Vintry Ward on Thames Street, facing the river; and baptized, he thought, near by at St. Martin's. Now with the passing of years the town had become vast, bursting its city walls, noisy with 40,000 Christian souls. A pleasant town, with green fields aplenty to the north and east. A well-curfewed, well-ruled town— he had helped to rule it. Its finest house of God was St. Paul's. Its best shops were proud with newfangled brick and even glass. It was fed by the swan-brightened Thames, from whose wharves he had so often watched the ships sail in and discharge upon the backs of the hill-clambering porters their wondrous un-English burthens. Over the river lay the great stone crown of London Bridge, with its twenty arches, its hundred and thirty-eight shops, its little two-storied chapel where surely his company would tarry and pray to Thomas à Becket before setting out on the long venturesome journey—all of threescore miles—to Canter- bury.

Yes, London was large. Still, an active man who liked to keep his eyes open could know it well, from the Tower with its cages of strange beasts to Westminster with its kings and counselors, from the marshy northern reaches of Moorfields where the boys skated or played prisoner's base, to the Thames that had flowed through so much of his life.

He had breathed its fine clear air—a century or so ago a

man was hanged for burning coal that made an evil smoke, and good riddance. Its streets were full of fine talk, for who would quarter himself in his house (unless perchance to read in a book) when all of God's good out-of-doors lay before him? He knew the streets—Watling Street where men were thick as the stars in the Milky Way, West Cheap, noisy with chaffering and the clink of coin of the realm, more and more of it with each passing day. At every chantry he had listened to the sound of the parson's Hail Marys, each one, as it should be, paid for in advance by some poor soul now pent in purgatory. In the innyards he had watched the miracle plays and in Cheapside the fine gaudy processions bringing home the Maypole on May Day.

He had idled (but to good purpose) in Paternoster Row, his eye upon the booksellers' stalls, quick to mark a precious bargain. God forgive the vanity, he now had near to sixty books, both great and small, snug in his chest by his bedside.

In his city-owned house over Aldgate, hard by the Thames, he and his good wife Philippa had looked to the west to the cross of St. Paul's and to the east at the woods of Essex. How often he had passed the time of day or night with William Duerhirst as that faithful porter opened or closed the great gate. How often, his day's work done, he had repaired home to sit as dumb as any stone with another book.

To these books he would add yet one more, but this of his own making, not Italianate or Frenchified as others he had idly scribbled, but cast in the fair English he heard around him in every London street, gaining daily on the

French of his youth, surely meant to grow into the common tongue of the realm.

All things were at the beginning. The wool trade flourished; the Thames rocked with foreign and English masts; the kingdom grew richer; Londoners laughed in every lane. It was April, wet with sweet showers, and men, though sinners, were wonderful and curious creatures.

Geoffrey Chaucer called his Canterbury pilgrims out of the inkhorn, he led them across London Bridge into Southwark, he gathered them at mine host's Tabard Inn. They began to talk. The world heard the first sounds of the literature of England.

1590?–1610?

The greatest man except Newton ever to walk London's streets must have known the town well. For twenty years he lived there. Anne and the children having been left behind in Stratford, he led a bachelor life in furnished lodgings: first in Bishopsgate Street where like any other law-abiding citizen he attended St. Helen's Church; then across the river in marshy, watery Southwark, handy to the Globe Theatre; then back again to the west part of town, in Silver Street, St. Olave's parish, where he stayed for a time with a theatrical costumer named Mountjoy.

We know what his active life was like. At twenty-eight he was already established as an actor. From that time until his retirement to Stratford he was a theater man, plunged daily into problems of finance, production, costuming, cosmetics, lighting, rehearsal. Like any other pro he had to learn the tricks of an exacting trade—how to tumble, to duel, to dance, to sing, probably even (for he played the Ghost, we are told) how to throw his voice.

But he was no Bohemian, no poor player strutting and fretting his hour upon the stage. London was a good place to make money in, and only wealth could win for him the estate of a gentleman. The theater business paid royally, and he was deep in it.

In his spare time he even wrote plays, most of which turned out hits. He had the knack of pleasing a variety of audiences: the great ones of the Court; the smart young dandies of Gray's Inn; the bluebloods of the great private houses; the honest kersey yeomen and burgesses of the provinces; the penny public that flocked to the Blackfriars in winter and in summer enriched the Watermen's Company that transported them down and across the Thames to the Globe.

The theater claimed most of his time, of course; but he could not help paying some attention to a greater show place than even the Globe—London itself. Like any other young author anxious to see whether his book was given proper display, he must have gone to St. Paul's churchyard to the sign of the White Greyhound to note how well *Venus and Adonis* was selling. He must have watched the mass executions at the Tower and, with an equally speculative eye, the bear-baiting at the Bear Garden just behind the Globe, and the cockfights and the processions and the street pageants. Cheapside he knew, and Bankside, and the scarred tough veterans, home from the wars, swaggering and boasting, a thousand Pistols and Bardolphs, in the streets. The taverns, too, he took his ease in. They were natural hang-outs for any actor who lived as he did in a furnished room: perhaps the Boar's Head on the south side of Eastcheap, perhaps the Mermaid in Bread Street where some say he outwitted in talk the magisterial Ben Jonson.

He sniffed the fine tangle of odors in Bucklersbury where the grocers and druggists and herbalists had their shops. He heard the chimes at midnight. At one in the morning he hearkened to the bellman on his morning rounds and perhaps chuckled as the notion of Dogberry and Verges crossed his practical playwright's mind. At five he watched the laggard scholars on their way to school. At nine he would note with professional interest the players' bills being set up, and look forward to the most important hour of his day, two in the afternoon, when the plays began. As with Chaucer, the Thames, "that long, broad, slippery fellow," flowed through his life. He marked again and again the turning of the tide, the moment in which Falstaff gave up the ghost.

A boom town, London, buzzing with conversation, trade, and the sense that it was the capital of a land shortly to be a Great Power; lively with big deals in real estate; growing in population; suffering almost every summer from the damnable plague that sometimes closed the theaters just when the box office was busiest; a fine town, a fine time to be alive in.

And yet, knowing it well, he dwelt in it for only part of the day or candle-starred night. Real enough, it was not as real as the city he was continually building in his mind, not as solid as Elsinore or Verona or Lear's heath or the Forest of Arden. There was something dreamlike about his connection with London. He seemed to have passed through it as he passed through the whole of his brief life, doing the suitable busy things—making money, working hard, gaining a reputation; yet in a way surveying London as though, with all its gorgeous palaces and solemn temples, it was but a baseless fabric, an insubstantial pageant. London, big enough for the successful theater-owner and playwright, was not big enough for Hamlet, Falstaff, and Othello. All things, if you saw them plain, became visions. London too.

1659–1669

To the Admiralty official, the Clerk of the Privy Seal, the Clerk of the Acts, the musician and experimental scientist, the playgoer and coffeehouse talker, the sight-seer and diner-out, the frequenter of Foxhall, the ever-ready wencher—to Pepys London was no vision. He valued London for the services it offered, as we today value a motor-car. He used London for the pleasure he could get out of it, as a wholehearted lecher will use a woman. Milton's *Paradise Lost* appeared in the middle of Pepys' heyday, in 1667. His own Paradise, rumorous, gay, politics-filled London, was never lost to him. He lived in it snugly, as though it were a warm, familiar private dwelling. In a phrase to be invented years later by another great Londoner, he possessed "the key of the street."

Almost ten years of Charles II's Restoration London pulse incessantly in the Diary he wrote in cipher, until the threat of blindness forced him to forbear and to betake himself, as his last sad entry has it, "to that course, which is almost as much as to see myself go into my grave."

He tells us the concrete things we want to know—where

he went, what he did, whom he spoke to, what he thought about it all. We see him in a thousand London streets, taverns, churches, houses great and small, theaters, amusement gardens, busy offices. He is forever on the move, the day is too short, there is always another good meal to eat, a joke to repeat, a round bottom to pinch, a new explanation to make to that poor wretch, his wife.

London is a fine show, even at its most dismal: he will go to Aldersgate in the fall of 1660 that he may see set upon that gate "the limbs of some of our new traitors"; or to Charing Cross "to see Major-General Harrison hanged, drawn and quartered; which was done there, he looking as cheerful as any man could do in that condition." Let it be a hanging or a coronation, a celebrated preacher or the cockpits in Shoe Lane, the Thames procession of the City Companies or the fine sight of the linen petticoats of my Lady Castlemaine at Whitehall Palace—he was the man, he enjoyed it, he was there.

You will find him at the Half Moon tavern in Bedford Street, at the Mitre in Wood Street ("very merry and had a very good dinner"—how much of the great diarist is in those eight words!), at the Cock in Fleet Street eating a lobster, at the Swan kissing the maid Sarah, at the Saracen's Head on Snow Hill consuming his share of a barrel of oysters.

He had more than one use for London's churches. In St. Dunstan's in Fleet Street one Sunday he flirted, alas unsuccessfully, while the minister delivered "an able sermon." He finds it worth while to chronicle a visit to Lord Lauderdale's house in Highgate for it was there and then that the noble Lord stated his preference for a cat's mew

over the best music in the world. He finds time for everything: to visit Bartholomew Fair and admire "the mare
that tells money"; to be elected a member of the Royal
Society; to watch the Great Fire of 1666 from the top of
Barking steeple in All Hallow's Barking Church in Mark
Lane and to help to save that noble edifice; as Master of
the Clothworkers' Company to present it with a silver
loving cup; to attend the theater at Drury Lane less to see
the play than to ogle pretty, witty Nell; and to work year
after year as a conscientious official to whom the Royal
Navy owes a permanent debt of gratitude.

He is the first notable English writer to perceive that
London could supply a great, a masterful theme. He used
the town. He wrote it down.

1737–1784

The connection between London and Dr. Johnson is
almost one of identity. Boswell and the great Doctor together have made it difficult for the literate to think of
London without thinking of Johnson, to think of Johnson
without thinking of London. He is the greatest public-
relations man the city has ever had, just as Shakespeare is
by far the greatest public-relations man England has ever
had. It was in London that Dr. Johnson lived forty-seven
of his seventy-five years. In his long life he touched upon
or dwelt in dozens upon dozens of its neighborhoods and
purlieus, from Little Britain (where at the tender age of
three he stayed with John Nicholson, like Johnson's father,
a bookseller) to Bolt Court, Fleet Street, where he died.

But what Johnson did for London has little to do with

longevity, little with local geography. Carlyle lived in
Cheyne Row, Chelsea, for exactly as many years as Johnson spent in London. Yet he is not, in the sense that Johnson is, a Londoner. Carlyle merely lived there; but Johnson
created a picture, an image of London which succeed-
ing generations will never be able to get out of their
heads.

Johnson was the first powerful personality in England
to come out flatly for the city as against the country and to
argue with conviction for London as the crown of all cities.
His love affair with London was conscious, deliberate, and
passionate. The image of London that he left remains clear
because his love was so deep and philosophic. It had a
quality not to be found in Pepys' gadabout casual affection.
Nor was it marked by any softness or sentimentality, as
readers of his satiric poem *London* (1738) will acknowl-
edge.

"When a man is tired of London," said the massive gen-
eralizer, "he is tired of life." Boswell tells us that Johnson's
love of London was so strong "that he would have thought
himself an exile in any other place, particularly if residing
in the country." Boswell's phrase for him is final: "this
permanent London object."

On May 16, 1763, in the shop of the bookseller Thomas
Davies, in Russell Street, Covent Garden, occurred one of
the crucial meetings in the history of London as well as
literature—Boswell's with Johnson. From that moment on
it was, as hindsight tells us, inevitable that a lasting image
of London should be projected, to be exceeded in intensity
only with the advent of Charles Dickens.

It is an odd circumstance that first-rate words, which are

but breath, make up a city's most enduring memorials and will help it to survive when all its solider artifacts, even great architecture, have done their best and failed. London calls up a clearer image than does Liverpool, not because more people live there or because more money is made there, but because more thoughts were thought there. A hamlet like Goethe's Weimar will evoke some response a thousand years from now, whereas New York, if it continues to neglect its chances to become a true culture center, will be remembered as but another dull megalopolis, like Thebes or Babylon. Human beings in the twentieth century still produce more interesting books about the Athens of Pericles than about the Chicago of today.

What Johnson did was to upgrade the image of London. He made it appear what it actually was, a capital of mental as well as material commerce. When he tells us that nothing yet contrived by man has produced so much happiness as has a good tavern, he is not wisecracking. He is stating the one unarguable advantage the city has over the country, namely that it provides social intercourse and thereby generates ideas.

Johnson fixed in our minds the notion of London as a city of books, writers, artists, actors, clubs, taverns, conversation, and ideas. That notion is still so powerful that the most nonliterary American tourist has at least an uneasy feeling that he *ought* to visit the Cheshire Cheese. He will have this feeling even when told the truth, that Johnson's connection with the tavern is most tenuous.

We may sum it up by saying that when you read the words "George III's London" not much happens in your head, unless you are a historian. But when you read the words "Johnson's London," something does happen. George III's London suggests little beyond a series of rather foolish political incidents. Johnson's London calls up a *city*, that is to say, civilization.

1775–1827

In 1827 there retired from his native London to the then countryside of Enfield a stammering, gin-loving, pipe-smoking, littlish man, his faintly Judaic face still pallid from thirty-three years of clerkship. Though he was to exist for seven years more, his career, a London career, was virtually over. He died in 1834, to be survived for thirteen years by the intermittently mad sister who had determined the jagged rhythm of his life. In their early years Mary had killed their mother and wounded their father, and she was to die insane. Charles Lamb, himself mentally unstable, lived out his days in bitter tragedy. Yet to this day his work and character distill a pomander sweetness. He is Cockneydom's sole saint.

This saint dwelt in a city his contemporary Shelley compared to Hell, but he never sniffed its sulfur nor felt its flames.

Lamb's love for London, deep as Johnson's, was of a different order. Some outward resemblances it did show. He, too, felt no love for the country. Living at Enfield his dreams carried him back to Fleet Market. Away from the sound of the rival bells, plangent on either side of the Thames, of St. Bride and Mary Overy, he grew uneasy. At Margate he would gladly have exchanged the sea gulls for the swans, descendants of Chaucer's swans, of the Thames. He was born in a crowd, he tells us. Loving the very smoke of London, he thought a man must have a rare recipe for melancholy who could be dull in Fleet Street. In the Strand he would often shed tears from "fulness of joy at so much life," and each morning at ten o'clock for three-and-thirty years would walk to his high stool at the East India House in Leadenhall Street and look up with unfading wonder at St. Paul's.

But he differed from Johnson and particularly from Pepys in that he discovered a new London. What was new about it lay in his perception that it was old. One cannot learn from Lamb's essays, or even his letters, much about the London that lay all contemporary about him. But he taught us to see a London thick with the past. It is no mean achievement.

From his writings you would hardly guess that for several years he spent his Sundays and holidays visiting his sister in a lunatic asylum; and, while the squabbles of the coachmen and the linkboys in the streets sound in his prose, they sound but faintly. If he walks in Pall Mall it is to recollect that once there he saw Nelson plain. He looks about him to see what is no longer present and to write a complaint of the decay of beggars. The Inner Temple, which he knew so well, brings to his mind the Old Benchers who once lived there, and when he thinks of the South Sea house, that relict of the Great Bubble, it is to recall some item of the past, like the artificial fountain that once played in a little green nook behind it. It is old actors, such as Elliston, he is eager to tell us about.

When he protests the institution of entrance fees for

Westminster Abbey, it is not the poor he is pleading for, but the stately monuments which will now lack sufficient admirers.

He writes of *Old China* and *Newspapers Five and Thirty Years Ago* and Christ's Hospital from 1782 to 1789. Covent Garden makes him think of the folio Beaumont and Fletcher he once dragged home late at night from Barker's. He is said to have wept when the two stiffly moving horological giants of St. Dunstan's in Fleet Street were removed. He loved the gardens of Gray's Inn because they were "altogether reverend and law-breathing." Passing a doorway, he marks it as all that is left of Garrick's Drury. He is quick to note the disappearance of the live sign of the tinman's shop, a cage with a squirrel.

This "speculative Lord Mayor of London," as he called himself, taught us to see a great city not only as something living, but as something continually dying, to see it as a concretion of the past, as history.

Lamb is London's most beautiful genius of the backward glance.

1822–1870

Around Christmas Day, 1822, the ten-year-old Charles Dickens left Chatham, took his seat timidly in the London coach, and was forwarded, carriage paid, to the Cross Keys, Wood Street, Cheapside. Even though a large part of his last decade was spent at Gadshill, his country place near Rochester, it is fair to say that from that moment until his death in 1870 London claimed Dickens, Dickens claimed London. He and Balzac are the two greatest imag-

inative re-creators of the modern metropolis the world has
ever seen; and he is the greater.

Many would be ready to argue that no man before or
since his time has known London as Dickens did. In a
sense there is almost as much London in Dickens as there
is in London. He describes so many places and so many
people that his novels and the city itself begin to seem
coextensive. I have said that when you think of Dr. Johnson you think of London. But when you think of Dickens
you are *in* London. Millions of people who have never
been within thousands of miles of Leicester Square are
filled with all kinds of emotions about London merely
because they have read Dickens.

Mr. Guppy in *Bleak House* called the fog "a London
particular." London fog has become Dickens' fog, for no
one else has described it so well. Think of a London bank
and you may very well be reminded automatically of Tell-
son's—which, by the way, is Child's, one of the old family
banks that developed from goldsmiths' shops; Pepys was
a depositor at Child's. Holborn recalls Oliver Twist. Go to
White Hart Yard, and you will think of the White Hart
Inn, and that will make you think of the first meeting of
Pickwick and Sam Weller, and you will be happier for the
recollection. Most of the old prisons of London are gone.
But Brixton and Holloway, Pentonville and Wandsworth
are meaningless syllables, whereas the Marshalsea brings
back the whole vast story of *Little Dorrit*, and the Fleet
means Jingle, Pickwick, Sam Weller, and Mrs. Bardell.

Dickens started to know London as a miserable, fright-
ened child when he walked from his Southwark attic to the
blacking factory at Hungerford Stairs. He never ceased to

explore it—not merely its public squares and theaters and churches and taverns, but its prisons, hospitals, madhouses, its slums and its sinister Thames-side arched vaults, the murder-filled alcoves of London Bridge, the frowsy Hanging Sword Alley where Jerry Cruncher lived.

His knowledge of London was, like Mr. Weller's, extensive and peculiar. "I thought I knew something of the town," said a contemporary of the youthful Dickens, "but after a little talk with Dickens I found that I knew nothing. He knew it all from Bow to Brentford."

My own feeling is that, slightly mad anyway, he was especially mad about London, that it obsessed him to the point of mania. He would walk "the black streets of London fifteen and twenty miles many a night when all sober folks had gone to bed." He lamed his friend Frank Stone once by walking him seventeen miles. London was his stimulant, his alcohol, his hashish; it spurred him on to uncover the visions that lay sleeping in his unconscious.

Dickens gives us London complete. For him it is not merely a great spectacle or place of social diversion. It is an arena of class conflict, a theater of suffering, a circus of comedy, a vast cockpit filled with frenzied ambitions and despairs. He saw it, and for the first time in English literature, as fit material for the exercise of the highest kind of creative imagination.

He turned London into dramatic poetry.

1914—

There is a passage somewhere in Lamb, I think in one of his letters: "Confusion blast all mercantile transactions,

all traffic, exchange of commodities, intercourse between
nations, all the consequent civilisation, and wealth, and
amity, and link of society, and getting rid of prejudices,
and getting a knowledge of the face of the globe; and
rotting the very firs of the forest, that look so romantic
alive, and die into desks!"

What Lamb was petulant about here, Dickens was to
see more clearly and passionately in the next generation,
and T. S. Eliot was to announce in our day in the grave
tones of a priest: that a city given over to the material has
surrendered its right to call itself a center of civilization
and will die, and its citizens will die with it, though its
body and their bodies may seem to persist.

T. S. Eliot removed to London in 1914. From that time
forward, in his poems and his plays, he has used the city
as a symbol, a symbol of what is wrong, what is hollow,
what is dying in the West. Eliot's word for London is
"Unreal" and his vision of the city is a vision of dullness,
decay, and death; of "one-night cheap hotels and sawdust
restaurants with oyster-shells"; of the muffled spirits who
in the early morning "are raising dingy shades in a thousand furnished rooms"; of "the damp souls of housemaids
sprouting despondently at area gates"; of multitudes
"weeping in a hundred A.B.C.'s"; of the wearily acquies-
cent typist and the degenerate Tarquin, "the young man
carbuncular . . . a small house agents' clerk"; of the whor-
ish Grishkin in her maisonette, giving promise of pneu-
matic bliss.

He wishes his Thames were Spenser's soft-running river,
bearing "no empty bottles, sandwich papers, silk handker-
chiefs, cardboard boxes, cigarette ends or other testimony

of summer nights"; but he knows the days of Elizabeth and Leicester in their gilded barge are over, that London Bridge is falling down, that London now is

> *the time kept City*
> *Where the River flows, with foreign flotations.*

Dickens' fog is romantic, Eliot's is frightening: it is yellow and smoky and rubs its back upon the windowpanes like a cat out of Poe. Under the brown fog of a winter dawn he sees in vision a crowd flowing over London Bridge

> *so many*
> *I had not thought death had undone so many.*

The hills of London are gloomy, its wind is the eructation of unhealthy souls, the air is faded. In the suburbs the Word is unspoken, in the land of lobelias and tennis flannels

> *The rabbit shall burrow and the thorn revisit,*
> *The nettle shall flourish on the gravel court,*
> *And the wind shall say: "Here were decent, godless people:*
> *Their only monument the asphalt road*
> *And a thousand golf balls."*

He broods over London as Chaucer and Shakespeare, Pepys and Johnson, Lamb and even Dickens, did not. He asks of its citizens the meaning of the city:

> *What will you answer? "We all dwell together*
> *To make money from each other"? or "This is a community"?*

Something, in Eliot's view, has happened to London—by which he means the West—since Chaucer's day. It has gained the whole world and lost its soul. By abandoning God it has become the Waste Land.

Our Seven Londons began with Chaucer and with the moment in which, filled with joy, he thought of April with her sweet showers piercing the dryness of March and bringing life to the land. We end with a great artist for whom London is not a city but an occasion for religious reflection and who begins his most famous poem with a bitter reminiscence of Chaucer:

> *April is the cruelest month, breeding*
> *Lilacs out of the dead land . . .*

Who speaks for London today? What pen is shaping for us a London image as memorable as that of Johnson or Dickens?

T. S. Eliot perhaps? His Dantean nightmare is a powerful image indeed. Yet who shall say Yes to it, recalling the rock cliff of passion against which the surf of German bombs broke in vain?

Yes, London still holds its millions of heroic hearts. But what writer of our day has had the cunning to wrap the city in a robe of glowing words?

It is a tricksy spirit, the *genius loci,* uneasy where the measures become too vast, the men too many. It seeks a habitation where the decibels are fewer and the pavement has an end. Megalopolis, like the saurian of old, defeats itself. It grows toward mindlessness—and it is upon minds that the imagination feeds. As the photograph loses definition by enlargement, so may the city lose what is great in what is big. Even now some feel this is true of our own New York. With what fervor one hopes it may never come to be true of that wondrous London whose streets still rumor the great ghosts of the writers who loved it.

ABOUT THE AUTHOR

CLIFTON FADIMAN was born in New York City in 1904, and got his A.B. from Columbia University in 1925. He has been a translator, a teacher, an advisor to Samuel Goldwyn, editor at Simon and Schuster, lecturer, and book review editor of *The New Yorker*. During these years writing—and editing such books as *Reading I've Liked, The Short Stories of Henry James, The American Treasury,* and other books and anthologies—played a concurrent part; and radio and TV chores grew into a memorable ten years as host of *Information Please,* M.C. of *This Is Show Business,* and conductor of the popular NBC radio series *Conversation.* Mr. Fadiman, a member of the Board of Judges of the Book-of-the-Month Club and essayist for *Holiday* magazine, keeps a busy schedule as a platform reader across the country.

This book was set in

Caledonia and Baskerville types by

Brown Brothers Linotypers

The paper is Crocker, Burbank's Hermes Antique

supplied by Whitehead and Alliger Company

It was printed and bound by

The Haddon Craftsmen

Typography and design are by

Lawrence S. Kamp

70
71
72
74
75
76
77
79
83
85
89